D1072245

Bilingual Education
in American Schools

EDUCATION INFORMATION GUIDE SERIES

Series Editor: Francesco Cordasco, Professor of Education, Montclair State College, Upper Montclair, New Jersey

Also in this series:

HIGHER EDUCATION IN AMERICA—*Edited by Franklin Parker**

THE HISTORY OF AMERICAN EDUCATION—*Edited by Francesco Cordasco, Marjorie Scilken Friedman, and David N. Alloway**

MEDICAL EDUCATION IN THE UNITED STATES—*Edited by Francesco Cordasco and David N. Alloway**

MUSIC EDUCATION—*Edited by Ernest E. Harris*

THE PHILOSOPHY OF EDUCATION—*Edited by Charles Albert Baatz**

PSYCHOLOGICAL FOUNDATIONS—*Edited by Charles Albert Baatz and Olga K. Baatz**

READING IN AMERICAN SCHOOLS—*Edited by Maria E. Schantz and Joseph F. Brunner**

SOCIOLOGY OF EDUCATION—*Edited by Francesco Cordasco and David N. Alloway*

WOMEN'S EDUCATION IN THE UNITED STATES—*Edited by Kay S. Wilkins**

*in preparation

The above series is part of the
GALE INFORMATION GUIDE LIBRARY

The Library consists of a number of separate series of guides covering major areas in the social sciences, humanities, and current affairs.

General Editor: Paul Wasserman, Professor and former Dean, School of Library and Information Services, University of Maryland

Managing Editor: Denise Allard Adzigian, Gale Research Company

Bilingual Education in American Schools

A GUIDE TO INFORMATION SOURCES

Volume 3 in the Education Information Guide Series

Francesco Cordasco

Professor of Education
Montclair State College
Upper Montclair, New Jersey

With

George Bernstein

Associate Professor of Education
Montclair State College
Upper Montclair, New Jersey

Gale Research Company
Book Tower, Detroit, Michigan 48226

Library of Congress Cataloging in Publication Data

Cordasco, Francesco, 1920-
  Bilingual education in American schools.

  (Education information guide series ; v. 3) (Gale
information guide library)
  Includes indexes.
  1. Education, Bilingual—United States. I. Bernstein, George, joint author. II. Title. III. Series.
LC3731.C667   371.9'7'0973   79-15787
ISBN 0-8103-1447-9

For
Carmela Cordasco and Elvira Romano
Exemplars of a Noble Tradition

VITAE

Francesco Cordasco, a cultural historian and sociologist, is a professor of education at Montclair State College, and has taught at New York University, the City University of New York, Long Island University, and the University of Puerto Rico. Cordasco has served as a consultant to the Migration Division, Commonwealth of Puerto Rico; to the U.S. Office of Education; and to federal, state, and community antipoverty programs. He is the author of books on ethnic communities in the United States, immigrant children, urban education, educational sociology, and bilingual schooling.

George Bernstein taught Hispanic students in the New York City public schools from 1958 to 1966. During the years 1959 to 1962, he also directed a volunteer course, Basic English for Adults, in Spanish Harlem. In the years 1967 to 1969, he was active in Montclair State College (N.J.) with programs for preparing teachers for New Jersey schools with Hispanic and other minority groups, and helping such pupils when they arrived at the Montclair State College campus. He has taught numerous courses which focused on Hispanic communities and their educational situation. He is presently a staff member of the Bilingual Education Program and School of Education Coordinator of the Latin American Area Studies Program at Montclair State College.

From the point of view of the relation of the school to children of foreign parentage, it is important to realize that they are inheritors of a foreign culture; that they are often a part of some foreign national community in America; and that their foreign cultural background operates unavoidably and insistently in their educational processes, be it in the school situation or in the general field of learning. Knowledge of this background is indispensable whether the function of the school is to achieve a satisfactory adjustment of individual students or whether the school focuses its aim upon the adjustment of entire groups; that is, whether the school operates according to the principles of the subject-minded school (academic or vocational) or whether it addresses itself to larger social aims such as assimilation, intercultural education, citizenship training, and so on.

Leonard Covello, THE SOCIAL BACKGROUND OF THE ITALO-AMERICAN SCHOOL CHILD (1944). Leiden, Netherlands: E.J. Brill, 1967.

CONTENTS

INTRODUCTION

No issue facing American educators has been more challenging than bilingual education, and none has stimulated more controversy. Advocacy of bilingual education has met opposition, at times intransigent, and the pros and cons of a bilingual educational policy have both been forcefully stated.

What is bilingual education? Bilingual education has been defined as instruction in two languages: the child's native language and English. In such an educational program a pupil receives instruction in academic subjects in both his native language and in English; concomitantly, the student learns about the history and culture associated with both languages, that is, bicultural education. Technically, this is "transitional" bilingual education, and its goal has been to help non-English speaking students to keep up with basic subjects (reading, mathematics, and so forth) in their native languages until they have been taught enough English to transfer them to regular English-speaking classrooms.

Most bilingual education programs in the United States are "transitional," and it is this type of bilingual education which has been encouraged by the U.S. Office of Education since the enactment of the federal Bilingual Education Act in 1968. Most state legislation mandating or allowing bilingual education (e.g., Massachusetts, New Jersey, Texas, Colorado, California, and so forth) has, also, called for "transitional" bilingual programs.

Since 1968 some half-billion dollars of federal funds have been committed to bilingual education; in Fiscal year 1978 some $125 million will have been made available from the U.S. Office of Bilingual Education. In Fiscal year 1977, HEW sponsored over six hundred bilingual projects in teacher training, curriculum development, and classroom projects, in some sixty-eight languages at a cost (including state funds) in excess of $200 million. This is a staggering sum, and the efforts in bilingual education have been enthusiastically praised, and at the same time bitterly condemned.

Critics of bilingual education have maintained that "the government has not demonstrated whether such instruction makes much difference in the students'

achievement, in their acquisiton of English, or in their attitudes toward school."
They have also argued against a philosophy of "affirmative ethnicity" which
would maintain the non-English language and its culture and would as a result,
in their view, impede the normal process of all students learning the common
English language and the common national history. The fears are largely un-
founded, and the answers to the questions surrounding bilingual education for
American children lie in both historical and contemporary perspectives.

Actually, bilingual education is not new in the United States; in a nation as
diverse in its origins as ours, this should not be surprising. English has not
always been the only language used in American schools. German immigrants
(whose progeny make up the largest ethnic group in America) established German-English bilingual schools in Cincinnati, Indianapolis, Hoboken (N.J.),
Cleveland, and many other cities: these were public schools, and German
was not only taught as a subject; it was used as a medium of instruction. Between 1880 and 1917, these schools flourished; they were eagerly supported by
a powerful and socially-stratified German community, and only the political
tensions of World War I ended their history. In Louisiana, French was used as
the medium of instruction, and in New Mexico, Spanish was so used; of course,
these were limited efforts and largely early and mid-nineteenth century phenomena, but they confirm a bilingual tradition in America. In New York City,
at different times and with different commitments, the public schools taught
children in Chinese, Italian, Greek, Yiddish, and French. In a real sense,
present-day efforts in bilingual education are a rediscovery of a respected and
traditional American educational practice. Why, then, the resistance by some
groups to bilingual education? The answer is complex.

It is not altogether untrue, as a national weekly recently affirmed, that "current bilingual policy is a curious hybrid of pedagogy and politics." Bilingual
education is a product of the social unrest which engulfed our institutions in
the 1960s. It could not have been otherwise, since bilingual education, in
its bicultural orientations, is a necessary concomitant of the new ethnic consciousness which has recently gripped the American imagination; flowing directly
from the black civil rights movement and new affirmations of identity, came
the bristling ethnicity which unleashed proclamations of ethnic pride in Mexican
Americans, Puerto Ricans, and in the progeny of earlier European immigrants--
Italians, Greeks, Jews, Poles, Slavs, and others. The preservation of languages is an important part of the ideology of the new ethnicity; and thus, bilingual education (in itself, an unassailable pedagogical technique) became em-
broiled in the controversy surrounding the new ethnicity, its ideologies, and
interventionist politics. And in these contexts, the resistance to bilingual and
bicultural education is not unrelated to dominant themes in American society
which have entertained, and continue to entertain, credence, for example,
interethnic rivalry, the Americanization movement, psychological testing and
race typologies, eugenics and hereditarian persuasions, and the "melting pot"
theory of assimilation. All of these issues are, and have been, highly controversial and emotionally disturbing episodes in our long history as a people;
and each of these themes (and a combination of any and all of them) have served
to obscure the very real pedagogic needs to which bilingual education addresses
itself.

There is a clear consensus among American educators that the purpose of bi-lingual education is to help children who have little or no command of English to succeed in school. In the landmark decision in Lau v. Nichols (1974), Associate Justice William O. Douglas (who delivered the opinion of the U.S. Supreme Court) said: "There is no equality of treatment merely by providing students with the same facilities, textbooks, teachers, and curriculum, for stu-dents who do not understand English are effectively foreclosed from any mean-ingful education. . . . Basic English skills are at the very core of what the schools teach. Imposition of a requirement that, before a child can effectively participate in the educational program, he must already have acquired those basic skills is to make a mockery of public education."

The contemporary contexts of bilingual schooling in the United States directly impinge on the ideologies that herald the energetic emergence of peoples who find in their cultures and languages the instrumentalities of an evolving enfran-chisement; and it would be hazardous to suggest otherwise. In many ways, the ideologies of race, culture, and language (if not new phenomena in Ameri-can history) have a crucial significance. How successful bilingual education proves in the United States will depend on how congruent its programs be-come with the aspirations of the ethnic communities to which the programs are addressed; on the awareness by American educators of the new American eth-nicity; on the very participation of ethnic communities in program formulation and evaluation; and on the cogency of those bilingual typologies that (in care-fully constructed bicultural frames) can best achieve desired objectives.

The present work is intended as a selective guide to the vast extant resources on bilingual education in the United States, its history, programs, curricula, administration, staff and teacher training, and the federal and state legislation which have governed its evolution as well as the indices of tests, evaluation, and measurement which have been employed. A brief register of titles on "English as a Second Language" has been included (chapter V), even though ESL (or more properly TESOL, i.e., Teaching English to Speakers of Other Languages) is not, technically, bilingual education. In American practice, ESL has become an ancillary component of transitional bilingual programs. Since language is integrally part of the larger cultural context in which a peo-ple is to be understood, many entries have been included which lie in ethno-cultural contexts, the sociology of ethnic and minority life in the United States, and in a broader frame, in the new disciplines defined in American ethnic historiography; the inclusion of investigations in linguistics (particularly, socio-linguistics), and related technical studies in language and multilingualism, afford dimensionally fuller perspectives in which bilingual practice in American schools is to be understood.

With few exceptions, English-language materials have been used; and in some instances, entries have been included on bilingual education outside the United States. Entries are listed in chronological order by publication date.

Francesco Cordasco

ACRONYMS AND ABBREVIATIONS

ABE	Adult Basic Education
ACTFL	American Council on the Teaching of Foreign Languages
BIA	Bureau of Indian Affairs
BBE	Bilingual Bicultural Education
CAL	Center for Applied Linguistics
EPDA	Education Professions Development Act
ERIC	Educational Resources Information Center
ESL	English as a second language
FL	Foreign language
FY	Fiscal year
FLES	Foreign languages, elementary schools
IRCD	Information Retrieval Center on the Disadvantaged
NACBE	National Advisory Council on Bilingual Education
NDEA	National Defense Education Act
SES	Socioeconomic status
TESOL	Teaching English to Speakers of Other Languages
WISC	Wechsler Intelligence Scale for Children

I. BIBLIOGRAPHIES AND GENERAL REFERENCES

1 Afendras, E.A., and Pianarosa, A. CHILD BILINGUALISM AND
SECOND LANGUAGE LEARNING: A DESCRIPTIVE BIBLIOGRAPHY.
Quebec: Les Presses de Universite Laval, 1975. 115 p.

2 Allen, Virginia F., and Forman, Sidney. ENGLISH AS A SEC-
OND LANGUAGE: A COMPREHENSIVE BIBLIOGRAPHY. New
York: Teachers College Press, Columbia University, 1967. Re-
print. New York: Arno Press, 1978. iii, 255 p.

> This bibliography is a subject-category listing of titles
> which constitute the special English as a Foreign or
> Second Language Library in the Teachers College,
> Columbia University, Library. The collection includes
> books, periodicals, films, filmstrips, phonograph records,
> tapes, charts, maps, games, models, flash cards, and
> related types of equipment. A new classification which
> was devised for the collection is used, arranging its
> entries (about fifteen hundred) under the broad, and
> further subdivided, categories of linguistics, language
> culture area, language learning, tests, and reference.

3 Altus, David M. AMERICAN INDIAN EDUCATION: A SELECTED
BIBLIOGRAPHY. Washington, D.C.: U.S. Government Printing Office,
1971. 112 p.

4 Andersson, Theodore, and Boyer, Mildred [V.], eds. BILINGUAL
SCHOOLING IN THE UNITED STATES. 2 vols. Austin, Texas:
Southwest Educational Development Laboratory, 1970. Texas: Introduction and supplementary bibliography by Francesco Cordasco.
Detroit: Blaine Ethridge, 1976. Volume 1 includes a massive,
annotated bibliography, pp. 149-243, and an index to the bibliography, pp. 245-76.

5 Babin, Patrick. BILINGUALISM: A BIBLIOGRAPHY. Cambridge, Mass.: Harvard Graduate School of Education, 1968. 30 p.

> This bibliography is a selected listing of books, monographs, journal articles, and bibliographies focusing on bilingualism.

6 Barnes, Regina. A SELECTED ERIC BIBLIOGRAPHY ON TEACHING ETHNIC MINORITY GROUP CHILDREN IN THE UNITED STATES OF AMERICA. ERIC-IRCD Urban Disadvantaged Series, no. 4. New York: Columbia University, Teachers College, ERIC Information Retrieval Center on the Disadvantaged, 1969. 26 p.

> This annotated bibliography includes a section on teaching Puerto Ricans.

7 Bengelsdorf, Winnie. ETHNIC STUDIES IN HIGHER EDUCATION: STATE OF THE ART AND BIBLIOGRAPHY. Washington, D.C.: American Association of State Colleges and Universities, 1972. Reprint. New York Times Bilingual Bicultural Education in the United States Series. New York: Arno Press, 1978. 261 p.

> This study conducted under a grant awarded by the National Endowment for the Humanities; "sought to identify and summarize recent material on ethnic studies in higher education and to determine the state of the art or trend of these studies." An analysis evaluates views of ethnicity; assesses the federal, state, and societal factors influencing ethnic studies; and includes a summary of findings. Pending research, general information, sociohistorical sources, reference and periodical sources are discussed and conclude with institutional lists of colleges and universities offering ethnic studies. All major ethnic groups are included (along with black, Chicano, Puerto Rican, and other Hispanic groups), with a concluding section on teacher training in ethnic studies.

8 Berry, Brewton. THE EDUCATION OF AMERICAN INDIANS: A SURVEY OF THE LITERATURE. Prepared for the Special Senate Subcommittee on Indian Education of the Committee on Labor and Public Welfare. Washington, D.C.: U.S. Government Printing Office, 1969. 121 p.

> The author deals with the history, problems, and causes of the problems in Native American education. An overview survey precedes the bibliography of 708 references.

9 Bobson, Sara. THE EDUCATION OF PUERTO RICANS ON THE MAINLAND: AN ANNOTATED BIBLIOGRAPHY. New York: Institute for Urban and Minority Education, Columbia University, 1975. vi, 81 p.

> This includes the following chapters: (1) "General Information," (2) "Historical Perspective and Background Information on Puerto Rico," (3) "Inservice Education and Inservice Workshops," (4) "Puerto Ricans and the Schools," (5) "Sociological Analysis," (6) "Spanish Language Texts," (7) "Bibliographies," and "Author Index."

10 Bravo, Enrique R., comp. ANNOTATED SELECTED PUERTO RICAN BIBLIOGRAPHY. New York: Columbia University, Urban Center, 1972. 237 p.

> A bilingual bibliography which includes those works considered to be classics, as well as those most relevant to the contemporary Puerto Rican experience, in the following areas: anthropology and sociology; political science, cultural development and national foundations; economics; education; geography; history; linguistics; literature; religion and philosophy; and Puerto Rico and the Hispanic world.

11 Buenker, John D., and Burckel, Nicholas C., eds. IMMIGRATION AND ETHNICITY: A GUIDE TO INFORMATION SOURCES. American Government and History Information Guide Series, vol. 1. Detroit: Gale Research Co., 1977. xii, 305 p.

> The following chapters are included in this bibliography: (1) "General Accounts," (2) "Old Immigration," (3) "New Immigration," (4) "Orientals," (5) "Recent Ethnics," (6) "Acculturation, Assimilation, Ethnicity, and Restriction," (7) "Centers, Repositories, Societies, Documents, and Journals."

12 CARTEL: ANNOTATED BIBLIOGRAPHY OF BILINGUAL BICULTURAL MATERIALS NO. 13. CUMULATIVE ISSUE. Austin, Tex.: Dissemination Center for Bilingual Bicultural Education, 1973. 210 p.

> Approximately four hundred books, curriculum guides, journals, and educational resource materials published between 1967 and 1973 are listed in this bibliography (annotated) of bilingual and bicultural materials on the Spanish-speaking, Native Americans, French, Portuguese, Chinese, and Russians.

13 Caskey, Owen L., and Hodges, Jimmy. A RESOURCE AND
REFERENCE BIBLIOGRAPHY ON TEACHING AND COUNSELING
THE BILINGUAL STUDENT. Lubbock, Tex.: School of Educa-
tion, Texas Technological College, 1968. 98 p.

This bibliography includes 733 references with some
annotations.

14 Charles, Edgar B., ed. MEXICAN-AMERICAN EDUCATION: A
BIBLIOGRAPHY. Prepared for National Conference on Educational
Opportunities for Mexican-Americans, 25-26 April 1968. Las
Cruces, N. Mex.: ERIC Clearinghouse on Rural Education and
Small Schools, 1968. 22 p.

This bibliography consists of a selected listing of 90
books, monographs, journal articles, and unpublished
papers on the education of the Mexican American,
with annotations.

15 Ching, D.C. "Reading, Language Development, and the Bilingual Child: An Annotated Bibliography." ELEMENTARY ENGLISH
46 (1969): 622-28.

16 Christiansen, Dorothy, comp. BIBLIOGRAPHY. BILINGUALISM:
TEACHING SPANISH-SPEAKING STUDENTS. New York: Center
for Urban Education, 1969. 10 p.

This bibliography is a partially annotated list of monographs, books, and articles on all aspects of bilingual
education.

17 Colorado, University of. Department of Sociology-Anthropology.
A SELECTED BIBLIOGRAPHY: HEALTH AND CULTURE OF
SPANISH-SPEAKING MIGRANT LABOR. Fort Collins, Colo.:
1966. 10 p.

18 Cook, Katherine M., and Reynolds, Florence E. THE EDUCATION
OF NATIVE AND MINORITY GROUPS: A BIBLIOGRAPHY,
1923-1932. U.S. Department of the Interior. Office of Education, Bulletin no. 12. Washington, D.C.: U.S. Government
Printing Office, 1933. 135 p.

This 573-item classified bibliography with succinct an-
notations, includes a subject and author index. Puerto
Rico, Hawaii, the Virgin Islands, the Philippines, the
Canal Zone, Samoa, and Guam are included.

19 Cooperative Children's Book Center. MATERIALS FOR THOSE
WITH A SPANISH-SPEAKING BACKGROUND. Madison, Wis.:
1969. 10 p.

Some one hundred fifty-one entries are listed in this annotated bibliography of books and audiovisual materials appropriate for persons with a Spanish-language heritage. The document contains titles grouped by geographical area of national origin and subgrouped by reading and interest levels. Countries: Mexico, Puerto Rico, South and Central America, and Spain are covered.

20 Cordasco, Francesco. ITALIANS IN THE UNITED STATES: A BIBLIOGRAPHY OF REPORTS, TEXTS, CRITICAL STUDIES AND RELATED MATERIALS. New York: Oriole Editions, 1972. xvi, 137 p.

This is a largely unannotated bibliography of some fourteen hundred entries which is intended "to furnish both a guide and framework for the study of the Italian experience in the United States."

21 _____. PUERTO RICANS ON THE UNITED STATES MAINLAND: A BIBLIOGRAPHY OF REPORTS, TEXTS, CRITICAL STUDIES AND RELATED MATERIALS. Totowa, N.J.: Rowman and Littlefield, 1972. xiv, 146 p.

A register of representative titles is arranged in six sections: (1) "General Bibliographies," (2) "The Island Experience," (3) "Migration to the Mainland," (4) "The Acculturation," (5) "The Mainland Experience: Education," (6) "The Mainland Experience: The Social Context."

22 _____. THE ITALIAN AMERICAN EXPERIENCE: AN ANNOTATED AND CLASSIFIED BIBLIOGRAPHICAL GUIDE. WITH SELECTED PUBLICATIONS OF THE CASA ITALIANA EDUCATIONAL BUREAU. New York: Burt Franklin and Co., 1974. xiv, 179 p.

This selective annotated bibliographical guide of 338 major entries, includes the texts of early studies (1931-34) of the Casa Italiana Educational Bureau: Leonard Covello, THE ITALIANS IN AMERICA; William B. Shedd, ITALIAN POPULATION IN NEW YORK; and John J. D'Alesandre, OCCUPATIONAL TRENDS OF ITALIANS IN NEW YORK CITY.

23 _____. IMMIGRANT CHILDREN IN AMERICAN SCHOOLS. A CLASSIFIED AND ANNOTATED BIBLIOGRAPHY WITH SELECTED SOURCE DOCUMENTS. Fairfield, N.J.: Augustus M. Kelley, 1976. 381 p.

This is a comprehensively dimensional bibliography of some fifteen hundred entries in a classified plan, for

the most part with annotations. The book is divided
into three parts: part 1, "Basic References, General
History, and Immigration"; part 2, "The Immigrant Child
and His World"; part 3, "Selected Source Documents."
It also includes "Bilingualism and Bilingual Education,"
pp. 171-79.

24 _____. PUERTO RICANS ON THE MAINLAND. The Balch Institute Historical Reading Lists, no. 13. Philadelphia: The Balch
Institute, 1976. 6 p.

This partially annotated list of titles is arranged for undergraduate, graduate, and advanced students.

25 _____. "Social Reform in American Education: A Bibliography
of Selected References." BULLETIN OF BIBLIOGRAPHY 33 (April-
June 1976): 105-10.

The article includes notices of immigrant children, bilingual education, and contemporary contexts.

26 _____. "Bilingual and Bicultural Education in American Schools:
A Bibliography of Selected References." BULLETIN OF BIBLI-
OGRAPHY 35 (April-June 1978): 53-72.

This article is a partially annotated list of some three
hundred fifty titles with a preliminary essay on bibliographical resources.

27 _____, advisory ed. BILINGUAL BICULTURAL EDUCATION IN
THE UNITED STATES. 37 vols. New York: Arno Press and New
York Times, 1978.

This core collection of documents, texts, and related
materials in bilingual-bicultural education draws from a
rich repository of materials. Included are the complete
texts of the historic hearings held before subcommittees
of the U.S. Senate and House of Representatives out of
which derived the enactment of the federal Bilingual
Education Act in 1968; and made available are the hearings before the House subcommittee which led to the
enactment of the Ethnic Heritage Program Act of 1970.
These government documents are invaluable primary
source materials for bilingual-bicultural education; and,
expanding the range of official government documents,
the collection includes reports on bilingual education
published under the aegis of the U.S. Commission on
Civil Rights; the first report to the president and the
Congress by the National Advisory Council on Bilingual
Education; HEARINGS which delineate the need for comprehensive bilingual manpower training; and the Bureau

of Indian Affairs' detailed proposals for bilingual education for American Indians and Eskimos. In the broad
frame of international perspective, the collection adds
the reports of the [Canada] Royal Commission on Bilingualism and Biculturalism; UNESCO documents on Vernacular Languages in Education, and Bilingualism in
Education; and the A STUDY OF BILINGUALISM IN
SOUTH AFRICA, an interpretative work with far-reaching
implications.

A wide range of doctoral disserations explores a multi-
tude of problems and needs in bilingual-bicultural education, and places these themes in historical focus. The
studies include analyses of language acquisition; descriptive studies of the supervision, evaluation, effectiveness,
and sociopsychological dimensions of bilingual education;
bilingualism and school achievement; research guidelines;
and profiles of urban immigrant school children, and the
origins of the community-oriented school.

28 _____, ed. ITALIAN AMERICANS: A GUIDE TO INFORMA-
TION SOURCES. Ethnic Studies Information Guide Series, vol.
2. Detroit: Gale Research Co., 1978. xix, 222 p.

Some two thousand entries are arranged under major cate-
gories: (1) "General Reference Works"; (2) "Social
Sciences"; (3) "History and Regional Studies"; (4) "Applied
Sciences"; (5) "Humanities." Entries on education of
Italian Americans can be found on pp. 77-84.

29 Cordasco, Francesco, and Covello, Leonard, comp. STUDIES OF
PUERTO RICAN CHILDREN IN AMERICAN SCHOOLS. A PRE-
LIMINARY BIBLIOGRAPHY. New York: Commonwealth of Puerto
Rico, Department of Labor, 1967. 25 p. Also in EDUCATION
LIBRARIES BULLETIN 31 (Spring 1968): 7-33; and JOURNAL OF
HUMAN RELATIONS 16 (1968): 264-85.

This unannotated bibliography lists works dealing with
Puerto Rican children and their experience in the mainland American schools. Unpublished and published materials are listed separately; some are in Spanish and a
number of them were produced by the New York City
Board of Education.

30 Cordasco, Francesco, et al. THE EQUALITY OF EDUCATIONAL
OPPORTUNITY: A BIBLIOGRAPHY OF SELECTED REFERENCES.
Totowa, N.J.: Littlefield, Adams and Co., 1973. 143 p.

This is primarily a bibliography of titles selected from
the vast literature spawned in the 1960s (and extending
into the next decade) which deals with the American

schools and the children of the poor--the minority child:
blacks, Puerto Ricans, Mexican Americans, Indians,
Appalachian poor, other ethnic minorities, and migrants.

31 Dossick, Jesse J. DOCTORAL RESEARCH ON PUERTO RICO
AND PUERTO RICANS. New York: New York University, School
of Education, 1967. 34 p.

This bibliography is a compilation of dissertations written since 1900, most of them in universities in the
United States. They are listed by author and title under twenty-one headings covering the fields of the natural sciences, the social and behavioral sciences, education, the arts and the humanities, and religion. About
one-third have been written in the field of education,
for the most part by Puerto Ricans.

32 ENGLISH AS A SECOND LANGUAGE IN ELEMENTARY SCHOOLS--
BACKGROUND AND TEXT MATERIALS. Washington, D.C.: Center for Applied Linguistics, 1967. 8 p.

This selective, annotated bibliography is a list of the
outstanding publications available in the field of teaching English as a second language in kindergarten and
elementary schools.

33 ERIC Clearinghouse on Early Childhood Education. BILINGUAL
EDUCATION FOR CHILDREN: AN ABSTRACT BIBLIOGRAPHY.
Urbana: College of Education, University of Illinois, 1975. 91 p.

This is a selective guide to recent ERIC documents on
bilingual education for children.

34 Goldberg, Gertrude S., and Gordon, Edmund W. PUERTO
RICAN MIGRANTS ON THE MAINLAND OF THE UNITED STATES.
New York: Yeshiva University, ERIC Clearinghouse on the Dis-
advantaged, 1968. 12 p.

This bulletin consists primarily of a review of research
which examines the social science literature dealing
with Puerto Ricans on the island as well as the mainland,
and two reviews, one of Oscar Lewis's LA VIDA, and
one of Piri Thomas's DOWN THESE MEAN STREETS.

35 Goldstein, Wallace L. TEACHING ENGLISH AS A SECOND
LANGUAGE: AN ANNOTATED BIBLIOGRAPHY. New York:
Garland Publishing, 1975. 218 p.

With an emphasis on the last ten years, the bibliography
is divided into seventeen topical sections: "Adult,"

"Audio-Lingual," "Audio-Visual," "Bilingual," "Curriculum," "Grammar," "Language Learning," "Methodology," "Reading," "Reference," "Socio-Cultural,"
"Spoken English," "Teacher Preparation," "Teaching
Aids," "Testing and Evaluation," "Texts," and "Writing."
In addition, it contains an author and a key-word index.

36 Gordon, Edmund W. DISADVANTAGED POPULATIONS. IRCD
Bulletin no. 3. New York: Yeshiva University, Project Beacon,
Ferkauf Graduate School of Humanities and Social Sciences, ERIC
Information Retrieval Center on the Disadvantaged, September,
1967. 8 p.

This bibliography contains a preface and is divided into
three main sections: (1) "Books"; (2) "Demographic and
Status Studies"; and (3) "Literature on Cultural and
Social Patterns." Also included are short book reviews
by Doxey Wilkerson of Kenneth Clark's DARK GHETTO
and by Clarence Senior of IMPERATIVE FOR CHANGE,
by Adelaide Jablonsky, ed.

37 Haller, Elizabeth S., comp. AMERICAN DIVERSITY: A BIBLI-
OGRAPHY OF RESOURCES ON RACIAL AND ETHNIC MINORI-
TIES FOR PENNSYLVANIA SCHOOLS. Harrisburg: Pennsylvania
State Department of Education, Bureau of General and Academic
Education, 1970. 250 p.

This bibliography was compiled to assist school personnel
in locating resources to implement the Curriculum Regulation adopted by the Pennsylvania State Board of Education in May 1968. The regulation requires that each
course in the history of the United States and of Pennsylvania taught in the elementary and secondary schools
include the major contributions made by blacks and other
racial and ethnic groups.

38 Harrigan, Joan, comp. MATERIALES TOCANTE LOS LATINOS:
A BIBLIOGRAPHY OF MATERIALS ON THE SPANISH-AMERICANS.
Denver: Colorado Department of Education, Division of Library
Services, October 1967. 36 p.

39 Haugen, Einar. BILINGUALISM IN THE AMERICAS: A BIBLIOG-
RAPHY AND RESEARCH GUIDE. University: University of Ala-
bama Press, 1956. 160 p.

A linguistic scholar presents under the auspices of the
American Dialect Society a synthesis of the extensive
literature in ten languages on the nature of the various
languages in the Western hemisphere, contact among

languages, the bilingual individual, and the bilingual
community. Attention is given to language attitudes and the
education of bilingual children, with special guidance
on approaches to research. The bibliography comprises
all the cited works plus starred titles in additional languages which were not consulted by Haugen. The
volume includes indexes of technical terms and of languages.

40 Herrera, Diane. PUERTO RICANS IN THE UNITED STATES. A
REVIEW OF THE LITERATURE. Austin, Tex.: Dissemination Cen-
ter for Bilingual Bicultural Education, 1973. 398 p. Reprint.
Detroit: Blaine Ethridge, 1978.

This is an extensive, annotated bibliography of over two thousand documents which covers the education of the Puerto
Rican child as well as the Puerto Rican experience on
the mainland (the latter from a psycho-socio-anthropologi-
cal perspective). Entries are complete through December
1972.

41 Hill, Marnesba D., comp. BIBLIOGRAPHY OF PUERTO RICAN
HISTORY AND LITERATURE. New York: City University,
Herbert H. Lehman College, 1972. 34 p.

This bibliography is a revised compilation of titles in
the Herbert H. Lehman College Library collection which
have a direct relationship to the area of Puerto Rican
studies. For easy reference, the bibliography is divided
into five broad categories: "Reference Books," "Biog-
raphy," "Education," "History and Social Science,"
"Language, Literature and the Arts."

42 HISPANIC AMERICANS IN THE UNITED STATES: A SELECTIVE
BIBLIOGRAPHY, 1963-1974. Washington, D.C.: U.S. Department of Housing and Urban Development, 1974. 28 p.

This bibliography includes: (1) general background, (2)
Mexican Americans, (3) Puerto Ricans and other Caribbean Spanish-speaking peoples, and (4) an author index.

43 Hopkins, Lee Bennett. LITERATURE ABOUT THE NEGRO AND
PUERTO RICAN CHILD. New York: Curriculum Consultation
Service, 1966. 4 p.

This annotated bibliography contains about twenty citations.

44 Hoyt, Anne K. BIBLIOGRAPHY OF THE CHEROKEES. North-
eastern State College Division of Library Science, Tahlequah,
Oklahoma. Bilingual Family School. Little Rock, Ark.: South
Central Region Educational Laboratory, 1969. 64 p.

Intended for those working with Cherokee young people,
this bibliography contains a comprehensive listing of
children's books about Cherokees and selective listings
of other related subjects such as folklore, education,
history, and language.

45 Jablonsky, Adelaide, comp. THE EDUCATION OF PUERTO
RICAN CHILDREN AND YOUTH: AN ANNOTATED BIBLIOG-
RAPHY OF DOCTORAL DISSERTATIONS. ERIC/IRCD Doctoral
Research Series, no. 6. New York: Columbia University, ERIC
Clearinghouse on the Urban Disadvantaged, 1974. 39 p.

This is an annotated bibliography which is organized
with the citations falling in three sections entitled:
"Studies of Puerto Rican Students on the Mainland,"
"Comparisons of Puerto Rican Students with Those of
Other Ethnic Groups," "Studies of Schools and Students
in Puerto Rico." Subject, author, and institution ac-
cess indexes are appended.

46 Kolm, Richard, ed. BIBLIOGRAPHY OF ETHNICITY AND ETH-
NIC GROUPS. Rockville, Md.: National Institute of Mental
Health, 1973. 250 p.

Intended as "a first step toward the development of an
ongoing comprehensive bibliography in the area of ethnicity," this bibliography includes in a general alphabetized list 451 annotated entries with some 1,000 additional unannotated entries.

47 Lado, Robert. ANNOTATED BIBLIOGRAPHY FOR TEACHERS OF
ENGLISH AS A FOREIGN LANGUAGE. U.S. Department of
Health, Education, and Welfare, Office of Education. Bulletin
1955, no. 3. Washington, D.C.: U.S. Government Printing
Office, 1955. 224 p.

This bibliography includes 730 items and covers the period from 1946 to 1953. It lists materials for the teacher
and the student, broken down according to the native
language background of the student.

48 Leopold, Werner F. BIBLIOGRAPHY OF CHILD LANGUAGE.
Northwestern University Studies, Humanities Series, no. 28.
Evanston, Ill.: Northwestern University Press, 1952. 115 p.

49 Link, Albert D., comp. MEXICAN AMERICAN EDUCATION:
A SELECTED BIBLIOGRAPHY WITH ERIC ABSTRACTS. Las Cruces:
ERIC Clearinghouse on Rural Education and Small Schools, New
Mexico State University, 1972. 345 p.

50 Lopez, Adalberto. "Puerto Ricans and the Literature of Puerto
Rico." JOURNAL OF ETHNIC STUDIES 1 (Summer 1973): 56-65.

This article is a brief critical review of available Puerto
Rican literature that is relevant for consideration by
Puerto Rican studies programs.

51 Mackey, William F. LE BILINGUISME CANADIEN: BIBLIOG-
RAPHIE ANALYTIQUE ET GUIDE DU CHERCHEUR. Quebec:
International Center for Research on Bilingualism, forthcoming.

Includes some five thousand titles limited to French-
English bilingualism in Canada.

52 _____, ed. BIBLIOGRAPHIE INTERNATIONALE SUR LE BILIN-
GUISME/INTERNATIONAL BIBLIOGRAPHY ON BILINGUALISM.
Quebec: Les Presses de Université Laval, 1972. xxviii, 337,
209, 203 p.

This basic bibliographical resource is a computer print-
out of an alphabetized and indexed checklist of 11,006
titles. See also SUPPLEMENT (1978) which lists an
additional nine thousand titles.

53 Malkoc, Anna Maria, comp. A TESOL BIBLIOGRAPHY: AB-
STRACTS OF ERIC PUBLICATIONS AND RESEARCH REPORTS
1969-1970. Washington, D.C.: Georgetown University, TESOL,
1971. 310 p.

54 Malkoc, Anna Maria, and Roberts, A.H. "Bilingual Education:
A Special Report from CAL-ERIC." ELEMENTARY ENGLISH 14
(May 1970): 713-25.

This article is a bibliographical overview with annotations and evaluations.

55 MATERIALS AND HUMAN RESOURCES FOR TEACHING ETHNIC
STUDIES: AN ANNOTATED BIBLIOGRAPHY. Boulder: Social
Sciences Education Consortium, 1975. xi, 275 p. Reprint. New
York Times Bilingual Bicultural Education in the United States
Series. New York: Arno Press/New York Times, 1978.

This bibliography is "An analysis and dissemination of
ethnic heritage studies curriculum materials," funded by

a U.S. Office of Education grant. The materials col-
lected relate to the experiences and lives of ethnic
peoples in the United States and includes materials on
blacks, Mexican Americans, and Puerto Ricans. It also
includes Afro-Americans, Asian Americans, and Pacific
Americans, British Americans, Central and Western
European Americans, East European Americans, Irish
Americans, Italian Americans, Jewish Americans, Latin
Americans and Caribbean Americans, Mediterranean
Americans, Mexican Americans, Native Americans and
Scandinavian Americans.

56 Mickey, Barbara H. A BIBLIOGRAPHY OF STUDIES CONCERN-
ING THE SPANISH-SPEAKING POPULATION OF THE AMERICAN
SOUTHWEST. Greeley: Colorado State College, Museum of
Anthropology, 1969. 42 p.

Largely anthropological in orientation, this bibliography
includes 544 entries and cites published and unpublished
materials.

57 Miller, Wayne. A COMPREHENSIVE BIBLIOGRAPHY FOR THE
STUDY OF AMERICAN MINORITIES. 2 vols. New York: New
York University Press, 1976.

Included in this bibliography are 29,300 entries of English-
language materials for most American minority groups.
A companion volume, A HANDBOOK OF AMERICAN
MINORITIES (xi, 225 p.) reprints the preliminary bibliographical essays for each of the minority groups in the
parent work.

58 Mobilization for Youth. "An Other-Directed Fantasy in a Puerto
Rican." THE ANNOTATED BIBLIOGRAPHY 1 (1962): 10-11.

This report of a cross-cultural research studies adolescents
who show superior effectiveness and creativity in the
academic, extracurricular and interpersonal spheres.

59 Moreland, Lilian. A SELECT BIBLIOGRAPHY ON BILINGUALISM.
Capetown, South Africa: University of Capetown, 1948. 37 p.

A partially annotated list of 161 items, this bibliography
emphasizes Belgium, Canada, Finland, Ireland, South
Africa, Switzerland, and Wales.

60 Navarro, Eliseo, comp. THE CHICANO COMMUNITY: A
SELECTED BIBLIOGRAPHY FOR USE IN SOCIAL WORK EDUCA-
TION. New York: Council on Social Work Education, 1971.
57 p.

61 New Mexico Department of Education. Cross-Cultural Education
Unit. BILINGUAL-BICULTURAL BIBLIOGRAPHY. Santa Fe:
New Mexico Department of Education, 1974. 38 p.

62 New York City. Board of Education. Bilingual Resource Center.
MATERIALS USED IN BILINGUAL PROGRAMS. New York: 1973.
17 p.

> This list of instructional materials used in bilingual pro-
> grams, includes textbooks, educational materials, and
> audiovisual aids used in the various school districts of
> New York City.

63 New York Public Library, New York. BORINQUEN: A BILIN-
GUAL LIST OF BOOKS, FILMS AND RECORDS ON THE PUERTO
RICAN EXPERIENCE. 3d ed. New York: Office of Branch
Libraries, New York Public Library, 1974. 43 p.

64 Ney, James W., and Eberle, Donnella K., comps. CAL and
ERIC Clearinghouse on Languages. "Bilingual/Bicultural Education." LINGUISTIC REPORTS 17 (January 1975): 1-44.

65 Nogales, Luis G., ed. THE MEXICAN AMERICAN: A SELECTED
AND ANNOTATED BIBLIOGRAPHY. 2d ed. Stanford: Stanford
University, Center for Latin American Studies, 1971. 162 p.

66 Ohannessian, Sirapi, ed., with assistance of Carol J. Kreidler,
Beryl Dwight, and Julia Sableski. REFERENCE LISTS OF MATE-
RIALS FOR ENGLISH AS A SECOND LANGUAGE. 2 vols.
Washington, D.C.: Center for Applied Linguistics, 1964-66.

> This comprehensive annotated bibliography covers mate-
> rials on the teaching of English as a second language
> produced between 1953 and 1963, and is divided into
> part 1: TEXTS, READERS, DICTIONARIES, TESTS and
> part 2: BACKGROUND MATERIALS, METHODOLOGY.
> See also entry no. 71.

67 Ortiz, Ana Maria, comp. BIBLIOGRAPHY ON HISPANO AMERI-
CAN HISTORY AND CULTURE. Springfield: Illinois State Commission on Human Relations, Department of Education Services,
1972. 25 p.

> This bibliography incorporates 145 entries written between
> 1945 and 1969 for children and students, teachers, li-
> brarians, parents, and people interested in learning about
> Hispano-Americans. Included are the following: (1) an
> introduction in English and Spanish, (2) 41 entries about

general history and culture, (3) 50 entries on the Puerto Rican experience, (4) 21 entries of selected reading materials on the Chicano and Mexican-American experience, and (5) 23 resource and story books for children. An addendum lists some recommendations for book purchasing.

68 Osborn, Lynn R. A BIBLIOGRAPHY OF NORTH AMERICAN INDIAN SPEECH AND SPOKEN LANGUAGE. Lawrence: University of Kansas; Communication Research Center, 1968. 55 p.

This comprehensive bibliography draws together citations to relevant materials concerning the spoken language of the North American Indian. It includes 132 theses and dissertations and 500 articles, books, and published reports from both domestic and foreign sources.

69 Padilla, Amaldo M., and Aranda, Paul. LATINO MENTAL HEALTH: BIBLIOGRAPHY AND ABSTRACTS. Washington, D.C.: U.S. Government Printing Office, 1974. 288 p.

This bibliography was done under contract with U.S. Department of Health, Education, and Welfare; the National Institute of Mental Health; and the Alcohol, Drug Abuse, and Mental Health Administration.

70 Pedreira, Antonio S. BIBLIOGRAFIA PUERTORRIQUENA, 1493-1930. Madrid: Imprenta de Hernando, 1932. Reissued with a foreword by Francesco Cordasco. New York: Burt Franklin, 1974. xxii, 707 p.

This vast repository of some ten thousand entries includes sections on "Bibliographical Sources"; "General Information"; "Natural History"; "Public Health"; "Social Economy"; "Political and Administrative History"; "Cultural Organization"; "History of Puerto Rico"; "Literary History"; and "Miscellaneous Works."

71 Pedtke, Dorothy, ed. REFERENCE LIST OF MATERIALS FOR ENGLISH AS A SECOND LANGUAGE: SUPPLEMENT. Washington, D.C.: Center for Applied Linguistics, 1969. 200 p.

72 Perlman, Shirley. BOOKS ABOUT PUERTO RICO AND PUERTO RICAN CHILDREN. New York: Mobilization for Youth, 1963. 21 p.

The first section contains a bibliography intended primarily for use with Puerto Rican children, both English and non-English speaking. Books in Spanish have also

been included. The second section is a teacher's guide
to using the bibliography within the curriculum.

73 Pietrzyk, Alfred, et al. SELECTED TITLES IN SOCIOLINGUIS-
TICS: AN INTERIM BIBLIOGRAPHY OF WORKS ON MULTILIN-
GUALISM LANGUAGE STANDARDIZATION, AND LANGUAGES
OF WIDER COMMUNICATION. Washington, D.C.: Center for
Applied Linguistics, 1967. 226 p.

The primary emphasis is on language in its relation to
sociological phenomena. It includes a bibliographic
listing relevant to the field, and general reference works
are included.

74 Pinero, Ivan. A BIBLIOGRAPHY OF BILINGUAL AND BICUL-
TURAL EDUCATION. New York: Bilingual Resource Center,
1975. 78 p.

Covers the period 1970-74.

75 Pochmann, H., comp., and Schultz, A., ed. BIBLIOGRAPHY
OF GERMAN CULTURE IN AMERICA TO 1940. Madison: University of Wisconsin Press, 1953. 483 p.

This massive bibliography on German Americans contained an index which lists 170 entries under the single
heading "German American Schools."

76 Randolph, H. Helen. URBAN EDUCATION 1963-1964: AN
ANNOTATED BIBLIOGRAPHY WITH A SUPPLEMENT. New York:
Center for Urban Education, 1968. 86 p.

For information on ethnic communities and the problem
of culture conflict as it relates to Puerto Ricans, see pp.
40-42.

77 Revelle, Keith. "A Collection for La Raza." LIBRARY JOURNAL
47 (15 November 1971): 3719-26.

Lists Spanish as well as English publications.

78 Salazar, Teresa Ann. "Bilingual Education Bibliography." Ed.D.
disseration, University of Northern Colorado, 1975. 127 p.

79 Sanchez, George I., and Putnam, Howard. MATERIALS RELAT-
ING TO THE EDUCATION OF SPANISH-SPEAKING PEOPLE IN
THE UNITED STATES: AN ANNOTATED BIBLIOGRAPHY. Latin
American Studies 17. Austin: University of Texas, Institute of
Latin American Studies, 1959. 76 p.

Concerned primarily with the education of Spanish-
speaking people in the United States who are of Mexican descent, this annotated bibliography will also be of
value to those working with other Spanish-speaking people and Puerto Ricans. The list cites selected books,
articles, monographs, bulletins, pamphlets, courses of
study, bibliographies, and unpublished theses and dissertations written between 1923 and 1954. There are 882
entries, which are cross-referenced under 53 headings
in the index.

80 Smith, Jessie Carney. "Minorities in the United States: Guide
to Resources." Nashville, Tenn.: George Peabody College for
Teachers, Peabody Library School, 1973. 133 p. Mimeographed.

This guide is a study of minority cultures through an introduction to the literature of certain minority groups in
the United States: Native Americans, blacks, Chinese,
Japanese, and Puerto Ricans. It is intended primarily
as a guide for libraries, library school students, library
schools, other educators, and other students who are interested in bibliographic and other resources for the
study of various minorities.

81 TEACHER TRAINING BIBLIOGRAPHY: AN ANNOTATED LISTING
OF MATERIALS FOR BILINGUAL-BICULTURAL EDUCATION.
Austin, Tex.: Dissemination and Assessment Center for Bilingual
Education, 1975. 61 p.

Included in this bibliography are seven major categories
in which some two hundred items are listed.

82 Texas, University of. Libraries. MEXICAN AMERICANS: A
SELECTED BIBLIOGRAPHY. Houston: The Library, 1972. 73 p.

83 Trejo, Arnulfo D., ed. BIBLIOGRAPHIA CHICANA: A GUIDE TO
INFORMATION SOURCES. Ethnic Studies Information Guide
Series, vol. 1. Detroit: Gale Research Co., 1975. xx, 193 p.

This comprehensive bibliography on Mexican Americans
is arranged under five major headings: (1) "General
Reference Works"; (2) "Humanities"; (3) "History"; (4)
"Applied Sciences"; and (5) "Social Sciences." Entries
on education of Mexican-American children are also included.

84 Trueba, Henry T. BILINGUAL BICULTURAL EDUCATION FOR
THE SPANISH SPEAKING IN THE UNITED STATES: A PRELIMI-

NARY BIBLIOGRAPHY. Champaign, Ill.: Stipes Publishing Co., 1977. 176 p.

This bibliography is arranged by topical index categories which "represent the major disciplinary and theoretical concerns of scholars in the field of bilingual education."

85 U.S. Cabinet Committee on Opportunities for Spanish Speaking People. THE SPANISH SPEAKING IN THE UNITED STATES: A GUIDE TO MATERIALS. Washington, D.C.: Government Printing Office, 1971. Reprint. Foreword by Francesco Cordasco. Detroit: Blaine Ethridge, 1975. xvi, 175 p.

This concise bibliographical guide lists some seventeen hundred entries, on Mexican Americans, Puerto Ricans, and Cubans.

86 U.S. Department of Labor. Migration Division. Commonwealth of Puerto Rico. BIBLIOGRAPHY ON PUERTO RICO AND PUERTO RICANS. New York: n.d. 6 p.

This bibliography is abstracted from an annotated bibliography by Clarence Senior.

87 U.S. Immigration Commission. REPORT OF THE IMMIGRATION COMMISSION. Washington, D.C.: U.S. Government Printing Office, 1911. Reprint. THE CHILDREN OF IMMIGRANTS IN SCHOOLS. Vols. 29-33. With new introductory essay by Francesco Cordasco. Metuchen, N.J.: Scarecrow Reprint New Corp., 1970.

This report is a vast repository of data on immigrant children (analyses of backgrounds, nativity, school progress, home environments, and so forth). In all, 2,036,376 school children are included (in both public and parochial schools in 37 cities). Also, data on 32,882 students in higher education and 49,067 public school teachers. "The purpose of the investigation was to determine as far as possible to what extent immigrant children are availing themselves of educational facilities and what progress they make in school work."

88 U.S. Inter-Agency Committee on Mexican American Affairs. THE MEXICAN AMERICAN: A NEW FOCUS ON OPPORTUNITY: A GUIDE TO MATERIALS RELATING TO PERSONS OF MEXICAN HERITAGE IN THE UNITED STATES. Washington, D.C.: 1969, 186 p.

89 Utah, University of. Library. CHICANO BIBLIOGRAPHY. Salt Lake City: 1973. 295 p.

90 Vivo, Paquita, ed. THE PUERTO RICANS. AN ANNOTATED BIBLIOGRAPHY. New York: R.R. Bowker Co., 1973. xv, 299 p.

   This selected bibliography attempts to cover the many diverse aspects of Puerto Rican life, including history, culture, education, music, science, social conditions, and many others. It covers the pre-Columbian era through contemporary political thought and economic development as well as the entire spectrum of thinking on Puerto Rican affairs, especially political.

91 Wales, University College of. LLYFRYDDIAETH. DWYIETHEG: BILINGUALISM: A BIBLIOGRAPHY WITH SPECIAL REFERENCE TO WALES. Aberystwyth: University College of Wales, Faculty of Education, 1960. 55 p.

   This research guide for bilingualism throughout the world contains 784 items listed in alphabetical order.

92 Wares, Alan C., comp. BIBLIOGRAPHY OF THE SUMMER INSTITUTE OF LINGUISTICS: 1935-1968. Santa Ana, Calif.: Summer Institute of Linguistics, 1968. 124 p.

   Containing 2,514 entries dealing with close to three hundred languages (not including separate dialects), this bibliography represents the work of more than 670 different authors. There are basically three types of output: general works, articles and monographs on specific languages, and educational materials written in a specific language.

93 Wasserman, Paul, and Morgan, Jean. ETHNIC INFORMATION SOURCES OF THE UNITED STATES. Detroit: Gale Research Co., 1976. 751 p.

   This bibliography contains data on some one hundred nationality, immigrant, and religious groups in the United States, excluding blacks, American Indians, and Eskimos.

94 "We Talk, You Listen: A Selected Bibliography." PERSONNEL AND GUIDANCE JOURNAL 50 (October 1971): 145-46.

   An adjunct to the articles contained in the same issue on ethnic groups, this bibliography is designed to assist readers, particularly counselors, in expanding their knowledge of such groups through readings by Chicanos, Indians, and Puerto Ricans.

95 Wilgus, Karna S., comp. LATIN AMERICAN BOOKS: AN ANNOTATED BIBLIOGRAPHY FOR HIGH SCHOOL AND COLLEGES. Rev. ed. New York: Center for Inter-American Relations, 1974. 82 p.

This annotated bibliography citing 479 books on Latin America, includes two new sections—one on Puerto Rico and Puerto Ricans in the United States, and one on Mexican Americans. Individual sections deal with general works, geography, history, art, music, literature, economics, politics, hemisphere relations, and sociology.

96 Williams, Frederick, and Naremore, Rita C. LANGUAGE AND POVERTY: AN ANNOTATED BIBLIOGRAPHY. Madison: University of Wisconsin, 1968. 42 p.

This bibliography contains 124 annotated entries. The following conclusion was reached: "A poverty environment has a socializing influence upon its population, an influence which manifests itself in distinctions of language and cognition, and these distinctions in turn serve in the definition and perpetuation of that population as a poverty culture."

97 Zirkel, Perry Alan. A BIBLIOGRAPHY OF MATERIALS IN ENGLISH AND SPANISH RELATING TO PUERTO RICAN STUDENTS. West Hartford, Conn.: University of Hartford, Migratory Children's Program, 1971. 51 p.

The contents of this bibliography are intended as resources for teachers and other persons concerned with improving the educational opportunities of Puerto Rican pupils on the mainland as well as on the island. It is organized in four sections: (1) "Books: Puerto Rican Culture in English, Puerto Rican Culture in Spanish, and Children's Fiction"; (2) "Audiovisual Materials: Films, Filmstrips, Recordings, and Others"; (3) "Research Studies"; and (4) "Bibliographies".

98 _____, comp. PUERTO RICAN PUPILS: A BIBLIOGRAPHY. West Hartford, Conn.: University of Hartford, 1973. 67 p.

This bibliography is intended as a resource for teachers and other persons concerned with improving the educational opportunities of Puerto Rican pupils on the mainland as well as those on the island. It includes books, audiovisual materials, self-contained research studies, and periodical articles.

II. GENERAL AND MISCELLANEOUS

99 Aarons, Alfred C.; Gordon, Barbara Y.; and Stewart, William A.[C.], eds. "Linguistic-Cultural Differences and American Education." FLORIDA FL REPORTER 7 (Spring-Summer 1969): 1-175.

100 Abraham, Willard. "The Bilingual Child, His Parents and THEIR School." EXCEPTIONAL CHILDREN 23 (November 1956): 51-52, 80.

   This article is a plea to the school, parents, and community to take better care of bilingual children, an important category of "exceptional children."

101 _____. "The Bilingual Child and His Teacher." ELEMENTARY ENGLISH 34 (November 1957): 474-78.

   This article describes the educational situation of Spanish-speaking children in Arizona.

102 Abrahams, Roger D., and Troike, Rudolph C., eds. LANGUAGE AND CULTURAL DIVERSITY IN AMERICAN EDUCATION. Englewood Cliffs, N.J.: Prentice-Hall, 1972. 156 p.

103 Adorno, William. "The Attitudes of Selected Mexican and Mexican American Parents in Regards to Bilingual/Bicultural Education." Ph.D dissertation, United States International University, 1973. 225 p.

   This dissertation is an assessment of parent understanding of bilingual education. Seventy-five parents in California were involved and favored their children knowing about American and Mexican cultures for both practical and idealistic reasons.

104 Aguirre, Adalberto, Jr., and Fernandez, Celestino. "Mexican Americans and Bicultural Education: A Sociological Analysis." ATISBOS: JOURNAL OF CHICANO RESEARCH 2 (Winter 1976-77): 15-26.

A study of bilingual-bicultural education in the process of being influenced by Anglo-American educational technology, this article maintains that inadequate concern has been shown for the sociocultural variables which affect Mexican-American educational attitudes.

105 Allen, Harold B. A SURVEY OF THE TEACHING OF ENGLISH TO NON-ENGLISH SPEAKERS IN THE UNITED STATES. New York: Teachers College Press, Columbia University, 1966. Reprint. New York Times Bilingual and Bicultural Education in the United States Series. New York: Arno Press, 1978. vi, 158 p.

Known generally as the TENES report, this survey and its voluminous data continue to be very useful and important. The report is based on 810 questionnaires, of a total of 1,683, sent to administrators in universities, colleges, and other agencies, requesting information on the teaching of English as a second language. The data sought included classification and number of personnel; policies for employing prospective teachers; actual preparation of teachers; structure and curriculum; number and foreign-language background of students; teaching aids available; use of commercial texts and tests; identification of problems and needs.

106 Anderson, Nels, ed. STUDIES IN MULTILINGUALISM. Leiden, Netherlands: E.J. Brill, 1969. 276 p.

107 Andersson, Theodore. "A New Focus on the Bilingual Child." THE MODERN LANGUAGE JOURNAL 49 (March 1965): 156-60.

This article suggests the need to correct present miseducation of Spanish speakers of the Southwest by the means of bilingual education, the principles of which could then be applied to language education in general.

108 _____. "The Bilingual in the Southwest." THE FLORIDA FL REPORTER 5 (Spring 1967): 3.

This brief statement was written in support of the Bilingual Education Act having to do with the Mexican-American child, often called a "bilingual," and "thoughtlessly, sometimes disparagingly, referred to by his teachers as a person 'who knows neither Spanish nor English.'"

109 _____. "Bilingual Elementary Schooling: A Report to Texas Educators." THE FLORIDA FL REPORTER 6 (Fall 1968): 3-4, 6, 25.

A concise statement on the principles of bilingual education this report suggests guidelines for bilingual programs.

110 _____. "Bilingual Education: The American Experience." THE MODERN LANGUAGE JOURNAL 55 (November 1971): 427-40.

111 _____. "Extending Bilingual Education into the Home." FOREIGN LANGUAGE ANNALS 8 (December 1975): 302-5.

This article states that parents, grandparents, and siblings can help develop the learning potential of pre-school children who are to participate in bilingual bicultural programs. Schools can help with materials and staff.

112 _____. "The Bilingual Child's Right to Read." JOURNAL OF THE NATIONAL ASSOCIATION FOR BILINGUAL EDUCATION 1 (May 1976): 17-21.

113 _____. "Popular and Elite Bilingualism Reconciled." HISPANIA 59 (September 1976): 497-98.

114 _____. "What Lessons Does Bilingual Education Hold for Foreign Language Teacher Trainers?" MODERN LANGUAGE JOURNAL 61 (April 1977): 159-60.

This article argues that foreign-language teachers would be better educators if they enjoyed the kind of training provided for bilingual teachers.

115 Arsenian, Seth. "Bilingualism in the Post-War World." PSYCHOLOGICAL BULLETIN 42 (February 1945): 65-68.

This article treats a variety of problems related to this "widespread phenomenon": (1) its measurement, (2) its relation to mental development, (3) its relation to language development, (4) its relation to school achievement ment, (5) its relation to speech and other motor functions, (6) its relation to personal and social adjustment, (7) its relation to learning a second language, and (8) its relation to the political state.

116 _____. BILINGUALISM AND MENTAL DEVELOPMENT: A STUDY OF THE INTELLECTUAL AND THE SOCIAL BACKGROUND OF BILINGUAL CHILDREN IN NEW YORK CITY. New York: Columbia University, Teachers College Press, 1973. Reprint. New York: AMS Press, 1973. vi, 164 p.

On Jewish and Italian immigrant children. Originally published as No. 712, Teachers College Contribution to Education.

117 Aspira. HEMOS TRABAJDO BIEN: A REPORT ON THE FIRST NATIONAL CONFERENCE OF PUERTO RICANS, MEXICAN-AMERICANS, AND EDUCATORS ON THE SPECIAL EDUCATIONAL NEEDS OF URBAN PUERTO RICAN YOUTH. New York: 1968. 78 p.

The proceedings consist primarily of brief summaries of conference workshops on: (1) teacher attitudes, (2) student attitudes, (3) curriculum and textbooks, (4) parent attitudes and community involvement, (5) the role of special efforts and programs, (6) preparation for postsecondary education, (7) positive self-identity and group life, (8) public politics and community power in education.

118 Aucamp, A.J. BILINGUAL EDUCATION AND NATIONALISM WITH SPECIAL REFERENCE TO SOUTH AFRICA. Pretoria, S. Africa: J.L. Van Schaik, 1926. Reprint. New York Times Bilingual Bicultural Education in the United States Series. New York: Arno Press, 1978. 247 p.

Originally a doctoral dissertation at Columbia University, this work is a detailed and documented study of the interrelationships of politics, society, language, and education, in historical context, in Wales, Scotland, and Ireland; and in the provinces of Ontario and Quebec, with particular stress on the rights of minorities. Aucamp also studies the controversial issue of French and Flemish (Dutch) instruction in Belgium, and the questions regarding the teaching of Afrikaans and English in South Africa. Of special significance are the conclusions which explore the concepts of nationalism, democracy, and internationalism in relation to governmental policy with regard to bilingual education. Appendixes include valuable source materials on school regulations concerning bilingual education in the countries discussed, and very comprehensive bibliographies.

119 Axelrod, Herman C. BILINGUAL BACKGROUND AND ITS RE-LATION TO CERTAIN ASPECTS OF CHARACTER AND RESPONSI-

BILITY OF ELEMENTARY SCHOOL CHILDREN. New York Times
Bilingual Bicultural Education in the United States Series. New
York: Arno Press, 1978. 192 p.

More than twelve hundred elementary school children
(with varying degrees of bilingual background) attending
public schools and representing three groups (Italian,
Jewish, and Polish) were selected for this study. All
were born in the United States and lived in predominantly
bilingual neighborhoods in New York City. Axelrod's
major aim in this investigation was "to study by means
of objective measures certain aspects of school conduct
and adjustment among bilingual children." The conclusions indicate that the "problem of bilingualism in the
United States involves much more than the use of two
languages. Bilingual background, viewed more broadly,
implies a bicultural background which may produce social
and emotional conflicts." It states that the inherent use
of two languages by the native-born child of immigrant
parents does not lead to maladjustment. In Alexrod's
view, "where a conscious and intelligent effort is made
by the parents and the school to harmonize and recon-
cile divergent elements in both cultures, the conflict
may be reduced or eliminated, and a major cause of
maladjustment removed." Originally Ph.D. dissertation,
Yeshiva University, 1951.

120 Badillo, Herman. "Politicas Y Realides de la Education Bilingue
en Norte-america." YELMO 8 (October-November 1972): 38-40.

Anglo-Americans, bilingual students, bilingualism,
minority groups, political attitudes, Puerto Ricans, and
Spanish speaking are discussed.

121 _____. "Bilingual Education." INTEGRATED EDUCATION 13
(May-June 1975): 166-67.

This article points out that there are not only the language problems faced by the Puerto Rican community,
but by those who are French (Haitian), Greek, and
Chinese speaking. The views were offered at a public
hearing of the New York City Commission on Human
Rights, May 1974.

122 Bauer, Evelyn. "Teaching English to North American Indians in
B.I.A. Schools." THE LINGUISTIC REPORTER 10 (August 1968):
1-3.

This article outlines the B.I.A. programs of the teaching of English as a second language, and stresses the
need for and progress toward bilingual education.

123 Bell, Paul W. "Bilingual Education in an American Elementary School." In LANGUAGES AND THE YOUNG SCHOOL CHILD. Edited by H.H. Steer, pp. 112-18. London: Oxford University Press, 1969.

This article is a description of the Coral Way Elementary School in Miami, Florida.

124 Berkson, Isaac B. THEORIES OF AMERICANIZATION: A CRITICAL STUDY. New York: Teacher's College Press, Columbia University, 1920. Reprint. New York: Arno Press, 1970. 240 p.

This study is an early, now classic, statement of the case for cultural pluralism, especially Jewish, in American education.

125 Bernal, Ernest M., Jr. "Concept-learning among Anglo, Black and Mexican-American Children Using Facilitation Strategies and Bilingual Techniques." Ph.D. dissertation, University of Texas, 1971. 123 p.

126 Berrol, Selma Cantor. IMMIGRANTS AT SCHOOL: NEW YORK CITY, 1898-1914. New York Times Bilingual Bicultural Education in the United States Series. New York: Arno Press, 1978. 438 p.

In this comprehensive study of immigrant Jewish and Italian children in New York City schools, Berrol provides invaluable historical backgrounds on the responses of American schools to the culturally different and language-minority child. The objectives of the study were to find out what changes were made in the educational structure of the city under the pressure of the Italian and Jewish immigrant groups, and to determine "if there were any clues to the viability of the New York City schools of today ascertainable in the developments of sixty years ago." Among the many new educational programs initiated during the period (intended largely to assimilate the immigrant child), Berrol discusses the "Grade C" classes, rudimentary beginnings of bilingual education, intended for the non-English child.

127 Betances, Samuel. "Puerto Ricans and Mexican Americans in Higher Education." RICAN 1 (May 1974): 27-36.

This report focuses on the problems which Mexican Americans, Puerto Ricans, and to a lesser degree, Cubans face in relating to higher education.

128 "Biculturalism and Education." THE JOURNAL OF EDUCATION
9 (January 1964): 1-112.

>   This collection of fifteen articles is on French-English
>   bilingualism in Canada.

129 BILINGUAL EDUCATION. Focus 2. Princeton, N.J.: Educational Testing Service, 1976. 19 p.

>   This book is a general overview of "an idea whose time
>   has come again: bilingual education."

130 Blossom, Grace A. "A New Approach to an Old Problem."
JOURNAL OF AMERICAN INDIAN EDUCATION 1 (January 1962):
13-14.

>   The article discusses the relationship between the shift
>   from "speaking" to "comprehension" vocabulary in upper-
>   grade texts and the widespread belief that retardation
>   for many bilingual Indian students starts at the fourth-
>   grade level.

131 Boody, Bertha M. A PSYCHOLOGICAL STUDY OF IMMIGRANT
CHILDREN AT ELLIS ISLAND. Baltimore: Johns Hopkins University Press, 1926. Reprint. New York: Arno Press, 1970. 163 p.

>   This monograph indicates the results of a psychological
>   survey of immigrant children testing the charge of innate
>   inferiority of recent nationalities. The author stationed
>   herself at Ellis Island in the years of heaviest migration,
>   1922 and 1923, to examine incoming children.

132 Botana, Joseph. "Community Involvement in Bilingual Programs."
ILLINOIS CAREER EDUCATION JOURNAL 33 (February 1975):
17-18.

133 Boyer, Mildred V. "Some Misconceptions About Teaching American Ethnic Children Their Mother Tongue." THE MODERN LAN-
GUAGE JOURNAL 48 (February 1964): 67-71.

>   The article points out that mother-tongue teachers of the
>   same ethnic background are regarded with sympathy by
>   their students; yet they rarely recognize or appreciate
>   an immigrant child's linguistic heritage.

134 _____. "Bilingual Schooling: A Dimension of Democracy."
TEXAS FOREIGN LANGUAGE ASSOCIATION BULLETIN 2 (December 1968): 1-6.

>   This address to the Texas Foreign Language Association,
>   Fort Worth, answers such questions as "What is bilingual
>   education, and what and whom is it for?"

135 Broman, Betty. "The Spanish-Speaking Five Year Old." CHILD-
HOOD EDUCATION 41 (1972): 362-64.

136 Brooks, Nelson H. "The Meaning of Bilingualism Today." FOR-
EIGN LANGUAGE ANNALS 2 (March 1969): 304-9.

> The article defines bilingualism as the habitual use of
> two languages by the same person and emphasizes the
> fact that in its purest form the two languages are quite
> separate.

137 Brophy, J.E. "Mothers as Teachers of Their Own Preschool Children: The influence of Socioeconomic Status and Task Structure
on Teaching Specificity." CHILD DEVELOPMENT 41 (1970):
79-94.

138 Cafferty, Pastora San Juan. "Puerto Rican Return Migration: Its
Implications for Bilingual Education." ETHNICITY 2 (March 1975):
52-65.

> The movement to and from Puerto Rico creates serious
> problems for Puerto Rican children who have to con-
> front two monolingual school systems.

139 Canada. Royal Commission on Bilingualism and Biculturalism.
PRELIMINARY REPORT. Book 1: THE OFFICIAL LANGUAGES.
Book 2: EDUCATION. New York Times Bilingual Bicultural
Education in the United States Series. New York: Arno Press,
1978. 773 p.

> Canada established a Royal Commission on Bilingualism
> and Biculturalism in 1963 whose publications constitute
> an invaluable repository of materials on the sociological,
> political, and educational challenges faced by modern
> states in dealing with the complex needs of language
> minorities; the findings of the Royal Commission include
> a vast assemblage of data of value to all societies dealing
> with the needs of ethnic minorities. The three reports
> selected from the Royal Commission's many publications
> constitute a compendious resource on all aspects of soci-
> etal bilingualism and biculturalism. The PRELIMINARY
> REPORT is a summary of the Commission's deliberations
> with a conspectus of preliminary conclusions; Book 1:
> GENERAL INTRODUCTION: THE OFFICIAL LANGUAGES
> is both a sociological and historical review of the origins,
> developments, and status of bilingualism and biculturalism
> in Canada; and Book 2: EDUCATION is a comprehensive
> treatise on bilingual-bicultural practice in modern Canada
> with reference to established policy and objectives to be
> achieved.

140 Candelaria, Cordelia. "The Future of Bilingual Multicultural Education." AGENDA 7 (March–April 1977): 30-33.

> Some of the main topics are cross-cultural training, the
> educational assessment of English as a second language
> and student evaluation.

141 Cannon, Garland. "Bilingual Problems and Developments in the
United States." PUBLICATIONS OF THE MODERN LANGUAGE
ASSOCIATION OF AMERICA 86 (1971): 452-58.

142 Cárdenas, Blandina. "Broadening the Concept of Bilingual Education." INTEGRATED EDUCATION 13 (May–June 1975): 171-72.

> Cárdenas, who holds the position of the consultant on
> Bilingual Education for Texans for Educational Excell-
> ence, points to some of the ways in which discrimina-
> tory practices are associated with languages and other
> forms of expression.

143 Cárdenas, Blandina, and Cárdenas, José A. THE THEORY OF
INCOMPATIBILITIES: A CONCEPTUAL FRAMEWORK FOR RE-
SPONDING TO THE EDUCATIONAL NEEDS OF MEXICAN
AMERICAN CHILDREN. San Antonio, Tex.: Intercultural De-
velopment Research Association, 1972. 41 p.

144 Carranza, Michael, and Ryan, Ellen Bouchard. "Evaluation Reactions of Bilingual Anglo and Mexican American Adolescents
toward Speakers of English and Spanish." INTERNATIONAL
JOURNAL OF THE SOCIOLOGY OF LANGUAGE 6 (1975): 82-
104.

145 Carrow, Sister Mary A[rthur]. "Linguistic Functioning of Bilingual
and Monolingual Children." JOURNAL OF SPEECH AND HEARING
DISORDERS 22 (1957): 371-80.

146 Carter, Ruth Barrera. "A Study of Attitudes: Mexican American
and Anglo American Elementary Teachers' Judgments of Mexican
American Bilingual Children's Speech." Ed.D. dissertation, University of Houston, 1976. 146 p.

> Fifty-two Anglo-American and forty-eight Mexican-
> American teachers reacted to each of nine speech sam-
> ples on the semantic differential instrument. The find-
> ings show there are statistically significant differences
> in teachers' attitudes toward speakers of minimally ac-
> cented, and highly accented English. The attitudes of
> Mexican-American teachers was more tolerant toward
> all types of speakers.

147 Carter, Thomas P. MEXICAN AMERICANS IN SCHOOL: A HISTORY OF EDUCATIONAL NEGLECT. New York: College Entrance Examination Board, 1970. 235 p.

148 Carton, Aaron S., et al. "Education of the Underprivileged. A Three-Part Section: Poverty Programs, Civil Rights, and the American School. SCHOOL AND SOCIETY 95 (18 February 1967): 108-10, 115-19.

149 Case, C.C. "Navaho Education: Is There Hope?" EDUCATIONAL FORUM 29 (November 1971): 129-32.

150 Caspar, M.G. "Education of Menominee Youth in Wisconsin." INTEGRATED EDUCATION 11 (January 1973): 45-51.

151 Castellanos, Diego. THE HISPANIC EXPERIENCE IN NEW JER-SEY SCHOOLS: AN ISSUE PAPER ON A TOPICAL SUBJECT IN EDUCATION. Trenton: New Jersey State Department of Education, Division of Research, Planning and Evaluation, 1972. 19 p.

   The report discusses the special problems of the His-panic population in New Jersey schools. It describes the joint efforts of the Department of Education, the Commissioner of Education, community groups, and schools to find ways to resolve the problems facing the Spanish speaking.

152 Center for Applied Linguistics. A HANDBOOK FOR STAFF DE-VELOPMENT WORKSHOPS IN INDIAN EDUCATION. Arlington, Va.: Center for Applied Linguistics, 1976. 58 p.

153 _____. BILINGUAL EDUCATION: CURRENT PERSPECTIVES. 5 vols. Arlington, Va.: Center for Applied Linguistics, 1977.

   This overview of information on all aspects of bilingual education, includes the following volumes: Vol. 1: SOCIAL SCIENCE, Vol. 2: LINGUISTICS, Vol. 3: LAW, Vol. 4: EDUCATION, and Vol. 5: SYNTHESIS (an overview of the first four volumes including a sub-ject index and working bibliography).

154 Chesarek, Rose. "Bilingual and Bicultural Indian Education in Montana." NORTHIAN 7 (Winter 1971): 1-3.

155 Chicago Board of Education. A COMPREHENSIVE DESIGN FOR BILINGUAL-BICULTURAL EDUCATION. Chicago: Board of Edu-cation. 1975. 112 p.

156 Christian, Chester C. [Jr.], and Sharp, John M. "Bilingualism in a Pluralistic Society." In THE ACTFL REVIEW OF FOREIGN LANGUAGE EDUCATION, vol. 4. Edited by Dale Lange and Charles James, pp. 341-75. Skokie, Ill.: National Textbook Co., 1972.

157 Colombiani, Serafina. "The Bilingual Pressure Cooker." JOURNAL OF THE NATIONAL ASSOCIATION FOR BILINGUAL EDUCATION 1 (May 1976): 13-16.

The article considers some of the types of stress which are experienced by those involved in bilingual education programs.

158 Columbia University. Institute of Field Studies. Teachers College. PUBLIC EDUCATION AND THE FUTURE OF PUERTO RICO: A CURRICULUM SURVEY, 1948-1949. New York: Teachers College Press, Columbia University, 1950. Reprint. New York: Arno Press, 1975. 614 p.

This exhaustive study of the educational system of Puerto Rico--the fullest ever undertaken--was conducted by the Institute of Field Studies, Teachers College, Columbia University. Basically historical and sociological, the study reviews the development of the island's educational system in light of problems which had reached critical proportions. Charts and tables are included.

159 Conn, Stephen. "At Ramah, New Mexico: Bilingual Legal Education." JOURNAL OF AMERICAN INDIAN EDUCATION 12 (January 1973): 3-10.

In a developing legal education program, dual identity as a member of the Navaho nation and as American citizen is stressed.

160 Cordasco, Francesco. "The Puerto Rican Child in the American School." CONGRESSIONAL RECORD 111 (19 October 1965): 2625-26.

The following topics are discussed: (1) migration, (2) Puerto Ricans and mainland schools, (3) how effectively to teach English as a second language, (4) how to promote a more rapid and effective adjustment of Puerto Rican parents and children to the community and the community to them.

161 _____. THE PUERTO RICAN CHILD IN THE AMERICAN SCHOOL. American Sociological Association. ABSTRACTS OF PAPERS. 61st annual meeting, 29 August - 1 September, Miami, 1966. Reprint. Washington, D.C.: American Sociological Association, 1966. 2 p.

Relegation to ghetto poverty life is the source of the Puerto Rican immigrant child's dilemma. The solution lies in allowing the child to retain his Puerto Rican identity in the process of acculturation--a more important and a more difficult task than helping the child acquire English. It recommends community-oriented schools.

162 _____. "The Puerto Rican Child in the American School." KANSAS JOURNAL OF SOCIOLOGY 2 (Spring 1966): 59-65.

The Puerto Rican child's school problems are a function of deprivation and the ghetto milieu. An unanswered, crucial question in the study is how to absorb Puerto Ricans into the wider community while maintaining their cultural identity.

163 _____. "Puerto-Rican Pupils and American Education." SCHOOL AND SOCIETY 95 (18 February 1967): 116-19.

The article strongly recommends that immediate and effective steps be undertaken to provide special education programs to meet the needs of the Puerto Rican population of American schools.

164 _____. "Bilingual Education Bill Hailed as Major Step in Breaking Down Language Walls." CONGRESSIONAL RECORD 113 (9 October 1967): 161.

A summary of the proceedings and debates of the 90th Congress, first session, dealing with the possible passage of the bilingual education bill.

165 _____. "The Challenge of the Non-English-Speaking Child in American Schools." SCHOOL AND SOCIETY 106 (30 March 1968): 198-201.

This article advocates bilingual schooling for preservation of cultural identity.

166 _____. "Educational Enlightenment out of Texas: Toward Bilingualism." TEACHERS COLLEGE RECORD 72 (May 1970): 608-12.

167 _____. "The Challenge of the Non-English-Speaking Child in American Schools." In EDUCATION AND THE MANY FACES OF THE DISADVANTAGED: CULTURAL AND HISTORICAL PERSPECTIVES, edited by William Brickman, pp. 119-25. New York: John Wiley and Sons, 1972.

The author proposes that poverty is the common denominator under which cultural differences, language handicaps, social disaffection are subsumed. At present, Spanish-speaking children are among the most neglected and in need of the most immediate attention--by means of reinforcing all aspects of their cultural strengths.

168 _____. "Puerto Ricans on the Mainland: The Educational Experience." JOURNAL OF HUMAN RELATIONS 20 (3d Quarter 1972): 344-78.

169 _____. "The Children of Immigrants in Schools: Historical Analogues of Educational Deprivation." JOURNAL OF NEGRO EDUCATION 42 (Winter 1973): 44-53.

See also, Colin Greer, THE GREAT SCHOOL LEGEND: A REVISIONIST INTERPRETATION OF AMERICAN PUBLIC EDUCATION (New York: Basic Books, 1972); and David K. Cohen, "Immigrants and Schools," REVIEW OF EDUCATIONAL RESEARCH 40 (February 1970): 13-27. Also, Francesco Cordasco, "The School and the Children of the Poor: A Bibliography of Selected References," BULLETIN OF BIBLIOGRAPHY 30 (July-September 1973): 93-101; and Francesco Cordasco, "The Challenge of the Non-English-Speaking Child in American Schools" (entry no. 165).

170 _____. "Spanish-Speaking Children in American Schools." INTERNATIONAL MIGRATION REVIEW 9 (Fall 1975): 379-82.

171 _____. BILINGUAL SCHOOLING IN THE UNITED STATES: A SOURCEBOOK FOR EDUCATIONAL PERSONNEL. New York: McGraw-Hill, 1976. xxviii, 387 p.

This source book includes materials on historical backgrounds, typology and definitions; linguistic perspectives; programs, practices, and staff development; an overview of court decisions and legislation affecting bilingual education; and selected programs and project descriptions in California, Florida, New Jersey, New Mexico, New York, Texas, Illinois, Oklahoma, and Montana.

172 _____. "Bilingual Education: An American Dilemma." THE IMMIGRATION HISTORY NEWSLETTER 10 (May 1978): 5-8.

This article is an overview of bilingual education in the United States, conflicting ideologies, and informational resources.

173 _____. "Bilingual Education Dramatizes Hopes of Millions." NEW JERSEY EDUCATION REVIEW 51 (March 1978): 16-17.

174 _____, ed. THE BILINGUAL–BICULTURAL CHILD AND THE
QUESTION OF INTELLIGENCE: A SOURCEBOOK. New York
Times Bilingual Bicultural Education in the United States Series.
New York: Arno Press, 1978. 275 p.

> A wide-ranging collection of investigations, spanning a
> half century, this volume assembles materials on the re-
> current question of intelligence and the bilingual-bicul-
> tural child. Included are investigations on the intelli-
> gence of immigrant children and the parents; early hered-
> itary oriented views; the perplexing issue of cross-cul-
> tural testing; the contemporary testing of Puerto Rican,
> Mexican, and other bilingual children; and, in a di-
> mensional sense, the overall effects of bilingualism on
> intelligence.

175 _____, ed. BILINGUAL EDUCATION IN NEW YORK CITY: A
COMPENDIUM OF REPORTS. New York Times Bilingual Bicul-
tural Education in the United States Series. New York: Arno
Press, 1978. 107, 36, 72 p.

> Gathered together in this compendium are three rare and
> unobtainable reports on educational programs for non-
> English-speaking students in New York City delineating
> official responses over the course of a generation. In-
> cluded are A PROGRAM OF EDUCATION FOR PUERTO
> RICANS IN NEW YORK CITY (1947); THE PUERTO
> RICAN PUPILS IN THE PUBLIC SCHOOLS OF NEW
> YORK CITY (1951); and BILINGUAL EDUCATION IN
> NEW YORK CITY (1971). The 1947 report is the first
> official response to the educational needs of the grow-
> ing number of non-English-speaking Puerto Rican stu-
> dents being encountered in the city's schools, and rec-
> ommends adaptation of "Grade C" classes, used in prior
> eras for immigrant children; the 1951 report, prepared
> under the auspices of the Mayor's Committee on Puerto
> Rican Affairs, is a detailed exposition of needs for bi-
> lingual resources and new community orientations; and
> the 1971 report is an overview of basic information
> needed for the recruitment and training of bilingual
> teachers. Cordasco's introduction places the reports in
> historical perspective and relates them to current needs
> and practices.

176 _____, ed. BILINGUALISM AND THE BILINGUAL CHILD:
CHALLENGES AND PROBLEMS. New York Times Bilingual Bi-
cultural Education in the United States Series. New York: Arno
Press, 1978. 355 p.

> Brought together in this volume are the complete texts
> of the papers assembled in THE MODERN LANGUAGE
> JOURNAL symposium on "Bilingualism and the Bilingual
> Child"; the text of "The Challenge of Bilingualism" pre-

sented at Northeast Conference on the Teaching of Foreign Languages (1965); the texts of the papers assembled
in the JOURNAL OF SOCIAL ISSUES on "Problems of
Bilingualism"; selections from the hugh corpus "Bilingualism in the Barrio" gathered together in THE MOD-
ERN LANGUAGE JOURNAL, in which bilingualism is
explored as a societal manifestation; and the complete
text of the special issue of THE CENTER FORUM which
the Center for Urban Education devoted to bilingualism,
an issue which includes materials on Mexican Americans,
excerpts from the Senate HEARINGS on the Bilingual
Education Act, notices of German public schools in the
United States, evaluative notes on ongoing programs,
and a valuable bibliography on teaching bilingual students.

177 Cortez, E[milio].G[regory]. "Puerto Rican Non-English Child:
What Can I Do?" LANGUAGE ARTS 53 (August 1976): 767-69.

178 Cotnam, Jacques. "Are Bilingualism and Biculturalism Nothing
But a Lure?" CULTURE 28 (June 1967): 137-48.

Discussed in this article is the French-Canadians' desire
for cultural survival.

179 Covello, Leonard. "Remarks of Dr. Leonard Covello Upon Acceptance of the Meritorious Service Medal of the Department of
State of the State of New York." CONGRESSIONAL RECORD
113 (March 1967): 2 p.

Highlighted in these remarks are the experiences of
Benjamin Franklin High School, a community-centered
school in East Harlem, from its beginnings in 1934 to
the present.

180 Covello, Leonard, et al. THE COMMUNITY SCHOOL IN A
GREAT METROPOLIS. New York: Migration Division, Depart-
ment of Labor, Commonwealth of Puerto Rico, 1966. 26 p. Also
in EDUCATION FOR BETTER LIVING: THE ROLE OF THE SCHOOL
IN COMMUNITY IMPROVEMENT, pp. 193-212. Washington,
D.C.: U.S. Department of Health, Education and Welfare, 1966.

This book discusses Benjamin Franklin High School, a
community school in East Harlem (Spanish Harlem).

181 Crispin, Benjamin J. "Role of School in Bilingual Bicultural Society." READING IMPROVEMENT 12 (Winter 1975): 251-52.

This article states that the problems in educating the
Mexican-American student can be dealt with more effectively by using a bilingual-bicultural approach.

182 _____. "Facilitation of Bilingual Bicultural Education." READ-
ING IMPROVEMENT 13 (Summer 1976): 96-97.

> This article states that bicultural education is essential for
> helping Mexican-American students.

183 Deane, Barbara, and Zirkel, Perry A[lan]. "The Bilingual Education
Mandate: It Says Schools Must 'Do Something,' Must Do It
Soon--And Probably Must Find the Money to Get It." AMERICAN
SCHOOL BOARD JOURNAL 163 (July 1976): 29-32.

> The article notes a lack of clarity about the kinds of
> bilingual programs that schools will be mandated to pro-
> vide. There is also no clarity about the sources of
> funds.

184 Deloria, Vine, Jr. "The Place of American Indians in Contemporary Education." AMERICAN INDIAN JOURNAL 2 (February
1976): 2-8.

185 Diebold, A. Richard, Jr. "The Consequences of Early Bilingualism
in Cognitive Development and Personality Formation." In THE
STUDY OF PERSONALITY: AN INTERDISCIPLINARY APPRAISAL,
edited by Edward Norbeck, Douglass Price-Williams, and William
M. McCord. pp. 218-45. Holt, Reinhart and Winston, 1968.

> Focuses on the emotional and intellectual psychology
> of the bilingual.

186 Diehl, Kemper. "San Antonio Classes Uses Two Languages."
SOUTHERN EDUCATION REPORT 3 (October 1967): 16-19.

> This article describes Spanish-English bilingual education
> in Carvajal Elementary School of the San Antonio Inde-
> pendent School District.

187 Dissemination Center for Bilingual Bicultural Education. GUIDE
TO TITLE VII ESEA BILINGUAL BICULTURAL PROJECTS, 1973-
1974. New York Times Bilingual Bicultural Education in the
United States Series. New York: Arno Press, 1978. viii, 254 p.

> A richly detailed repository of data, this GUIDE fur-
> nishes broad descriptions of 211 bilingual bicultural pro-
> grams funded under Title VII of the Elementary and
> Secondary Education Act for fiscal year 1973-74. The
> programs were funded in thirty-two states and territories
> furnishing bilingual bicultural education to 128,767
> school children. Each program is described in the form
> of an abstract. Programs are arranged alphabetically
> by state, then by city or town, and by project title or
> district number. The abstracts are invaluable for an
> assessment of the national effort on bilingual-bicultural

education including narrative statements regarding staff
development, management activities, instructional materials used, instructional content areas, classroom organization, parental and community involvement activities,
and a description of evaluation components. The Dissemination Center is funded by the U.S. Office of Education. The GUIDES began publication in 1972-73;
unfortunately, the valuable abstracts provided in 1973-74
were discontinued and subsequent guides are only di-
rectory and statistical registers.

188 Dissemination Center for Bilingual Bicultural Education. PRO-
CEEDINGS. NATIONAL CONFERENCE ON BILINGUAL EDU-
CATION. Sponsored by the Texas Education Agency in Coopera-
tion with Education Service Center Region XIII in Austin and the
United States Office of Education, ESEA, Title VII. New York
Times Bilingual and Bicultural Education in the United States
Series. New York: Arno Press, 1978. xiii, 339 p.

The proceedings include the text of papers by outstanding bilingual education consultants from throughout the
United States presented at the conference (14-15 April
1972) at the Lyndon B. Johnson Library, University of
Texas in Austin. The purpose of the Conference was
"to give impetus to the implementation and continued
development of bilingual programs throughtout the nation." The papers deal with many aspects of the bilingual curriculum, skills-teaching methodology, cultural
implications, psychological aspects of the teaching-
learning process, literature, tests and measurements, and
related topics.

189 Drake, Diana. "Bilingual/Bicultural Education." EDUCATIONAL
FORUM 40 (January 1976): 199-204.

This article recommends educational programs that will
help children understand the world's diversity.

190 Dumont, Robert V., Jr. "Cherokee Children and Their Teacher."
SOCIAL EDUCATION 33 (January 1969): 70-72.

191 Edelman, Martin. "The Contextualization of School Children's
Bilingualism." MODERN LANGUAGE JOURNAL 53 (March
1969): 179-82.

The topics discussed in this article are: "Bilingual Students," "Bilingualism," "English (Second Language),"
"Language Proficiency," "Language Research," "Language Usage," "Puerto Ricans," "Spanish Speaking,"
and "Word Recognition."

192 Edwards, E.J. "Current Issues in Bilingual Education." ETH-NICITY 3 (March 1976): 70-81.

This article states that some issues in bilingual education are related to establishing and running effective programs, while others are rooted in questions concerning the purposes of bilingual education.

193 Epstein, Erwin Howard. "Value Orientation and the English Language in Puerto Rico; Attitude Toward Second Language Learning Among Grade Pupils and Their Parents. Ph.D. dissertation, University of Chicago, 1966. 58 p.

194 Epstein, Noel. LANGUAGE, ETHNICITY, AND THE SCHOOLS: POLICY ALTERNATIVES FOR BILINGUAL-BICULTURAL EDUCATION. Washington, D.C.: George Washington University, Institute for Educational Leadership, 1977. 104 p.

The book questions whether a bilingual system of education is the best for teaching children who are deficient in English. Included is a rebuttal by José A. Cárdenas.

195 Ervin-Tripp, Susan [M.]. "Becoming a Bilingual." Working Paper no. 9, Language-Behavior Research Laboratory. Berkeley: Institute of International Studies, University of California, 1968. 28 p.

The author brings to bear some of the considerations affecting age of learning and the milieu to suggest new directions for research.

196 Fisher, John C. "Bilingualism in Puerto Rico: A History of Frustration." THE ENGLISH RECORD 21 (April 1971): 19-24.

197 Fishman, Joshua A. "The Status and Prospects of Bilingualism in the United States. THE MODERN LANGUAGE JOURNAL 49 (March 1965): 143-55.

This article discusses cultural pluralism, bilingualism, and biculturalism. It suggests that a commission on bilingualism and biculturalism be established at the federal, state, and local levels.

198 _____. "Bilingualism, Intelligence, and Language Learning." THE MODERN LANGUAGE JOURNAL 49 (April 1965): 227-36.

199 _____. "Some Contrasts Between Linguistically Homogeneous and Linguistically Heterogeneous Politics." SOCIOLOGICAL INQUIRY 36 (1966): 146-58.

200 _____. "The Politics of Bilingual Education." In BILINGUALISM AND LANGUAGE CONTACT. Edited by James E. Alatis, pp. 47-58. Washington, D.C.: Georgetown University Round Table on Languages and Linguistics, 1970.

201 _____. "Attitudes and Beliefs About Spanish and English Among Puerto Ricans." VIEWPOINTS 47 (March 1971): 51-72.

> The article discusses "Attitudes," "Biculturalism," "Bi-lingualism," "Community Attitudes," "Dialects," "English," "Puerto Rican Culture," "Puerto Ricans," "Spanish."

202 _____. BILINGUAL EDUCATION: AN INTERNATIONAL SOCIOLOGICAL PERSPECTIVE. Rowley, Mass.: Newbury House, 1976. xiii, 208 p.

> This book includes the following topics: (1) "Point of View," (2) "International Findings," and (3) "Appendixes."

203 _____. LANGUAGE LOYALTY IN THE UNITED STATES: THE MAINTENANCE AND PERPETUATION OF NON-ENGLISH MOTHER TONGUES BY AMERICAN ETHNIC AND RELIGIOUS GROUPS. The Hague: Mouton, 1966. 478 p.

> This book is an invaluable repository of formal language-maintenance resources and institutions in American society. Fishman and his colleagues define the framework of their investigations in very broad terms: the study of language loyalty in the United States encompasses American ethnic historiography; the twin processes of deethnization and the concomitant conflicts in the enforced acculturation that accompanies assimilation; and the history of immigrant language maintenance. Comprehensive in its coverage with special attention to German, French, Spanish, and Ukrainian groups, LANGUAGE LOYALTY IN THE UNITED STATES is a basic document for the "study of the self-maintenance efforts, rationales, and accomplishments of non-English speaking immigrants on American shores." In the introduction, Einar Haugen observes: "Joshua Fishman has done us all a great service in building up a more positive image of the immigrant in this book. He has brought to light a facet of the immigrant's life in this country which has remained unknown and unheralded even by most historians of immigration, let alone historians of America."

204 _____. BILINGUALISM IN THE BARRIO. FINAL REPORT. 2 vols. New York: Yeshiva University, 1968.

This two-volume collection of studies attempts to measure and describe the sociolinguistic norms of a Puerto Rican bilingual community. The target population of 431 individuals in a single neighborhood in Jersey City identify with the large Puerto Rican community of the greater New York area. The individual studies, all written to be understood independently, are grouped into background studies and sociologically, psychologically, and linguistically oriented sections.

205 _____. "Bilingualism in the Barrio." THE MODERN LANGUAGE JOURNAL 53 (March 1969): Special Issue on Bilingualism. Included are the following articles; Fishman, Joshua A. "The Measurement and Description of Widespread and Relatively Stable Bilingualism," pp. 152-56; Fishman, Joshua A., and Casiano, Heriberto, "Puerto Ricans in Our Press," pp. 157-62; Cooper, Robert L., and Greenfield, Lawrence "Word Frequency Estimation as a Measure of Degree of Bilingualism," pp. 163-66; Cooper, Robert L., and Greenfield, Lawrence, "Language Use in a Bilingual Community," pp. 166-72; Cooper, Robert L., "Two Contextualized Measures of Degree of Bilingualism," pp. 172-78; Edelman, Martin, "The Contextualization of School Children's Bilingualism," pp. 179-82; Berney, Tomi D., and Cooper, Robert L., "Semantic Independence and Degree of Bilingualism in Two Communities," pp. 182-85.

206 _____. "Bilingualism in the Barrio." THE MODERN LANGUAGE JOURNAL 53 (April 1969): Special Issue on Bilingualism. Includes: Findling, Joav, "Bilingual Need Affiliation and Future Orientation in Extragroup and Intragroup Domains," pp. 227-31; Ronch, Judah; Cooper, Robert L.; and Fishman, Joshua A., "Word Naming and Usage Scores for a Sample of Yiddish-English Bilinguals," pp. 232-35; Cooper, Robert L.; Fowles, Barbara L.; and Givner, Abraham, "Listening Comprehension on a Bilingual Community," pp. 235-41; Silverman, Stuart H., "The Evaluation of Language Varieties," pp. 241-44; Fertig, Shelton, and Fishman, Joshua A., "Some Measures in the Interaction Between Language Domain and Semantic Dimension in Bilinguals," pp. 244-49; Silverman, Stuart H., "A Method for Recording and Analyzing the Prosodic Features of Language," pp. 250-54; Terry, Charles E., and Cooper, Robert L., "A Note on the Perception and Production of Phonological Variation," pp. 254-55; Fishman, Joshua A. "Some Things Learned; Some Things Yet to Learn," pp. 255-58.

207 Flores, Solomon Hernandez. THE NATURE AND EFFECTIVENESS OF BILINGUAL EDUCATION PROGRAMS FOR THE SPANISH-SPEAKING CHILD IN THE UNITED STATES. New York Times Bilingual Bicultural Education in the United States. New York: Arno Press, 1978. 188 p.

This book is a review of bilingual programs in elementary schools in New York City, Miami (Florida), Del Rio, Laredo and San Antonio (Texas) in which the programs were examined from standpoints of philosophical, sociological, psychological, and linguistic considerations. A major objective of the study was to test the operational theories and practices in bilingual education programs for the three major Spanish-speaking groups in the United States: Puerto Ricans, Cubans, and Mexican Americans. Hernandez Flores concludes that "the general feeling among most educators of the non-English speaking is that we are at last near a solution for the educational problems of these children." Included are recommendations for school policy, materials, methodology, evaluation, teacher training, and research, with guidelines for setting up exemplary bilingual education programs.

208 Foerster, Leona M., and Little Soldier, Dale. "Open Education and Native American Values." EDUCATIONAL LEADERSHIP 32 (October 1974): 41-45.

209 Forbes, Jack D. MEXICAN-AMERICANS. A HANDBOOK FOR EDUCATORS. Berkeley, Calif.: Far West Laboratory for Educational Research and Development, 1967. 41 p.

The author presents sixteen suggestions for the teacher and administrator of Mexican-American programs to begin acquiring insights into the background of Mexican culture and thinking.

210 Gaarder, A. Bruce. "Conserving Our Linguistic Resources." PUBLICATIONS OF THE MODERN LANGUAGE SOCIETY OF AMERICA 80 (May 1965): 19-23.

An appeal in favor of bilingual education for bilingual children in an attempt to preserve the ethnic heritage of non-English-mother-tongue children in the United States is emphasized in this article.

211 _____. "The Challenge of Bilingualism." In FOREIGN LANGUAGE TEACHING: CHALLENGES TO THE PROFESSION, edited by G. Reginald Bishop, Reports of the Working Committees of the Northeast Conference on the Teaching of Foreign Languages. New York: Modern Language Association, 1965.

212 _____. "Bilingualism." In A HANDBOOK FOR TEACHERS OF SPANISH AND PORTUGUESE. Edited by Donald D. Walsh, pp. 149-72. Lexington, Mass.: D.C. Heath, 1969.

This authoritative summary deals with the "relationship between natural and artificial bilingualism, and the extent to which the teacher of foreign language must concern himself with more and more aspects of the total phenomenon of bilingualism. . . ." (p. 149).

213 _____. "Linkages Between Foreign Language Teaching and Bilingual Education." BULLETIN OF THE ASSOCIATION OF DEPARTMENTS OF FOREIGN LANGUAGE 6 (March 1975): 8-11.

The article discusses the distinctions between folk bilingualism and elitist bilingualism, and bilingual education is concerned with the former. One main problem that needs to be faced is how second language teaching and bilingual education can be brought closer together.

214 _____. "Bilingual Education: Central Questions and Concerns." NEW YORK UNIVERSITY EDUCATION QUARTERLY 6 (Summer 1975): 2-6.

This article maintains that social and political factors outside the school are preponderant in affecting the problems of bilingual education.

215 _____. BILINGUAL SCHOOLING AND THE SURVIVAL OF SPANISH IN THE UNITED STATES. Rowley, Mass.: Newbury House, 1977. vii, 238 p.

This book is a series of essays dealing with the rationale, school organization, teaching methods, preparation of teachers, and community relationships, for bilingual education, and for the Spanish language, essays on its dialects, teaching Spanish to its native speakers, collective bilingualism, cultural pluralism, and relationships between English and Spanish.

216 Gallardo, Jose M., ed. PROCEEDINGS OF THE CONFERENCE ON EDUCATION OF PUERTO RICAN CHILDREN ON THE MAINLAND. San Juan, P.R.: Department of Education, 1970. Reprint. New York: Arno Press, 1975. 175 p.

This is the published proceedings of an invitational conference held from 18 October through 21 October 1970 by the Commonwealth of Puerto Rico Department of Education.

217 Garcia, Ramiro. "Bilingual Education: Progress under Pressure." UCLA EDUCATOR 18 (Winter 1976): 36-40.

Outlined are some of the advances made by bilingual education.

218 Green, Shirley E. THE EDUCATION OF MIGRANT CHILDREN. Washington, D.C.: National Education Association, Department of Rural Education, 1954. 179 p.

This book, written under the sponsorship of the National Council of Agricultural Life and Labor, studies migrant education in various parts of the United States. In the Southwest, conditions among migrant children of Seguin, Texas, receive special study.

219 Grubb, Susan. "Back of the Yards' Goes Bilingual." AMERICAN EDUCATION 12 (March 1976): 15-18.

This article describes a bicultural program which has been started in Chicago's old stockyard district.

220 Hamilton, Andrew. "The Old Equalizer." AMERICAN EDUCA-TION 11 (March 1975): 6-10.

This article states bilingual education has been present in American society for a considerable time but the novelty in recent years is that it is supposed to play a role in educational opportunities for minority youth.

221 Harris, Dixie Lee. "Education of Linguistic Minorities in the United States and the U.S.S.R." COMPARATIVE EDUCATION REVIEW 6 (February 1963): 191-99.

The article compares general and educational treatment by the USSR of its linguistic minorities, and the U.S. native Indian and Eskimo tribes. It also provides a thorough comparison of two schools, one in each coun-try.

222 Harrison, Selig S. THE MOST DANGEROUS DECADES: AN INTRODUCTION TO THE COMPARATIVE STUDY OF LANGUAGE POLICY IN MULTI-LINGUAL STATES. New York: Language and Communication Research Center, Columbia University, 1957. 102 p.

This study is concerned with the influence of multilin-gualism on national unity. The comprehensive classified bibliography focuses on the Soviet Union, Switzerland, the Philippines, and Sub-Saharan Africa.

223 Haugen, Einar. "Problems of Bilingualism." LINGUA: INTER-NATIONAL REVIEW OF GENERAL LINGUISTICS 2 (August 1950): 271-90.

This article contains valuable information about Pennsyl-vania Germans, New England Portuguese, American Indians, English loanwords in Norwegian, and general commentary on the bilingual in the United States.

224 _____. "Bilingualism: Definition and Problems." Cambridge: Harvard University, February 1968. 16 p.

225 Havighurst, Robert J. THE NATIONAL STUDY OF AMERICAN INDIAN EDUCATION. Chicago: University of Chicago Press, 1970. 270 p.

226 Hechinger, Fred. "Combating Lingui-Chauvinism: A Biracial, Bilingual Program in Ohio." SATURDAY REVIEW 2 (8 March 1975): 46–47.

227 Henniger, Daniel, and Esposito, Nancy. "Regimented Non-Education, Indian Schools." THE NEW REPUBLIC 84 (15 February 1969): 18–21.

A depressing picture of the schools is painted in this article, including the more negative data regarding educational failure and environmental rigidity in which American Indians are educated.

228 Holland, William R. "Language Barrier as an Educational Problem of Spanish-Speaking Children." EXCEPTIONAL CHILDREN 27 (September 1960): 42–44.

229 Hornby, Peter A. ed., BILINGUALISM: PSYCHOLOGICAL, SOCIAL, AND EDUCATIONAL IMPLICATIONS. New York: Academic Press, 1977. 167 p.

This work includes the proceedings of a Canadian-American conference on bilingualism held 12–13 March 1976 on the Plattsburgh campus of the State University of New York.

230 Ibarra, Herbert. "Teaching Spanish to the Spanish Speaking." FOREIGN LANGUAGE ANNALS 2 (March 1969): 310–15.

The story of a typical Mexican immigrant family in the Southwest with emphasis on the educational opportunities offered to the children is depicted in this article.

231 Illinois State Advisory Committee for the United States Commission on Civil Rights. BILINGUAL/BICULTURAL EDUCATION--A PRIVILEGE OR A RIGHT? A REPORT. Washington, D.C.: Government Printing Office, 1974. Reprint. New York Times Bilingual Bicultural Education in the United States Series. New York: Arno Press, 1978. vii, 117 p.

Prepared as a report for the U.S. Commission on Civil
Rights, this document is the result of a two-year investigation by the Illinois Advisory Committee to the U.S.
Commission on Civil Rights on the educational experiences of Hispanics in Illinois. The report is an extra-
ordinarily detailed text on the major failings in Illinois
to meet the educational needs of the non-English-speaking child. The Illinois Advisory Committee prepared
the report as a set of recommendations to implement
Illinois Public Act 78-727 which required that bilingual
education be offered to language minority students. The
committee's recommendations are valuable for the articu-
lation of a national policy in bilingual-bicultural education, and are largely congruent with the recommendations for bilingual-bicultural education made by the
parent commission in its study of Mexican-American educational needs in the five Southwestern states of Arizona,
California, Colorado, New Mexico, and Texas.

232 Inclan, Rosa G. de. "School-Community Relations." JOURNAL
OF THE NATIONAL ASSOCIATION FOR BILINGUAL EDUCA-
TION 1 (December 1976): 73-77.

The teacher who is bilingual and bicultural has a responsibility for acting as liaison between the parents
and their children in relationship to the school and
teachers.

233 Jacobson, Kathleen. "Bilingual/Bicultural Education: Why?
For Whom? What? How? MINNESOTA LANGUAGE REVIEW
.3 (December 1974): 2-9.

Among the aspects of bilingual education treated are
teacher qualifications, curriculum and materials, and
the identification of bilingual children.

234 Jensen, J. Vernon. "Effects of Childhood Bilingualism." ELE-
MENTARY ENGLISH. 39 (February-April 1962): 132-43; 358-
66.

A study of childhood bilingualism including a 200-item
bibliography.

235 Johnson, Laura. "Bilingual Bicultural Education: A Two Way
Street." THE READING TEACHER 29 (December 1975): 231-39.

The differences between ESL and bilingual-bicultural
programs are given, along with some of the materials
and methods of exemplary programs.

236 John-Steiner, Vera [P.], and Osterreicher, Helgi. "Learning Pueblo Style." NOTES FROM WORKSHOP CENTER FOR OPEN EDU-CATION 5 (Spring 1976): 21-26.

> This study of the cognitive styles of Indian and non-Indian children includes some recollections of college students.

237 Jordan, Riverda H. "Retention of the Foreign Language in the Home." JOURNAL OF EDUCATIONAL RESEARCH 3 (1921): 35-42.

> This article reveals that the Germans and Danes are foremost in the acquisition of the English language and that the disposition on the part of the parents to use the native language among themselves is less marked among Danish, German, and Jewish families than among the Slavs, Spaniards, Greeks, and Hungarians.

238 Kashinsky, M., and Wiener, M. "Tone in Communication and the Performance of Children from Two Socioeconomic Groups." CHILD DEVELOPMENT 40 (1969): 1193-202.

239 Keller, Gary D.; Teschner, Richard V.; and Viera, Silvia. BI-LINGUALISM IN THE BICENTENNIAL AND BEYOND. New York: Bilingual Press, 1976. 250 p.

240 Keller, Gary D., and Van Hooft, Karen S. BILINGUALISM AND BILINGUAL EDUCATION IN THE UNITED STATES: A CHRONOLOGY FROM THE COLONIAL PERIOD TO 1976. New York: Bilingual Press, 1976. 16 p.

241 Kjolseth, Rolf. "Bilingual Education Programs in the United States: For Assimilation or Pluralism?" In THE LANGUAGE EDUCATION OF MINORITY CHILDREN. Edited by Bernard Spolsky, pp. 94-121. Rowley, Mass.: Newbury House, 1972.

242 Kloss, Heinz. "Bilingualism and Nationalism." THE JOURNAL OF SOCIAL ISSUES 23 (April 1967): 39-47.

> This article analyses the relationship between nationalism and bilingualism with many examples taken from various parts of the world.

243 _____. THE AMERICAN BILINGUAL TRADITION. Rowley, Mass.: Newbury House, 1977. xiii, 347 p.

> This history of the bilingual tradition in the United States is based on the author's earlier studies, DAS

VOLKSGRUPPENRECHT IN DEN VEREINIGTEN STAATEN,
2 vols. (1940-42); and DAS NATIONALITATENRECHT
DER VEREINIGTEN STAATEN (1963).

244 Kobrick, J.W. "The Compelling Case for Bilingual Education."
SATURDAY REVIEW 39 (29 April 1972): 54-57.

245 [LaFontaine, Hernan]. "An Interview with Hernan LaFontaine."
RICAN 1 (May 1974): 37-43.

Discussed in this article is bilingual-bicultural education in New York City.

246 Lambert, Wallace E. "Behavioral Evidence for Contrasting Norms
of Bilingualism." In REPORT OF THE TWELFTH ANNUAL ROUND
TABLE MEETING ON LINGUISTICS AND LANGUAGE STUDIES.
Edited by Michele Zarechnol, pp. 73-80. Georgetown University
Monograph Series on Languages and Linguistics, no. 14. Washington,
D.C.: Georgetown University, 1961.

This article discusses the psychological approach to bilingualism, to complement the traditional linguistic approach.

247 Lambert, Wallace E., and Tucker, Richard C. BILINGUAL EDU-
CATION OF CHILDREN: THE ST. LAMBERT EXPERIMENT.
Rowley, Mass.: Newbury House, 1972. 194 p.

248 Leach, John [Nathaniel]. VIEWPOINTS ON BILINGUALISM.
Panama: Impresora Panama, 1974. 27 p.

A summary of definitions, methods, content, and scope
of bilingual education is presented in this book.

249 Leppke, Ronald Dean. Perceptual Approaches for Disadvantaged
Anglo-American and Mexican-American Students. Ed.D. dissertation, University of the Pacific, 1967. 157 p.

One assumption used in this dissertation was that a concept of a sense modality hierarchy may account for the
apparent nonverbal or motoric learning orientation of
Mexican Americans. Both low socioeconomic and Mexican-American groups seem to be more motoric in their
learning orientations.

250 Levenson, Dorothy. "Many Languages Are Spoken Here."
TEACHER 93 (October 1975): 68-70.

Discussed in this article are the many ways teachers
can help students in class learn even if there are many
languages spoken.

251 Loasa, Luis M. "Viewing Bilingual Multicultural Educational
Television: An Empirical Analysis on Children's Behaviors During
Television Viewing." JOURNAL OF EDUCATIONAL PSYCHOL-
OGY 68 (April 1976): 133-42.

A report of behavior among early elementary school
children while they were looking at two multicultural
programs designed for children is offered in this article.

252 Lopez, David E. "The Social Consequences of Chicano Home/
School Bilingualism." SOCIAL PROBLEMS 24 (December 1976):
234-46.

This article states that home and school bilingualism do
not have necessary positive or negative effects on attainment. Bilingualism has social consequences only when
there is interaction with groups and individual status.

253 Lorber, Fred. "A Demonstration Prevocational Program." In
EMPLOYMENT AND EDUCATIONAL SERVICES IN THE MOBILI-
ZATION FOR YOUTH EXPERIENCE. Edited by Harold H.
Weissman, pp. 72-89. The New Social Work Series. New York:
Association Press, 1969.

This paper describes a prevocational training program
(Division of Employment Opportunities) for recent Puerto
Rican immigrant youth, based on the premise that these
youngsters are a relatively homogeneous group in regard
to employment problems. The program, coordinated by
a Puerto Rican, involved teaching English, group counseling, promotion of warm social relationships leading
to work training leading to job placement. Author reports success (no statistics).

254 Lovas, John C. "Language Planning in a Multilingual Community
in the United States." In NEW DIRECTIONS IN SECOND
LANGUAGE LEARNING, TEACHING AND BILINGUAL EDUCA-
TION. Edited by Marina K. Burt and Heidi C. Dulay, pp. 113-
22. Washington, D.C.: TESOL, 1975.

Argues that in American society there is no recognition
of the right of a non-English-speaking community to
maintain or develop itself; and calls for a "community
of spirit" which would lead to community self-study so
people could determine for themselves what is important

to them in their language code and language use so
they could more effectively determine how professional
language planners could help them.

255 Love, Harold D. "Bilingualism in Southwest Louisiana." JOUR-
NAL OF EDUCATIONAL RESEARCH 56 (November 1962): 144-47.

Discusses French-speaking children in Southwest Louisiana.

256 Lowie, Robert H. "A Case of Bilingualism." WORD 1 (December 1945): 249-59.

An autobiography of a German-English bilingual immigrant from Austria.

257 Luhman, Reid A. The Social Bases of Thinking and Speaking:
A Study of Bilingual Chicano Children. Ph.D. dissertation, University of Kansas, 1974. 244 p.

258 Mackey, William F. "Toward a Redefinition of Bilingualism."
JOURNAL OF THE CANADIAN LINGUISTIC ASSOCIATION 2
(March 1956): 4-11.

The author incorporates and elaborates on his article on
"Bilingualism and Education" (PEDAGOGIE ORIENTA-
TION 2 [1952]: 135-47.), with an expansion of defini-
tions.

259 _____. "The Description of Bilingualism." CANADIAN JOUR-
NAL OF LINGUISTICS 7 (1962): 51-85.

The author extends further the definition of bilingualism
and, encouraged by his colleagues at the 1960 International Seminar on Bilingualism in Education, held in
Aberystwyth, he provides a framework for describing
bilingualism.

260 _____. BILINGUALISM AS A WORLD PROBLEM. Montreal:
Harvest House, 1967. 146 p.

261 _____. "The Description of Bilingualism." In READINGS IN
THE SOCIOLOGY OF LANGUAGES. Edited by Joshua A.
Fishman, pp. 554-84. The Hague: Mouton, 1968.

262 _____. BILINGUAL EDUCATION IN A BINATIONAL SCHOOL:
A STUDY OF EQUAL LANGUAGE MAINTENANCE THROUGH
FREE ALTERNATION. Rowley, Mass.: Newbury House, 1972.
185 p.

This is a study of the John F. Kennedy Schule in Ber-
lin, Germany.

263 _____. THEORY AND METHOD IN THE STUDY OF BILIN-
GUALISM. Oxford: Oxford University Press, 1976. 183 p.

264 Mackey, William F., and Andersson, Theodore. BILINGUALISM
IN EARLY CHILDHOOD. Rowley, Mass.: Newbury House,
1977. x, 443 p.

The proceedings of a conference on child language includes the following: (1) "Theory and Method," (2)
"Early Language Learning," (3) "Family Bilingualism,"
(4) "Bilingualism and Society," (5) "Planning Pre-School
Language Learning," (6) "Planning the Primary Curriculum," (7) "Case Studies of School Bilingualism," and
(8) "Policy and Research."

265 Mackey, William F., and Beebe, Von Nieda. BILINGUAL
SCHOOLS FOR A BICULTURAL COMMUNITY: MIAMI'S ADAP-
TATION TO THE CUBAN REFUGEES. Rowley, Mass.: Newbury
House, 1977. xiv, 223 p.

This book is a case study of the Miami (Florida) school
system's development of a bilingual school model.

266 Mackey, William F., and Ornstein, Jacob, eds. THE BILINGUAL
EDUCATION MOVEMENT: ESSAYS ON ITS PROGRESS. El
Paso: Texas Western Press, 1977. 153 p.

The essays of this book are divided into a section that
emphasizes educational and language factors and another
which points to the political and social dimensions of
bilingual education.

267 Mackey, William F., and Verdoodt, Albert eds. THE MULTI-
NATIONAL SOCIETY: PAPERS OF THE LJUBLJANA SEMINAR.
Rowley, Mass.: Newbury House Publishers, 1975. ix, 388 p.

This book is a collection of essays on minority rights,
antidiscrimination laws, ethnic diversity, and cultural
identity.

268 Macnamara, John. "The Effects of Instruction in a Weaker Language." THE JOURNAL OF SOCIAL ISSUES 23 (April 1967):
121-35.

The attainment of bilingual students in general subjects
taught through their second language is discussed in this
article.

269 Malherbe, Ernst G. THE BILINGUAL SCHOOL: A STUDY OF
BILINGUALISM IN SOUTH AFRICA. London: Longmans, Green
and Co., 1946. Reprint. New York Times Bilingual Bicultural
Education in the United States Series. New York: Arno Press,
1978. 127 p.

An important interpretative work, Malherbe's study has
far-reaching implications on the problems of bilingualism,
if even limited to the controversy over bilingualism
(English and Afrikaans) in South Africa. The study and
its research conclusions were part of a survey of bilingualism in which 18,000 pupils in representative schools
were tested. Malherbe, who was director of Census and
Statistics of the Union of South Africa, characterized
the study as "the most comprehensive piece of research
of its kind ever conducted on bilingualism in South
Africa or in other countries," and concluded that bilingual education helps the process of learning.

270 Mandera, Franklin Richard. AN INQUIRY INTO THE EFFECTS
OF BILINGUALISM ON NATIVE AND NON-NATIVE AMERI-
CANS, VIEWED IN SOCIOPSYCHOLOGIC AND CULTURAL
TERMS. New York Times Bilingual Bicultural Education in the
United States Series. New York: Arno Press, 1978. 165 p.

In Mandera's important study, he undertook the description of the identity and characteristics of bilinguals;
the examination, analysis and critical evaluation of the
workings of bilingualism: the examination of the theoretical bases for interpreting the effects of bilingualism,
and the examination of the effects of the sociopsychological and cultural experiences on the behavior of bilinguals. The conclusions demonstrate that all bilinguals
and their American-born offspring were subjected to over-
whelming pressures by the dominant American society to
be Americanized and assimilated; that free mass education, accompanied by sociocultural conditioning, played
a determining role in the destruction of bilingualism;
and that since 1924 there was a shift toward total Americanization seeking to stamp out cultural diversity and
to drive the ethnic minorities to the acceptance of
American society based on a common language and culture.

271 Manuel, Herschel T. SPANISH-SPEAKING CHILDREN IN THE
SOUTHWEST: THEIR EDUCATION AND THE PUBLIC WELFARE.
Austin: University of Texas Press, 1965. 222 p.

This book is an authoritative study of the many educational problems of the Mexican Americans.

272 Margolis, Richard J. THE LOSERS: A REPORT ON PUERTO
RICANS AND THE PUBLIC SCHOOLS. New York: Aspira,
1968. 21 p.

This report is on visits to a number of schools and the
educational plight of Puerto Rican children.

273 Mitzman, Barry. "Si se Puede--It Can Be Done." CHANGE 8
(May 1976): 16-19.

Mitzman traces the evolving program of the Colegio
Cesar Chavez in Mt. Angel, Oregon, which is directed
toward the needs of Chicano students.

274 Morrison, J. Cayce, director. THE PUERTO RICAN STUDY,
1953-57. New York: Board of Education, 1958. Reprint. With
an introductory essay by Francesco Cordasco. New York: Oriole
Editions, 1972. xxiii, 265 p.

The report was published by the Board of Education of
the City of New York in 1958. It was the result of a
heavily funded four-year study of the problems of the
education and adjustment of Puerto Rican children, and
by interference, all Spanish-speaking groups in the public schools of the United States.

275 National Advisory Council on Bilingual Education. ANNUAL
REPORT. Washington, D.C.: National Institute of Education,
1976. vi, 169 p.

The fullest report yet published by the NACBE, includes:
(1) "Recommendations," (2) "History, Growth and Future
Potention of the Bilingual/Multicultural Approach,"
(3) "Needs of the Bilingual Population," (4) "Office of
Bilingual Education: Administration," (5) "Federal Level
Programs," (6) "State and Local Developments," (7)
"Research and Development," (8) "Future Plans," (9)
appendixes: "Council Data"; "Digest of Public Hear-
ings." See also, ANNUAL REPORT (1975), and AN-
NUAL REPORT (1977).

276 National Conference on Bilingual Education. PROCEEDINGS.
14-15 April 1972. Austin, Tex.: Dissemination Center for Bilingual Bicultural Education, 1972. 400 p.

Included in the proceeding are complete texts of speeches
presented. The topics include the following: "Teaching Spanish to English Speaking Children," "Bilingual
Education Programs," "Teacher Training," "Curriculum
Development," and "Future of Bilingual Education."

277 National Service Center. Philadelphia. BILINGUAL EDUCATION: ETHNIC PERSPECTIVES. Proceedings for conference held 28 October 1977. Philadelphia: Community College of Pennsylvania, 1978. 141 p.

278 Northeast Conference on the Teaching of Foreign Languages. "The Challenge of Bilingualism." Report of Working Committee 2. In FOREIGN LANGUAGE TEACHING: CHALLENGES TO THE PROFESSION, edited by G. Reginald Bishop, pp. 54-101. New York: Modern Language Association, 1965.

   This report is essential for information concerning the rationale behind bilingual schooling. A group of recognized experts anaylzes bilingualism problems in the United States and unanimously advocates bilingual education for bilingual children, and proposes guidelines for the realization of bilingual programs.

279 Ogletree, Earl J., and Garcia, David. EDUCATION OF THE SPANISH SPEAKING URBAN CHILD: A BOOK OF READINGS. Springfield, Ill.: Charles C Thomas, 1975. xxv, 474 p.

280 Oksaar, Els. "Bilingualism." In CURRENT TRENDS IN LINGUISTICS. Edited by Thomas Sebeck, pp. 476-511. The Hague: Mouton, 1972.

281 Olim, E.G. "Maternal Language Styles and Cognitive Behavior." JOURNAL OF SPECIAL EDUCATION 4 (1970): 53-68.

282 Olneck, Michael R., and Lazerson, Marvin. "The School Achievement of Immigrant Children: 1900-30." HISTORY OF EDUCATION QUARTERLY 14 (Winter 1974): 453-82.

   This article is a comparison of the children of the foreign-born to the children of white, native-born parents on measures of school attendance and school continuance; considers in detail Southern Italians and Russian Jews.

283 Onativia, Oscar V., and Donoso, Maria Alejandra Reyes. "Basic Issues in Establishing a Bilingual Method." READING TEACHER 30 (April 1977): 727-34.

   This essay discusses a bilingual approach to language learning is used where the students use comparative "analogical language" which is between both languages.

284 Ontario Institute for Studies in Education. WORKING PAPERS
ON BILINGUALISM - TRAVAUX DE RECHERCHES SUR LE BI-
LINGUALISME. Toronto: 1973. 142 p.

285 Ortega, Luis., ed. INTRODUCTION TO BILINGUAL EDUCA-
TION/INTRODUCCION A LA EDUCATION BILINGUE. New
York: Las Americas-Anaya, 1975. 261 p.

The articles included are on the question of bilingual
education for Puerto Ricans, politics and bilingualism
and the development of teaching materials. Statistical
data are provided.

286 Overlan, S. Francis., et al. PAPERS PRESENTED AT THE NA-
TIONAL EQUAL EDUCATION INSTITUTE. St. Louis: National
Equal Education Institute, March 1973. 124 p.

Included in this anthology on equal education are two
papers dealing directly with Puerto Ricans: (1) "Puerto
Ricans and Education," a report prepared by the Puerto
Rican Congress, and (2) "Training Classroom Personnel
in Dealing with Bilingual/Bicultural Children."

287 Padilla, Amado M. "Bilingual Schools: Gateways to Integration
or Roads to Separation." THE BILINGUAL REVIEW 4 (January-
August 1977): 52-67.

This article states that bilingual education provides a
viable means of diminishing ethnic separateness. Without life opportunities, ethnolinguistic minorities must
remain isolated. Bilingual education should help move
students into the mainstream.

288 Pasquariello, Anthony. "En Busca de Compression y Direccion:
La Educacion Bilingue y Bicultural/A Cause in Search of Com-
prehension and Direction: Bilingual and Bicultural Education."
HISPANIA 56 (March 1973): 27-34.

289 Peebles, Robert Whitney. LEONARD COVELLO: A STUDY OF
AN IMMIGRANT'S CONTRIBUTION TO NEW YORK CITY. New
York Times Bilingual Bicultural Education in the United States
Series. New York: Arno Press, 1978. 414 p.

Leonard Covello spent nearly a half-century in educational service in the New York City schools, and was
a leading advocate of bilingual-bicultural education.
In the East Harlem Italian and Puerto Rican ghetto, as
principal of Benjamin Franklin High School, Covello
created the first successful community-oriented school.

Peebles's dissertation is a dimensionally rich biographical
study, drawing on all of Leonard Covello's activities in
behalf of the immigrant child, educational innovations
which provided the beginnings of bicultural education,
and the struggle for the implementation of pluralistic
models in American educational practice, all of which
are singularly relevant to contemporary problems in
American urban education.

290 Peña, Albar A[ntonio]. "Bilingual Education: The What, the Why and
the How." JOURNAL OF THE NATIONAL ASSOCIATION FOR
BILINGUAL EDUCATION, May 1976, pp. 27-33.

291 Petrello, Barbara A. THE NEW YORK-NEW JERSEY BILINGUAL
JOB MARKET: ITS IMPLICATIONS FOR FOREIGN LANGUAGE
EDUCATION. Ed.D dissertation, Rutgers University, 1977.
179 p.

Although eleven languages were cited in the survey,
Spanish, French, and German were requested most frequently, with Spanish accounting for 44 percent of all
job openings. Statistical evidence supports the need for
a career-oriented component in foreign-language education.

292 Pialorsi, Frank [Paul], ed. TEACHING THE BILINGUAL: NEW METH-
ODS AND OLD TRADITIONS. Tucson: University of Arizona
Press, 1974. vii, 263 p.

This book includes the following chapters: "Bicultural
Understanding," "Theoretical Bases," "The School Program."

293 Pike, Kenneth L. "Toward a Theory of Change and Bilingualism."
STUDIES IN LINGUISTICS 25 (Summer 1960): 1-7.

This article discusses setting up a frame of reference to
discuss the relationships between a change of system in
general and the status of the languages of the bilingual
or the dialects or styles of the monolingual.

294 Pitler, Barry. "Chicago's Korean American Community." INTE-
GRATED EDUCATION 15 (July-August 1977): 44-47.

Chicago has two bilingual programs in its schools for
Koreans.

295 Polacca, Kathryn. "Ways of Working with the Navahos Who
Have Not Learned the White Man's Ways." JOURNAL OF
AMERICAN INDIAN EDUCATION 2 (October 1962): 6-16.

296 Puerto Rican Community Development Project. New York City.
     BRIEF HISTORY OF THE PUERTO RICAN COMMUNITY DEVEL-
     OPMENT PROJECT. New York: Puerto Rican Forum, 1966.
     5 p.

> This book is a statement of the intent and organization
> of the Puerto Rican Community Development Project,
> Inc., designed by Manuel Diaz. The project contracts
> existing local groups, committing them to carry out
> self-help activities with project funds.

297 _____. SUMMARY OF THE PUERTO RICAN COMMUNITY
     DEVELOPMENT PROJECT. New York: The Puerto Rican Forum,
     1966. 33 p.

> Described in this book are the following aspects of the
> Puerto Rican Community Development Project: block
> organization structure and supportive services, which
> focus on (1) job and economic opportunity, (2) consumer
> program, (3) education and child guidance, (4) chil-
> dren's court services, (5) family rehabilitation program,
> (6) foster care program, (7) housing program, (8) legal
> services and (9) mobile theater.

298 "The Puerto Rican Experience." NEW JERSEY EDUCATION RE-
     VIEW 47 (May 1974): 26-29.

> This article, based on an educational research study,
> "The Puerto Rican Experience," presented the opinions
> of superintendents and principals concerning attitudes
> on bilingual programs for Puerto Rican students.

299 Puerto Rican Forum. THE PUERTO RICAN COMMUNITY DEVEL-
     OPMENT PROJECT: A PROPOSAL FOR A SELF-HELP PROJECT
     TO DEVELOP THE COMMUNITY BY STRENGTHENING THE
     FAMILY, OPENING OPPORTUNITIES FOR YOUTH AND MAK-
     ING FULL USE OF EDUCATION. New York: 1964. 145 p.

> For this project, the following areas were researched:
> a comprehensive social profile of the community, the
> community's social structure, socioeconomic status,
> leadership and values, and existing Puerto Rican organi-
> zations.

300 _____. BASIC OCCUPATIONAL LANGUAGE TRAINING (BOLT).
     FINAL REPORT. New York: 1969. 121 p.

> This eighteen-month phase of a continuing demonstration
> project was designed to develop and test a program of
> English-literacy training for Puerto Rican workers.

301 _____. PROJECT BOLT--FINAL REPORT FOR THE EXPERIMEN-
TAL AND DEMONSTRATION PHASE OF THE BASIC OCCUPA-
TIONAL LANGUAGE TRAINING PROGRAM. New York: 1971.
94 p.

This program teaches English-language skills to Spanish-
speaking people, and Spanish-language skills to English-
speaking people.

302 Raffler-Engel, Walburga von. "Investigation of Italo-American
Bilinguals." ZEITSCHRIFT FUR PHONETIK SPRACHWISSENSCHAFT
UND KOMMUNIKATIONSFORSCHUNG 14 (1961): 127-30.

A technical analysis of the speech patterns of Italian
Americans is discussed.

303 Ramirez, Manuel, and Castaneda, Alfredo. CULTURAL DEMOC-
RACY, BICOGNITIVE DEVELOPMENT, AND EDUCATION. New
York: Academic Press, 1974. 287 p.

304 Ramirez, Manuel, et al. SPANISH-ENGLISH BILINGUAL EDU-
CATION IN THE UNITED STATES: CURRENT ISSUES, RESOURCES,
AND RESEARCH PRIORITIES. Arlington, Va.: Center for Ap-
plied Linguistics, 1977. 80 p.

305 Reyes, Vinicio H. BICULTURAL-BILINGUAL EDUCATION FOR
LATINO STUDENTS: A CONTINUOUS PROGRESS MODEL.
New York Times Bilingual Bicultural Education in the United
States Series. New York: Arno Press, 1978. 314 p.

The two-fold purpose of this study was "to provide a
rationale for bilingual education based on historical developments and the sociocultural characteristics of
Spanish-speaking students in Chicago; and to propose a
model for a continuous progress, two-way, integrated,
maintenance type, total, bicultural-bilingual program
that would incorporate up-to-date educational strategies
beginning with the Early Childhood Bilingual Readiness
Center and continuing with the Bilingual Middle School,
and the Bilingual High School." The model developed
includes a curriculum for each unit and charts of the
organizational structure; the concept of a multilingual-
multicultural magnet school; teacher training components; and the development of relevant instructional materials.

306 Rich, Leslie. "Transforming Francisco." AMERICAN EDUCATION
10 (March 1974): 6-11.

Puerto Rican students in a Teacher Corps Project reveal
the magic that can result by having Spanish-speaking
children.

307 Rodgers, Ron, and Rangel, Diego. "Learning for Two Worlds."
AMERICAN EDUCATION 8 (November 1972): 28-32.

The authors discuss a bilingual center in Chicago serving youngsters whose families have immigrated to the
United States. The center seeks to harmonize the native
culture with the adopted one.

308 Rodriguez, Ray. "Bilingual/Career Education." ILLINOIS CA-
REER EDUCATION JOURNAL 33 (February 1975): 7-8.

309 Roemer, Robert E. "The Polarities of Bilingual, Cross-Cultural
Education." CALIFORNIA JOURNAL OF TEACHER EDUCATION
2 (Winter 1975): 49-61.

310 Salganik, Laura Hersh. "Fox Point: The History of a Portuguese
Bilingual Program." INEQUALITY IN EDUCATION 19 (February
1975): 47-50.

311 Sanchez, George I. CONCERNING SEGREGATION OF SPAN-
ISH-SPEAKING CHILDREN IN THE PUBLIC SCHOOLS. Inter-
American Educational Occasional Papers, no. 9. Austin: Uni-
versity of Texas Press, 1951. 75 p.

This book sets forth in summary form the various aspects
of the segregation of Spanish-speaking children legally,
educationally, and morally.

312 Saville-Troike, Muriel R. BILINGUAL CHILDREN: A RESOURCE
DOCUMENT. Bilingual Education Series, no. 2. Washington,
D.C.: Center for Applied Linguistics, 1973. 149 p.

A discussion of the linguistic diversity and profiles of
bilingual children.

313 Saville[-Troike], Muriel R., and Troike, Rudolph C. A HANDBOOK
OF BILINGUAL EDUCATION. Washington, D.C.: Center for Applied
Linguistics, 1971. 71 p.

This handbook is a guide for establishing and implementing bilingual education programs.

314 Seaman, Paul David. "Modern Greek and American English in
Contact: A Socio-Linguistic Investigation of Greek-American

Bilingualism in Chicago." Ph.D. dissertation, Indiana University, 1965. 451 p.

Besides the thorough linguistic analysis of the speech of Greek-Americans, a demographic analysis in this thesis gives a brief history of Greek immigration to the United States, and outlines the geographical distribution of a half-million Americans of Greek descent.

315 Seda, Eduardo. "Bilingual Education in a Pluralistic Context." RICAN 1 (May 1974): 19-26.

This work discusses the rationale for bilingual education and for ethnic studies in a culturally pluralistic society.

316 Seller, Maxine. "The Education of Immigrant Children in Buffalo, New York, 1890-1916." NEW YORK HISTORY 57 (April 1976): 183-99.

The author contrasts the Italian experience with that of Polish and Jewish immigrants.

317 Shaw, Frederick. "Bilingual Education: An Idea Whose Time Has Come." NEW YORK AFFAIRS 3 (Fall 1975): 94-111.

Bilingual education is not new in the United States, but earlier assimilationism is dominant. Miami's Coral Way School's approach was a success in having both Spanish and English as the target languages.

318 Shender, Karen Joseph. "Bilingual Education: How Un-American Can You Get." LEARNING 5 (October 1976): 32-41.

Shender presents views on bilingual education at the elementary level, experiences in setting up a bilingual program, some ideas on the Lau v. Nichols decision and possible future directions for bilingual education.

319 Singer, Harry. "Bilingualism and Elementary Education." MODERN LANGUAGE JOURNAL 40 (December 1956): 444-58.

Analyzes the meaning of bilingualism, the language proficiency of bilinguals, their mental development, school achievement and emotional adjustment; then advocates the teaching of foreign languages in the elementary schools.

320 Sirgado, Isabel Cid. "Bilingual Education: Is It Here to Stay? JOURNAL OF THE NATIONAL ASSOCIATION FOR BILINGUAL EDUCATION 1 (May 1976): 35-37.

A brief discussion of the role college educators can play in bilingual education programs is discussed in this article.

321 Soffietti, James P. "Bilingualism and Biculturalism." THE JOURNAL OF EDUCATIONAL PSYCHOLOGY 46 (April 1955): 222-27.

Soffietti attempts to solve the problem of the definition of bilingualism and proposes that the research worker be able to distinguish between four basic culture-language types.

322 Soriano, Jesse M., and McClafferty, James. "Spanish-Speakers of the Midwest: They Are American Too." FOREIGN LANGUAGE ANNALS 2 (March 1969): 316-24.

This article is a study of the educational problems of the Spanish-speaker of the Midwest, which are different from those of his Southwest counterpart. A description of the Title III, ESEA Program in developing bilingual and bidialectal instructional materials in Ann Arbor, Michigan is included.

323 Sotomayor, F. "Se hable ingles y Espanol: A Bilingual Class in Action." CIVIL RIGHTS DIGEST 6 (Summer 1974): 27-31.

324 Souflee, Frederick, and Schmidt, Graciela. "Educating for Practice in the Chicano Communities." JOURNAL OF EDUCATION FOR SOCIAL WORK 10 (February 1974): 75-84.

Helping Mexican Americans is improved by developing bicultural models.

325 Southwest Council for Bilingual Education. BILINGUAL EDUCATION IN THREE CULTURES. Annual Conference Report. Las Cruces, N. Mex.: 1968. 147 p.

326 Southwest Council of Foreign Language Teachers. "Reports: Bilingual Education: Research and Teaching." Edited by Chester Christian. Fourth Annual Conference, 10-11 November 1967. El Paso, Tex.: 1967. 88 p. Mimeographed.

An account of contemporary bilingual education in the United States is covered in the reports. The first report deals with areas of needed research and a description of bilingual programs in American schools abroad; the second analyzes the problem of reading content in a foreign language; the third is an account of bilingual programs operating in the Southwest or of the need of them.

327 Southwest Council on the Education of Spanish-Speaking People. "Proceedings. Fifty Annual Conference." 18-20 January 1951. Los Angeles: George Pepperdine College, 1951. 101 p. Mimeographed

Covers problem areas of Spanish-speaking groups including education, sociology, business opportunities, culture patterns, and so forth.

328 Spang, Alonzo. "Eight Problems in Indian Education." JOURNAL OF AMERICAN INDIAN EDUCATION 10 (October 1970): 1-4.

329 Spoerl, Dorothy Tilden. "The Academic and Verbal Adjustment of College Age Bilingual Students." THE JOURNAL OF GENETIC PSYCHOLOGY 64 (March 1944): 139-57.

The article concludes that at college level there are no lasting effects due to bilingualism in childhood which are apparent in academic records, vocational choices, or English ability: if there was a handicap, it has been stabilized by the first year of college.

330 Spolsky, Bernard, ed. THE LANGUAGE EDUCATION OF MINORITY CHILDREN: SELECTED READINGS. Rowley, Mass.: Newbury House, 1973. 200 p.

This book includes the following chapters: (1) "Multilingualism in the United States," (2) "Bilingualism and Bilingual Education," (3) "Language Education in Practice."

331 Spolsky, Bernard, and Cooper, Robert L., eds. FRONTIERS OF BILINGUAL EDUCATION. Rowley, Mass.: Newbury House, 1977. 326 p.

This book is a companion volume to the editors' CASE STUDIES IN BILINGUAL EDUCATION (1978). It includes essays on language education policy, bilingualism and bilingual education, the sociology of bilingual education, linguistic perspectives, educational perspectives, psychological perspectives, philosophical perspectives, evaluation of bilingual education, and bilingual education and language planning.

332 _____. CASE STUDIES IN BILINGUAL EDUCATION. Rowley, Mass.: Newbury House, 1978. vii, 544 p.

This book is an overview of bilingual education around the world, including black English, Yiddish, and American Indian programs in the United States. See, particularly, George M. Blanco, "The Implementation of Bilingual Bicultural Programs in the United States," pp. 454-99.

333 Sutherland, Iris Rose. "A Study of Puerto Rican Parents' Views on Bilingual Bicultural Education." Ed.D. disertation, 1975, University of Illinois, Urbana-Champaign. 112 p.

334 Swain, Merrill, ed. BILINGUAL SCHOOLING: SOME EXPERIENCES IN CANADA AND THE UNITED STATES. Toronto: Ontario Institute for Studies in Education, 1972. vii, 102 p.

This book is a report on a bilingual education conference held at the institute, 11-13 March 1971.

335 Swanson, Maria M. "Bilingual Education: The National Perspective." In THE ACTFL REVIEW OF FOREIGN LANGUAGE EDUCATION, vol. 5. Edited by Gilbert A. Jarvis, pp. 75-127. National Textbook Co., 1974.

336 Teel, D. "Preventing Prejudice Against Spanish-Speaking Children." EDUCATIONAL LEADERSHIP 12 (November 1954): 94-98.

The author suggests a school program to eliminate prejudice against Spanish-speaking people, with emphasis in basic principles of curriculum making.

337 Teruel, Manual. "Negotiating Change in the Boston Public Schools: Bilingual Education." Ed.D. dissertation, Harvard University, 1973. 167 p.

The author explores conditions in the Puerto Rican community and relates them to the conditions of the Boston school system.

338 Texas Education Agency. AN ORIENTATION TO BILINGUAL EDUCATION IN TEXAS: A TRAINING MANUAL. Austin, Tex.: 1976. 186 p.

339 Texas Education Agency. Regional Educational Agencies Project in International Education. ADDRESSES AND REPORTS PRESENTED AT THE CONFERENCE ON DEVELOPMENT OF BILINGUALISM

IN CHILDREN IN VARYING LINGUISTIC AND CULTURAL HERITAGES. Edited by W.R. Goodson. Austin: 1967. 123 p.

Reports on various Texas cities, Guatemala, New Mexico, Germany, with addresses and statements by several experts in the field are included.

340 Thonis, Eleanor Wall. LITERACY FOR AMERICA'S SPANISH SPEAKING CHILDREN. Newark, Del.: International Reading Association, 1976. 69 p.

The author attempts to synthesize what is known about several important areas of bilingual education.

341 Tiffany, Warren I. EDUCATION IN NORTHWEST ALASKA. Rev. ed. Juneau: Bureau of Indian Affairs, 1966. 71 p.

This account deals not only with this specific geographic section, but reflects the economic, political, and social as well as educational development of the whole state from the era of Russian occupation to the period of young statehood.

342 Tireman, Lloyd S. TEACHING SPANISH-SPEAKING CHILDREN. Albuquerque: University of New Mexico Press, 1951. 252 p.

This is a survey of bilingualism in the world; it studies bilingualism separately in different countries and in general as a social phenomenon. Conclusions of studies are applied to design a pattern for the education of Spanish-speaking children.

343 Travieso, Lourdes. "Puerto Ricans and Education." JOURNAL OF TEACHER EDUCATION 26 (Summer 1975): 128-30.

This article is a study of the interrelationship between Puerto Rican culture and education. Attention is given to the work of the courts in fostering bilingual-bicultural education.

344 Troike, Rudolph C., and Modiano, Nancy, eds. PROCEEDINGS. First Inter-American Conference on Bilingual Education. Arlington, Va.: Center for Applied Linguistics, 1975. 401 p.

The presentations of thirty scholars in a broad range of perspectives, models, and methods in bilingual education are included in this publication.

345 Trueba, Enrique T. "Issues and Problems in Bilingual Bicultural Education Today." JOURNAL OF THE NATIONAL ASSOCIATION FOR BILINGUAL EDUCATION 1 (December 1976): 11-19.

The article states that bilingual and bicultural education is the most important recent development in American education. Such an approach could be the answer
to helping many ethnic children with their developmental and cognitive problems.

346 Tsu, John B. "Chinese Bilingual Education and Chinese Language
Teaching." JOURNAL OF THE CHINESE LANGUAGE TEACHERS
ASSOCIATION 12 (February 1977): 44-54.

The article offers a brief history of the Chinese bilingual program, types of Chinese bilingual education,
teaching Chinese as a first language, and views of
language transfer and maintenance.

347 Turner, Paul R., ed. BILINGUALISM IN THE SOUTHWEST.
Tuscon: University of Arizona Press, 1973. xv, 352 p.

This book includes the following chapters: (1) "Mexican Americans," (2) "American Indians," (3) "Suggestions for Further Research."

348 Ulibarri, Horacio. EDUCATIONAL NEEDS OF THE MEXICAN-
AMERICAN. Prepared for the National Conference on Educa-
tional Opportunities for Mexican-Americans, 25-26 April 1968,
Austin, Texas. Las Cruces, N. Mex.: ERIC Clearinghouse on
Rural Education and Small Schools, March 1968. 20 p.

The author examines the educational needs of the Mexican American in relation to occupational success, citizenship participation, and personality factors.

349 Ulibarri, Mari-Luci. "Ambiente Bilingue: Professionals, Parents,
and Children." JOURNAL OF MEXICAN AMERICAN STUDIES
1 (Spring-Summer 1972): 130-35.

The article states that bilingual education should be
viewed as a component of bicultural education if we are
to move toward cultural equality.

350 Ulin, Richard Otis. THE ITALO-AMERICAN STUDENT IN THE
AMERICAN PUBLIC SCHOOL: A DESCRIPTION AND ANALYSIS
OF DIFFERENTIAL BEHAVIOR. New York: Arno Press, 1975.
201 p.

Ulin studied the academic and school-related performance
of a selected group of Italian-American second- and third-
generation boys in a Massachusetts high school.

351 United Kingdom. Department of Education and Science. National Commission for UNESCO. BILINGUALISM IN EDUCATION: REPORT ON AN INTERNATIONAL SEMINAR, ABERYSTWYTH, WALES, 20 August-25 September, 1960. London: Her Majesty's Stationery Office, 1965. Reprint. New York Times Bilingual Bicultural Education in the United States Series. New York: Arno Press, 1978. v, 234 p.

As a compendium of presentations by authorities on all aspects of bilingualism, this collection of papers is an invaluable repository of documents on the linguistic, social, cultural, psychological, historical, and educational issues which constitute bilingualism, and its challenges in the modern world. The report, sponsored under the auspices of UNESCO, derives from the International Seminar on Bilingualism in Education convened at Aberystwyth, Wales on 20 August through 2 September 1960. The range of the seminar's inquiries are defined in the "Inaugural Address" by Ernst G. Malherbe which opened the seminar, and which is published as the first of the presentations. Other papers include "The Linguistic Aspect of Bilingualism," "Social and Psychological Aspects of Bilingualism," "Social and Cultural Aspects of Bilingualism," and "Bilingualism--Some Aspects of Its History." These are followed by the REPORT of the seminar which includes conclusions and recommendations with a valuable appended bibliography.

352 United Nations Educational Scientific and Cultural Organization. THE USE OF VERNACULAR LANGUAGES IN EDUCATION. Paris: UNESCO, 1953. Reprint. UNESCO Monographs on Fundamental Education, no. 8. New York Times Bilingual Bicultural Education in the United States Series. New York: Arno Press, 1978. 154 p.

This report is a compendium of materials derived from an international conference of specialists on the use of the mother tongue as a medium of instruction all over the world. A comprehensive global survey of vernaculars is followed by discussions on various issues involved in mother tongue instruction, the need for learning a second language, and the problems of multilingual areas. The report also presents brief case histories illustrating challenges and needs in Mexico, Egypt, Indonesia, New Guinea, the Gold Coast (Ghana), the Philippines, and East Europe.

353 U.S. Bureau of Indian Affairs. BILINGUAL EDUCATION FOR AMERICAN INDIANS. Washington, D.C.: Government Printing Office, 1971. Reprint. Curriculum Bulletin no. 3. New York

General and Miscellaneous

Times Bilingual Bicultural Education in the United States Series. New York: Arno Press, 1978. iii, 102 p.

Published as a curriculum bulletin, this important collection of materials includes a broad view of past and present activities in bilingual education for American Indians and Eskimos; the history of language instruction in American Indian schools and of bilingual education in Bureau of Indian Affairs schools; the Bilingual Education Act and its effect on the American Indian; statements on bilingual education and a summary of pertinent research in bilingual education; bilingual programs for Navaho children, and classroom techniques for bilingual teachers; a partially annotated bibliography of books and articles on bilingualism written between 1953 and 1971; and appendixes providing a glossary and linguistic principles for describing language.

354 U.S. Commission on Civil Rights. A BETTER CHANCE TO LEARN: BILINGUAL-BICULTURAL EDUCATION. Washington, D.C.: U.S. Government Printing Office, 1975. iv, 254 p.

The U.S. Commission on Civil Rights, an independent, bipartisan agency established by the U.S. Congress in 1957, prepared this report "to provide educators and the general public with information about bilingual-bicultural education as a means for equalizing educational opportunity for language minority students." The report includes the following topics: (1) historical overview of language minorities and education, (2) language minority students and equal education opportunity, (3) bilingual-bicultural education and program structures, and (4) appendixes: (a) constitutionality of the right to equal education opportunity, (b) federal policy on bilingual education, and (c) state policy on bilingual education. The report is one of the best introductions to bilingual-bicultural educational practice in the United States; unfortunately, as a commission special report, its circulation and availability have been limited.

355 _____. MEXICAN-AMERICAN EDUCATION STUDY. Reports 1-5. Washington, D.C.: Government Printing Office, 1971-73. Reprint. New York Times Bilingual Bicultural Education in the United States Series. New York: Arno Press, 1978. 102, 101, 86, 53, 68 p.

In the proliferating literature on Mexican Americans and the Chicano heritage, none is more important than the detailed reports which constitute the MEXICAN-AMERICAN EDUCATION STUDY published by the U.S. Commission on Civil Rights. Bilingual and bicultural edu-

66

cational needs of Mexican Americans are the twin themes
which are recurrent in the reports, which were published
under the following titles: (1) ETHNIC ISOLATION OF
MEXICAN AMERICANS IN THE PUBLIC SCHOOLS OF
THE SOUTHWEST; (2) THE UNFINISHED EDUCATION:
OUTCOMES FOR MINORITIES IN THE FIVE SOUTH-
WESTERN STATES; (3) THE EXCLUDED STUDENT: EDU-
CATIONAL PRACTICES AFFECTING MEXICAN AMERI-
CANS IN THE SOUTHWEST; (4) MEXICAN AMERICAN
EDUCATION IN TEXAS: A FUNCTION OF WEALTH;
(5) TEACHERS AND STUDENTS: DIFFERENCES IN
TEACHER INTERACTION WITH MEXICAN AMERICAN
AND ANGLO STUDENTS.

356 U.S. Congress. House of Representatives. Committee on Education
and Labor. General Subcommittee on Education. BILINGUAL EDU-
CATION PROGRAMS, HEARINGS. . ., H.R. 9840 and H.R.
10224. 90th Cong., 1st sess. Washington, D.C.: Government
Printing Office, 1967. Reprint. New York Times Bilingual
Bicultural Education in the United States Series. New York:
Arno Press, 1978. viii, 584 p.

This is a companion volume to the Senate HEARINGS.
The House HEARINGS (28 and 29 June 1967) supplement
and extend the Senate HEARINGS, and H.R. 9840 and
H.R. 10224 were more comprehensive in their proposals
for bilingual education than S.428. Like the Senate
HEARINGS, the House HEARINGS contain a staggering
amount of materials delineating all aspects of bilingual
schooling in the United States.

357 U.S. Congress. House of Representatives. General Subcommittee on
Education and Labor. UNITED STATES ETHNIC HERITAGE STUDIES
CENTERS, HEARINGS., H.R. 14910. 91st Cong., 2d sess.
Washington, D.C.: Government Printing Office, 1970. Reprint.
New York Times Bilingual Bicultural Education in the United
States Series. New York: Arno Press, 1978. vii, 363 p.

This work includes the text of the HEARINGS (16, 17,
18, 24, and 26 February; 4, 5, and 19 March; and 6
May 1970) out of which derived the enactment of the
Ethnic Heritage Program by the Congress as Title IX of
the Elementary and Secondary Education Act. In en-
acting Title IX (23 June 1972), the Congress observed
". . .it is the purpose of this title to provide assistance
designed to afford to students opportunities to learn
about the nature of their own culture heritage and to
study the contributions of the cultural heritages of the
other ethnic groups of the Nation." The text of the
HEARINGS constitutes an invaluable source for materials

on many of the ethnic groups in the United States with
special reference to bicultural education, the need for
the preservation of ethnic archives, and for new evaluations of the immigrant experience in America.

358 U.S. Congress. Senate. CUBAN REFUGEE PROBLEM. HEAR-
INGS BEFORE THE SUBCOMMITTEE TO INVESTIGATE PROBLEMS
CONNECTED WITH REFUGEES AND ESCAPEES OF THE COM-
MITTEE ON THE JUDICIARY, 89th Cong., Part 1: Washington,
D.C., 23, 24, 29, and 30 March 1966; Part 2: New York,
13 April 1966; Part 3: Newark, N.J., 15 April 1966. Wash-
ington, D.C.: Government Printing Office, 1966. 304 p.

Part 1 presents testimony and statistics dealing with the
resettlement problem, the memorandum of understanding
between Cuba and the United States, conditions in
Cuba, effectiveness of the refugee program, issues re-
flected in the mail to Congress, and the inability of
Cubans to practice their profession or skill. Part 2
focuses on the New York situation and part 3 on the
New Jersey situation. (Part 3 is entitled CUBAN
REFUGEE PROGRAM.)

359 U.S. Congress. Senate. Committee on Labor and Public Welfare. BILINGUAL EDUCATION: STATEMENT OF DR. FRAN-
CESCO CORDASCO. HEARINGS BEFORE THE SPECIAL SUB-
COMMITTEE ON BILINGUAL EDUCATION, 90th Congress, 1st
session, 1967. Washington: Congress of the United States, Senate Committee on Labor and Public Welfare, 1967. 7 p.

The following issues are discussed: (1) the American
common school and the children of poverty, (2) the bilingual child and the American school, and (3) proposed
legislation.

360 _____. BILINGUAL EDUCATION, HEALTH, AND MANPOWER
PROGRAMS. JOINT HEARING BEFORE THE SUBCOMMITTEE
ON EDUCATION AND SPECIAL SUBCOMMITTEE ON HUMAN
RESOURCES, 93d Cong., 1st sess. Washington, D.C.: Govern-
ment Printing Office, 1973. Reprint. New York Times Bilingual
Bicultural Education in the United States Series. New York:
Arno Press, 1978. iv, 151 p.

The Hearings, which were conducted in Los Angeles,
constitute important source materials out of which the
provisions for comprehensive bilingual manpower training
proposals emerged, and the needs for bilingual vocational
training were defined. The hearings were chaired by
Senator Claiborne Pell, and testimony and statements

were submitted from a wide range of individuals actively engaged in a variety of bilingual training settings, for example, East Los Angeles Skill Center, the Bilingual Community Adult School of Los Angeles, the East Los Angeles Health Task Force, and the East Los Angeles Occupational Center. Also included are excerpts from articles and miscellaneous publications, and demographic data.

361 U.S. Congress. Senate. Committee on Labor and Public Welfare. Special Subcommittee on Bilingual Education. BILINGUAL EDU-CATION, HEARINGS. . .90th Cong., 1st sess. on S.428, Part 1 and Part 2. Washington, D.C.: Government Printing Office, 1967. Reprint. New York: Arno Press, 1978. 681 p.

This volume is the text of the historic hearings (18, 19, 26, 29, 31 May and 24 June and 21 July 1967) out of which derived the enactment of the Bilingual Education Act by the Congress as Title VII of the federal Elementary and Secondary Education Act recognizing "the special education needs of the large numbers of children of limited English speaking ability in the United States," and declaring "it to be the policy of the United States to provide financial assistance to local educational agencies to develop and carry out new and imaginative elementary and secondary school programs designed to meet these special educational needs." The hearings constitute a vast compendium of data, information, materials, and statements exploring the backgrounds of an articulated national policy for bilingual education.

362 U.S. Congress. Senate. Committee on Labor and Public Welfare. Subcommittee on Education of the "Quality Educator for American Indians: A Report on Organizational Location." Washington, D.C.: Government Printing Office, May 1967. 11 p.

Gives details concerning the responsibility for Indian education within the federal government. Contains a description of past and present governmental educational policies with pertinent data as to school enrollment, legislation, financing, and so forth. The report also makes a series of recommendations regarding research, planning, and programs.

363 U.S. Congress. Senate. Select Committee on Equal Educational Opportunity. EQUAL EDUCATIONAL OPPORTUNITY FOR PUERTO RICAN CHILDREN, part 8. Washington, D.C.: Government Printing Office, 1970. Reprint. New York: Arno Press, 1975. 3683-973 p.

HEARINGS BEFORE THE SELECT COMMITTEE ON

EQUAL EDUCATIONAL OPPORTUNITY OF THE UNITED
STATES SENATE, 91st. Cong., 2d sess. Washington,
D.C., 23, 24 and 25 November 1970.

364 U.S. Office of Education, Bureau of Research. INTERPRETATIVE
STUDIES ON BILINGUAL EDUCATION. Washington, D.C.:
Government Printing Office, 1969. Reprint. New York Times
Bilingual Bicultural Education in the United States Series. Edited
by Horacio Ulibarri. New York: Arno Press, 1978. 154 p.

This publication includes an important analysis of the
literature on bilingual education and a summary of research with a list of projects and ongoing programs with
some evaluative assessments. Particularly valuable is
an annotated bibliography. The project was undertaken
under the auspices of the Bureau of Research, U.S.
Office of Education, and completed during 1968-69,
and had as its major objective "implications for educational practice and administration, and research in the
areas of bilingual-bicultural education."

365 Valette, Rebecca M. "Some Reflections on Second-Language
Learning in Young Children." LANGUAGE LEARNING 14
(1964): 91-98.

366 Vasquez, Hector. "Civil Rights at the Crossroads." INTEGRATED
EDUCATION 13 (May-June 1975): 168-70.

The director of the Puerto Rican Forum in testimony before the New York City Commission on Human Rights in
May 1974 says that strategically placed bilingual schools
encourage parents to send their children for an education.

367 Vasquez, José A. "Bilingual Education's Greatest Potential: Enrichment for All." JOURNAL OF THE NATIONAL ASSOCIA-
TION FOR BILINGUAL EDUCATION 1 (May 1976): 23-26.

Some of the changes that are necessary in order for bilingual education to be of benefit to everyone are discussed.

368 Viereck, Louis. GERMAN INSTRUCTION IN AMERICAN
SCHOOLS. Annual Report of the U.S. Commissioner of Education, 1900-01, vol. 1. Reprint. Introduction by George Bernstein. New York Times Bilingual Bicultural Education in the
United States Series. New York: Arno Press, 1978. 177 p.

Itself one of the most comprehensive accounts of German language instruction in the United States for the two-hundred-year period it covers, Viereck's monograph includes a wealth of material on the German bilingual school systems in Cincinnati, Baltimore, Indianapolis, Cleveland, and other American cities, and appeared in a German edition as well (ZWEI JAHRUNDERTE DER UNTERRICHT IN DEN VEREINIGTEN STAATEN [Braunschweig: Vieweg, 1903]). George Bernstein's new introduction written for this edition places the report in historical development, and notes significant trends since the report was prepared.

369 Vilomec, V. MULTILINGUALISM. Leiden, Netherlands: Sythoff, 1963. 262 p.

370 Von Maltitz, Frances Willard. LIVING AND LEARNING IN TWO LANGUAGES: BILINGUAL-BICULTURAL EDUCATION IN THE UNITED STATES. New York: McGraw-Hill, 1975. xiii, 221 p.

This book is an overview of the progress and development of bilingual education in the United States.

371 Von Raffler, Walburga. "Studies in Italian-English Bilingualism." Ph. D. dissertation, Indiana University, 1953. 129 p.

372 Walsh, Donald D. "Bilingualism and Bilingual Education: A Guest Editorial." FOREIGN LANGUAGE ANNALS 2 (March 1969): 298-303.

Walsh, a foreign language teacher, advocates progressive bilingual education in order to have "brighter, more tolerant" children, who would be "more perceptive about their own culture and the other than are otherwise comparable monolinguals."

373 Waubaunsee, A. John. INDIAN CONTROL OF SCHOOLS AND BILINGUAL EDUCATION. Arlington, Va.: Center for Applied Linguistics, 1976. 148 p.

373 West, Michael. "Bilingualism." ENGLISH LANGUAGE TEACHING 12 (April-June 1958): 94-97.

Suggests that bilingualism is an inevitable disadvantage and points out its ill effects, suggesting measures for mitigating its evils.

375 Wilson, Robert D. "Bilingual Education for Navaho Students: Strategies for Teaching the Nature of Coordinate Bilingualism as Part of the General Objective, Learning How to Learn." Unpublished paper delivered at the Conference of Teaching English to Speakers of Other Languages, Chicago, 7 March 1969.

> Presents the rationale and general objectives for the curriculum materials the author is developing with the Bureau of Indian Affairs.

376 Wollfradt, K.W. "Die Statistik des Deutsch-Amerikanischen Schulwesens." DEUTSCHER PIONIER 18 (1886): 50-55.

377 Woodford, Protase. "Bilingual-Bicultural Education: A Need for Understanding." In THE ACTFL REVIEW OF FOREIGN LANGUAGE EDUCATION. Vol. 6. Edited by Gilbert A. Jarvis, pp. 397-433. Skokie, Ill.: National Textbook Co., 1974.

378 Wranosky, Ernest J., ed. TEACHING THE BILINGUAL CHILD: A HANDBOOK FOR TEACHERS. Corpus Christi, Tex.: Flour Bluff Public Schools, 1953. 67 p.

379 Wright, Lawrence. "Bilingual Education." RACE RELATIONS REPORTER 4 (September 1973): 14-19.

> This article includes the following chapters: "Mexican Americans," "Bilingual Education," "Bilingual Schools," "Puerto Ricans," "School Integration," "Staff Utilization," "Remedial Reading," "Compensatory Education," "Court Litigation."

380 _____. "The Bilingual Education Movement at the Crossroads." PHI DELTA KAPPAN 46 (November 1973): 183-86.

381 Yamamoto, Kaoru. "Bilingualism: A Brief Review." MENTAL HYGIENE 48 (July 1964): 468-77.

> This article is a general summary and review of the literature dealing with bilingualism: bilingualism and verbal intelligence; studies of English-Yiddish, -Gaelic, -Italian, -Chinese, -Spanish bilingual children; and bilingualism and later emotional development.

382 Yarborough, Ralph M. "Bilingual Education As a Social Force." FOREIGN LANGUAGE ANNALS 2 (March 1969): 325-27.

> This article discusses the implications of the Bilingual Education Act. Based on an address before the joint

conventions of the Modern Language Association and the
American Council on the Teaching of Foreign Languages,
New York, 28 December 1968.

383 Yu, Connie Young. "The 'Others': Asian Americans and Educa-
tions." CIVIL RIGHTS DIGEST 9 (February 1976): 44-51.

Among topics discussed in this article are language difficulties which limit how much Asian-American parents
can help in shaping educational policy, textbook discrimination, and the growth of bilingual education.

384 Zintz, Miles V. "What Teachers Should Know About Bilingual
Education." In INTERPRETIVE STUDY ON BILINGUAL EDUCA-
TION. Edited by Horacio Ulibarri and James G. Cooper. Albuquerque: University of New Mexico, College of Education,
1969. 60 p.

Special emphasis is placed on cross-cultural education,
problems in second-language learning, classroom methodology, special aspects of vocabulary, and the bilingual school. Several valuable bibliographies are in-
included; some are annotated.

385 Zobel, Jan. "The Mexican-American School Child." ILLINOIS
SCHOOLS JOURNAL 50 (Summer 1970): 103-13.

The article states that changes are needed in language
teaching, curricula enrichment and inservice teacher
education, so the education of Mexican-American children will be more functional.

III. HISTORICAL AND SOCIOCULTURAL PERSPECTIVES

386 Alloway, David N., and Cordasco, Francesco. MINORITIES AND
THE AMERICAN CITY: A SOCIOLOGICAL PRIMER FOR EDUCA-
TORS. New York: David McKay, 1970. x, 124 p.

387 Aran, Kenneth, et al. PUERTO RICAN HISTORY AND CULTURE.
A STUDY GUIDE AND CURRICULUM OUTLINE. New York:
United Federation of Teachers, 1973. 151 p.

   These materials are designed primarily for junior and
   senior high schools. They can be taught independently,
   combined to form minicourses, or integrated into con-
   ventional American history or American studies courses.

388 Arndt, Richard. "La Fortalecita: A Study of Low-Income Mexican Americans and Implications for Education." Ph.D. dissertation, University of New Mexico, 1970. 240 p.

389 Berle, Beatrice B. 80 PUERTO RICAN FAMILIES IN NEW YORK
CITY. New York: Columbia University Press, 1958. Reprint.
New York: Arno Press, 1975. 331 p.

   This is a study of health and related problems of eighty
   Puerto Rican families living in a New York City slum.
   The eighty families were chosen from a group of families with sickness. A few of the topics are migration,
   family organization, housing, language and communication, and welfare. The reprint includes a new chapter
   by the author.

390 Bishops' Committee for the Spanish Speaking. San Antonio, Texas.
PROCEEDINGS OF THE ELEVENTH CONFERENCE OF THE NA-
TIONAL CATHOLIC CONFERENCE FOR SOCIAL SERVICES. San
Antonio, Tex.: National Catholic Conference for Social Services,
1962. 104 p.

This is a report of a conference on the aspects of the
problems of Spanish-speaking migrants and residents of
Mexican, Puerto Rican, and Cuban origin.

391 Bongers, Lael Shannon. "A Developmental Study of Time Perception and Time Perspective in Three Cultural Groups: Anglo-
American, Indian-American, and Mexican-American." Ph.D. dissertation, University of California, Los Angeles, 1971. 183 p.

392 Browning, Harley, and McLemore, S. Dale. A STATISTICAL
PROFILE OF THE SPANISH-SURNAME POPULATION OF TEXAS.
Population Series no. 1. Austin: Bureau of Business Research,
University of Texas, 1964. 83 p.

The number, growth, geographical distribution, basic
population characteristics, education, employment opportunities, occupation, and income of the Spanish-
surname population of Texas is compared with four other
southwestern states.

393 Brussell, Charles B. DISADVANTAGED MEXICAN AMERICAN
CHILDREN AND EARLY EDUCATIONAL EXPERIENCE. Austin,
Tex.: Southwest Educational Development Corp., 1968. 105 p.

"The study is divided into four major areas of interest--
history and demography, social characteristics, intelligence and intellectual functioning of Spanish-speaking
children, and implications for early educational experiences for disadvantaged Mexican-American children. A
fifth section contains brief descriptions of a number of
current projects designed for Mexican-American children. A bibliography is included for each section."

394 Burger, Henry C. ETHNO-PEDAGOGY: A MANUAL IN CUL-
TURAL SENSITIVITY WITH TECHNIQUES FOR IMPROVING CROSS-
CULTURAL TEACHING BY FITTING ETHNIC PATTERNS. Albuquerque, N. Mex.: Southwestern Cooperative Educational Laboratory, June 1968. 193 p.

395 Burma, John H. SPANISH-SPEAKING GROUPS IN THE UNITED
STATES. Durham, N.C.: Duke University Press, 1954. Reprint.
Detroit: Blaine Ethridge, 1974. 214 p.

396 _____, ed. MEXICAN AMERICANS IN THE UNITED STATES:
A READER. Cambridge, Mass.: Schenkman Publishing Co.,
1970. 487 p.

397 Cahman, Werner J. "The Cultural Consciousness of Jewish Youth." JEWISH SOCIAL STUDIES 14 (July 1952): 195-208.

This article presents results from a study of a group of nonorthodox but otherwise ideologically undefined and unaffiliated Jewish teenagers in the Brownsville section of Brooklyn, in order to contribute to the reformulation of the values of Judaism and Jewish culture in the new frame of reference developed since the creation of Israel.

398 Cantu, Ismael Sierra. "The Effects of Family Characteristics, Parental Influence, Language Spoken, School Experience, and Self-Motivation on the Level of Educational Attainment of Mexican Americans." Ph.D. dissertation, University of Michigan, 1975. 134 p.

Mexican Americans born between 1940 and 1952 who attended Mercedes, Texas, schools were chosen for this study. One recommendation is that schools provide competent bilingual-bicultural teachers and revise curriculum to meet the needs of Mexican Americans.

399 Cárdenas, Blandina, and Cárdenas, José A. "Chicano--Bright-Eyes, Bilingual, Brown, and Beautiful." TODAY'S EDUCATION 41 (February 1973): 49-51.

400 Cárdenas, René. "Three Critical Factors that Inhibit Acculturation of Mexican Americans." Ph.D. dissertation, University of California, Berkeley, 1970. 221 p.

401 Carter, Thomas P. "A Negative Self-Concept of Mexican American Students." SCHOOL AND SOCIETY 96 (30 March 1968): 217-19.

402 Center for Applied Linguistics. STYLES OF LEARNING AMONG AMERICAN INDIANS: AN OUTLINE FOR RESEARCH. Report and recommendations of a conference held at Stanford University, 8-10 August 1968. Washington, D.C.: Center for Applied For Linguistics, February 1969. 36 p.

This work includes the proceedings of a meeting of specialists in psycholinguistics who study child language, child psychology, Indian cultural anthropology, and related fields, organized to outline feasible research projects to investigate the ways in which the styles of learning employed by Indian groups may be related to the school achievement of the Indian student.

403 Chenault, Lawrence R. THE PUERTO RICAN MIGRANT IN NEW YORK CITY. New York: Columbia University Press, 1938. Reprint. Foreword by Francesco Cordasco. New York: Russell and Russell, 1970.

404 Child, Irvin L. ITALIAN OR AMERICAN? THE SECOND GENERATION IN CONFLICT. New Haven, Conn.: Yale University Press, 1943. Reprint. Introduction by Francesco Cordasco. New York: Russell and Russell, 1970. 208 p.

 This book is a comprehensive study of the acculturation of Italian immigrants.

405 Christian, Chester C., Jr. "The Acculturation of the Bilingual Child." THE MODERN LANGUAGE JOURNAL 49 (March 1965): 160-65.

 Here the effect that insistence on spoken English has on bilingual children is studied. The problem of confusion and frustration which exists when a child learns one language and culture from his parents and then must learn another language and culture when he enters school is discussed.

406 Christian, Jane M. "The Navajo: A People in Transition." Part 1. SOUTHWESTERN STUDIES 2 (Fall 1964): 3-35; Part 2 (Winter 1965): 39-71.

407 Christian, Jane M., and Christian, Chester C., Jr. "Spanish Language and Culture in the Southwest." In LANGUAGE LOYALTY IN THE UNITED STATES: THE MAINTENANCE AND PERPETUATION OF THE NON-ENGLISH MOTHER TONGUE BY AMERICAN ETHNIC AND RELIGIOUS GROUPS. Edited by Joshua A. Fishman, pp. 280-317. The Hague: Mouton and Co., 1966.

 This article contains a history of Spanish-speaking peoples in the development of the Southwest; a profile of the contemporary Mexican Americans; a sociocultural analysis with emphasis on language and its relationship to society and culture.

408 "The Church and the Irish Language." ECCLESIASTICAL REVIEW 5 (October 1891): 279-89.

 The essay describes attempts to have the Irish language and history introduced into American schools. See also, T. O'Neill, "The Decay of the Celtic Languages," CATHOLIC WORLD 34 (January 1882): 563-73; and

Joseph T. Tracy, "Church, State and School," CATH-
OLIC WORLD 50 (January 1890): 530-39.

409 Ciarlantini, Franco. "Italian in American Schools." ATLAN-
TICA 9 (July 1930): 14-15.

The author discusses the teaching of Italian in American
public and private schools.

410 Cintrón de Crespo, Patria. "Puerto Rican Women Teachers in
New York, Self-Perception and Work Adjustment as Perceived in
Themselves and by Others." Ed.D. dissertation, Columbia Univer-
sity Teachers College, 1965. 281 p.

411 Cooper, Paulette, ed. GROWING UP PUERTO RICAN. New
York: Arbor House, 1972. 216 p.

412 Cordasco, Francesco. "Nights in the Gardens of East Harlem:
Patricia Sexton's East Harlem." JOURNAL OF NEGRO EDUCA-
TION 34 (Fall 1965): 450-51.

413 _____. "The Puerto Rican Family and the Anthropologist."
TEACHERS COLLEGE RECORD 68 (May 1967): 672-74.

This article reviews of Oscar Lewis's A PUERTO RICAN
FAMILY IN THE CULTURE OF POVERTY: SAN JUAN
AND NEW YORK. New York: Random House, 1966.

414 _____. JACOB RIIS REVISITED: POVERTY AND THE SLUM IN
ANOTHER ERA. New York: Doubleday, 1968. xxii, 418 p.

Included in this work are materials on immigrant children
(Jewish and Italian) in American schools.

415 _____. "Another View of Poverty: Oscar Lewis' LA VIDA."
PHYLON: THE ATLANTA UNIVERSITY REVIEW OF RACE AND
CULTURE 29 (Spring 1968): 88-92.

416 _____. "Leonard Covello and the Community School." SCHOOL
AND SOCIETY 98 (Summer 1970): 298-99.

417 _____. "The Children of Columbus: Recent Works on the
Italian American Experience." PHYLON: THE ATLANTA UNI-
VERSITY REVIEW OF RACE AND CULTURE 4 (September 1973):
295-98.

418 _____. "The Children of Immigrants in Schools: Historical
Analogues of Educational Deprivation." JOURNAL OF NEGRO
EDUCATION 42 (Winter 1973): 44–53.

419 _____, ed. THE CHILDREN OF IMMIGRANTS IN SCHOOLS.
Vols. 29–33. Report of the Immigrant Commission. 41 vols.
Washington, D.C.: U.S. Government Printing Office, 1911.
Reprint. Metuchen, N.J.: Scarecrow Reprint Corp., 1970.

420 _____, comp. THE PUERTO RICANS, 1493–1973: A CHRONOL-
OGY AND FACT BOOK. Ethnic Chronology Series, no. 11.
New York: Oceana Publications, 1973. 137 p.

Included in this work are materials from the important
and generally unavailable report of the U.S. and Puerto
Rico Commission on the Status of Puerto Rico. Sections
deal with the history of Puerto Rico, migrations to the
mainland, the Puerto Rican community in New York
City, and education on the mainland.

421 _____, advisory ed. THE ITALIAN AMERICAN EXPERIENCE.
39 vols. New York: Arno Press/New York Times, 1975.

422 _____, advisory ed. THE PUERTO RICAN EXPERIENCE. 33
vols. New York: Arno Press/New York Times, 1975.

423 _____, ed. PUERTO RICANS AND EDUCATIONAL OPPORTUN-
ITY. New York: Arno Press, 1975. 190 p.

One of the major problems facing the Puerto Rican community in the United States is the meaningful education
of its children. Collected in this original anthology
are the following: (1) a report on the Puerto Rican
graduates (June 1961) of Morris High School in New
York City, one of the few studies of this kind, (2) a
report to the Congressional Committee on Education and
Labor on education in Puerto Rico in the early 1960s
(and its concomitant problems for the mainland experience), (3) a graphic chronicle of visits to American
schools revealing the educational plight of Puerto Rican
children, (4) the text of the report of the First National
Conference on the Special Needs of Puerto Rican Youth,
and (5) a provocative discussion of the Bilingual Education Act enacted by the Congress in 1967 and its failure
to serve the needs of Puerto Rican children. Charts and
tables are included.

424 _____, ed. STUDIES IN ITALIAN AMERICAN SOCIAL HIS-
TORY. ESSAYS IN HONOR OF LEONARD COVELLO. Totowa,
N.J.: Rowman and Littlefield, 1975. xvii, 264 p.

425 Cordasco, Francesco, and Bucchioni, Eugene. THE PUERTO RICAN
COMMUNITY AND ITS CHILDREN ON THE MAINLAND: A
SOURCEBOOK FOR TEACHERS, SOCIAL WORKERS AND OTHER
PROFESSIONALS. Metuchen, N.J.: Scarecrow Press, 1972. xiii,
465 p.

426 _____. THE PUERTO RICAN EXPERIENCE: A SOCIOLOGICAL
SOURCEBOOK. Totowa, N.J.: Littlefield, Adams and Co.,
1973. 386 p.

This anthology of Puerto Rican life both on the mainland and in Puerto Rico covers the following areas:
island background, the migration, life on the mainland,
and education on the mainland.

427 _____. THE ITALIANS: SOCIAL BACKGROUNDS OF AN
AMERICAN GROUP. New York: Augustus M. Kelley, 1974.
xx, 598 p.

428 Cordasco, Francesco, and Galattioto, Rocco. "Ethnic Develop-
ment in the Interstitial Community: The East Harlem (New York
City) Experience." PHYLON: THE ATLANTA UNIVERSITY RE-
VIEW OF RACE AND CULTURE 31 (Fall 1970): 302-12.

429 Cordova, Ignacio R. THE RELATIONSHIP OF ACCULTURATION,
ACHIEVEMENT AND ALIENATION AMONG MEXICAN AMERI-
CAN SIXTH-GRADE STUDENTS. Las Cruces: N. Mex.: Educational Resources Information Center, New Mexico State University,
1969. 24 p.

The author maintains that low achievement is a symptom
of alienation and that educators must alter the system to
permit biculturalism.

430 Cornwell, Elmer E., Jr. "Party Absorption of Ethnic Groups:
The Case of Providence, Rhode Island." SOCIAL FORCES 38
(March 1960): 205-10.

This article confirms the hypothesis that the American
political party has been an important factor in the integration of successive waves of immigrants into the American political community.

431 Cortes, Carlos E., advisory ed. THE MEXICAN AMERICAN.
21 vols. New York: Arno Press/New York Times, 1974.

432 Covello, Leonard. "The Italians in America." ITALY-AMERICA
MONTHLY 1 (15 July 1934): 11-17.

433 _____. "A High School and Its Immigrant Community." JOUR-
NAL OF EDUCATIONAL SOCIOLOGY 9 (February 1936): 333-46.

   East Harlem (New York City) Italian immigrant community and its Benjamin Franklin High School are described.

434 _____. "Language as a Factor in Integration and Assimilation."
MODERN LANGUAGE JOURNAL 36 (February 1939): 211-17.

435 _____. THE SOCIAL BACKGROUND OF THE ITALO-AMERI-
CAN SCHOOL CHILD. A STUDY OF THE SOUTHERN ITALIAN
FAMILY MORES AND THEIR EFFECT ON THE SCHOOL SITUA-
TION IN ITALY AND AMERICA. Edited with an introduction
by Francesco Cordasco. Leiden, Netherlands: E.J. Brill, 1967;
Totowa, N.J.: Rowman and Littlefield, 1972. xxxii, 488 p.

   This work is a revision of Ph.D. dissertation written at
   New York University, 1944. A major study of ethnicity, of the context of poverty, of a minority's children, and the challenges to the American school. Part
   1: "Social Background in Italy," Part 2: "The Family
   as the Social World of the Southern Italian Contadino
   Society," Part 3: "Italian Family Mores and Their Educational Implications," and Part 4: "Summary and Conclusions."

436 Covello, Leonard, with Guido D'Agostino. THE HEART IS THE
TEACHER. New York: McGraw-Hill, 1958. Reprint. Intro-
duction by Francesco Cordasco. Totowa, N.J.: Littlefield,
Adams and Co., 1970. 275 p.

   The romanticized autobiography of Leonard Covello, who
   has devoted his talent and experience to solving the
   educational problems of migrant children in New York,
   Italians and Puerto Ricans in particular.

437 Dadabhay, Yusuf. "Circuitous Assimilation Among Rural Hindustanis in California." SOCIAL FORCES 33 (December 1954): 138-
41.

   The author shows that the assimilation of East Indian
   immigrants follows the pattern of that of Mexican Americans, whose subculture is more immediately accessible
   to them than is the dominant American culture.

438 Del Campo, Philip E. "An Analysis of Selected Features in the Acculturation Process of the Mexican American School Child." Ph.D. dissertation, International University, 1970. 178 p.

439 Dickeman, Mildred. "The Integrity of the Cherokee Students." In THE CULTURE OF POVERTY: A CRITIQUE. Edited by Eleanor Leacock, pp. 140-79. New York: Simon and Schuster, 1971.

440 Doob, C.F. "Family Background and Peer Group Development in a Puerto Rican District." SOCIOLOGICAL QUARTERLY 11 (1970): 523-32.

441 Downs, James F. "The Cowboy and the Lady: Models as a Determinant of the Rate of Acculturation Among the Piñon Navajo." KROEBER ANTHROPOLIGICAL SOCIETY PAPERS 29 (Fall 1963): 53-67.

442 Drotning, Phil. "Norway in Wisconsin." AMERICAN-SCANDINAVIAN REVIEW 28 (Summer 1950): 149-54.

443 Dyke, R.B., and Witkin, H.A. "Family Experiences Related to the Development of Differentiation in Children." CHILD DEVELOPMENT 36 (1965): 21-55.

444 Eggan, Dorothy. "Instruction and Affect in Hopi Cultural Continuity." SOUTHWESTERN JOURNAL OF ANTHROPOLOGY 12 (1956): 347-70.

445 Ellis, Frances H. "Historical Account of German Instruction in the Public Schools of Indianapolis 1869-1919." THE INDIANA MAGAZINE OF HISTORY 50 (June 1954): 119-138; 50 (December 1954): 357-80; 52 (September 1956): 251-76.

446 Epstein, Erwin [Howard] , ed. POLITICS AND EDUCATION IN PUERTO RICO. Metuchen, N.J.: Scarecrow Press, 1970. 275 p.

447 Ervin-Tripp, Susan [M.] "Learning and Recall in Bilinguals." AMERICAN JOURNAL OF PSYCHOLOGY 74 (September 1961): 446-51.

  Italian bilinguals were tested for recall of pictorial material using English and Italian during learning and during recall.

448 Fellows, Donald Keith. "Puerto Ricans." In A MOSAIC OF AMERICA'S ETHNIC MINORITIES, edited by Donald K. Fellows, pp. 169-95. New York, N.Y.: John Wiley and Sons, 1972.

This essay is a brief historical and sociological description of Puerto Ricans from colonial times to the present. It takes into account geography, political changes, religion, family patterns on the island; reasons, patterns of migration (to New York City), acculturation, religion on the mainland, and recent occupational diversification. There is question as to whether Puerto Ricans will follow a culturally pluralistic pattern or adopt American ways.

449 Fishman, Joshua A. "Degree of Bilingualism in a Yiddish School and Leisure Time Activities." JOURNAL OF SOCIAL PSYCHOLOGY 36 (1952): 155-65.

450 _____. "The Ethnic Group School and Mother Tongue Maintenance in the United States." SOCIOLOGY OF EDUCATION 27 (Summer 1964): 306-17.

451 _____. HUNGARIAN MAINTENANCE IN THE UNITED STATES. Bloomington: Indiana University Press, 1966. 58 p.

Past and present Hungarian language maintenance efforts in the United States are appraised in this work.

452 Fishman, Joshua A., and Casiano, Heriberto. "Puerto Ricans in Our Press." THE MODERN LANGUAGE JOURNAL 53 (March 1969): 157-62.

"This study reports on the treatment of Puerto Ricans in four New York City dailies, two published in English and two in Spanish." It seeks to answer certain questions dealing with attitude and language maintenance.

453 Fitzpatrick, Joseph P. PUERTO RICAN AMERICANS: THE MEANING OF MIGRATION TO THE MAINLAND. Englewood Cliffs, N.J.: Prentice-Hall, 1971. 192 p.

454 Ford, Richard Clyde. "The French-Canadians in Michigan." MICHIGAN HISTORY MAGAZINE 27 (Spring 1943): 243-57.

455 Frey, J. William. "Amish 'Triple Talk'" AMERICAN SPEECH 20 (April 1945): 85-98.

A technical discussion of the Pennsylvania Dutch-High German English trilingualism existing among the Amish communities of Lancaster County, Pennsylvania, among others is included in this work.

456 Gabet, Yvonne, Y. "Birth-Order and Achievement in Anglo, Mexican American and Black Americans." Unpublished Ph.D. dissertation, University of Texas. 1971. 188 p.

457 Garbarino, M.S. "Seminole Girl: The Autobiography of a Young Woman Between Two Worlds." TRANSACTION 7 (1970): 40-46.

458 Garcia, A.B., and Zimmerman, B.J. "The Effect of Examiner Ethnicity and Language on the Performance of Bilingual Mexican American First Graders." JOURNAL OF SOCIAL PSYCHOLOGY 87 (1972): 3-11.

459 Gardner, R.C. "Attitudes and Motivation: Their Role in Second Language Acquisition." TESOL QUARTERLY 2 (1968): 141-50.

460 Gavillan-Torres, Eva M. "The Forgotten Rican: The Puerto Rican Community on the Mainland." HARVARD GRADUATE SCHOOL OF EDUCATION ASSOCIATION BULLETIN 20 (Spring-Summer 1976): 10-12.

Most bilingual programs have given a good deal of attention to island culture, and not allowed sufficient attention to be given to mainland Puerto Rican life. Models are needed to demonstrate how to proceed with the latter concern.

461 Georges, Robert A. "The Greeks of Tarpon Springs: An American Folk Group." SOUTHERN FOLKLORE QUARTERLY 29 (June 1965): 129-41.

462 Gerber, Malcolm. "Ethnicity and Measures of Educability: Differences among Rural Navajo, Pueblo, and Rural Spanish American First Graders on Measures of Learning Style, Hearing Vocabulary, Entry Skills, Motivation, and Home Environment Processes." Ph.D. dissertation, University of Southern California, 1968. 202 p.

463 Gerhard, E.S. "The History of Schwenkfelder Schools." SCHWENKFELDIANA 1 (1943): 5-21.

464 Giles, [W.]H., et al. "Dimensions of Ethnic Identity: An Example from Northern Maine." JOURNAL OF SOCIAL PSYCHOLOGY 100 (October 1976): 11-19.

465 Glazer, Nathan, and Moynihan, Daniel P. BEYOND THE MELTING POT: THE NEGROES, PUERTO RICANS, JEWS, ITALIANS AND IRISH OF NEW YORK CITY. 2d ed. Cambridge, Mass.: M.I.T. Press, 1970. 363 p.

466 Goldman, R., and Sanders, J.W. "Cultural Factors and Hearing." EXCEPTIONAL CHILDREN 35 (1969): 489-90.

467 Gonzales, E., and Ortiz, L. "Social Policy and Education Related to Linguistically and Culturally Different Groups." JOURNAL OF LEARNING DISABILITIES 10 (June-July 1977): 332-38.

468 Goodenough, Ward. "Multiculturalism as the Normal Human Experience." ANTHROPOLOGY AND EDUCATION 7 (1976): 4-6.

469 Gottlieb, David, and Heinsohn, Annie L., eds. AMERICA'S OTHER YOUTH: GROWING UP POOR. Englewood Cliffs, N.J.: Prentice-Hall, 1971. 216 p.

The contents of part 1, "Puerto Rican Youth," include excerpts from C. Mayerson's "Two blocks apart: Jan Gonzales and Peter Quinn," E. Padilla's "Up from Puerto Rico," P. Sexton's "Spanish Harlem," and P. Montgomery's "Poverty on the Lower East Side. . . ."

470 Graves, Nancy B. "City, Country and Child Rearing: A Tri-culture Study of Mother-Child Relationships in Varying Environments." Ph.D. dissertation, University of Colorado, 1971. 303 p.

471 Greene, John F., and Zirkel, Perry [Alan]. "The Family Background of Puerto Rican Students: An Analysis of Educationally Relevant Variables." Mimeographed. 1971. 23 p.

The purpose of this study was to construct a data base concerning the home background of Puerto Rican students as it relates to present and potential educational programs. The focus was on parental perceptions of educationally relevant variables in the hopes of improving the planning and implementation of educational programs by school and community groups to better the needs of Puerto Rican people.

472 Gross, Feliks. "Language and Value Changes Among the Arapaho." INTERNATIONAL JOURNAL OF AMERICAN LINGUISTICS 17 (1951): 10-17.

This article discusses language as an index of culture change, the functional distribution of language, the distribution of the use of Arapaho and English within the family, and the transformation of values as these factors pertain to this Indian group.

473 Guinn, R. "Value Clarification in the Bicultural Classroom." JOURNAL OF TEACHER EDUCATION 28 (January-February 1977): 46-47.

The inclusion of bicultural curricula has never been more beneficial or more critical than when used with Mexican-American students. The teacher preparing in bicultural studies that use value clarification could do undergraduate specialization in cross-cultural education, linguistic communication skills, application of educational psychology to the bilingual learner, and directed teaching in the bicultural classroom.

474 Ham, Edward Billings. "Journalism and the French Survival in New England." NEW ENGLAND QUARTERLY 11 (March-December 1938): 89-107.

This article is an extensive survey of the Franco-American press.

475 _____. "French National Societies in New England." NEW ENGLAND QUARTERLY 12 (June 1939): 315-32.

This article outlines one aspect of the Franco-Americans' struggle "to preserve some semblance of racial integrity," the Franco-American fraternal societies.

476 _____. "French Patterns in Quebec and New England." NEW ENGLAND QUARTERLY 27 (December 1945): 435-47.

477 Hamon, E. LES CANADIENS-FRANÇAIS DE LA NOUVELLE-ANGLETERRE. Quebec: Hardy, 1891. 483 p.

French Canadians of New England are discussed in this work.

478 Harris, D.L. "Education of Linguistic Minorities in the United States and the USSR." COMPARATIVE EDUCATION REVIEW 6 (1963): 191-98.

479 Haugen, Einar. "The Struggle Over Norwegian." NORWEGIAN-AMERICAN STUDIES AND RECORDS 17 (1952): 1-35.

480 Havighurst, Robert J. "The American Indian: From Assimilation to Cultural Pluralism." EDUCATIONAL LEADERSHIP 31 (April 1974): 585-89.

481 Hawaii. Department of Education. Office of Research. "Survey of Non-English Speaking Students Attending the Public Schools in Hawaii." Research Report no. 58. Honolulu: Department of Education, 23 May 1968. 92 p.

482 Helm, June, ed. SPANISH-SPEAKING PEOPLE IN THE UNITED STATES: PROCEEDINGS OF THE 1968 ANNUAL SPRING MEETING OF THE SOCIETY. Seattle: University of Washington Press, 1968. 215 p.

483 Henderson, R.W. "Environmental Stimulation and Intellectual Development of Mexican American Children." Ph.D. dissertation, University of Arizona, 1966. 176 p.

484 Henderson, R.W., and Merritt, G.C. "Environmental Backgrounds of Mexican American Children with Different Potentials for School Success." JOURNAL OF SOCIAL PSYCHOLOGY 75 (1969): 101-6.

485 Hermenet, Argelia Maria Buitrago. ETHNIC IDENTIFICATION OF PUERTO RICAN SEVENTH GRADERS. Ed.D. dissertation, University of Massachusetts, 1971. 375 p.

486 Herskovits, Melville J. "Some Comments on the Study of Culture Contact." AMERICAN ANTHROPOLOGIST 43 (January-March 1941): 1-10.

> The article describes contact studies stating that the "concept of acculturation is beginning its cycle of development."

487 Hertzig, Margaret E. "Aspects of Cognitive Style in Young Children of Differing Social and Ethnic Backgrounds." In COGNITIVE STUDIES II: DEFICITS IN COGNITION. Edited by J. Hellmuth, pp. 184-201. New York: Brunner/Mazel, 1971.

488 Hilger, Sister Inez. ARAPAHO CHILD LIFE AND ITS CULTURAL BACKGROUND. Smithsonian Institution, Bureau of American Ethnology, Bulletin no. 148. Washington, D.C.: U.S. Government Printing Office, 1952. 187 p.

489 Hirata, Lucie Cheng. "Youth, Parents, and Teachers in China-
town: A Triadic Framework of Minority Socialization." URBAN
EDUCATION 10 (October 1975): 279-96.

490 Hofman, John E. "The Language Transition in Some Lutheran
Denominations." In LANGUAGE LOYALTY IN THE UNITED
STATES, by Joshua A. Fishman et al., pp. 127-55. The Hague:
Mouton, 1964.

This essay discusses language transition in German- and
Norwegian-speaking Lutheran parishes.

491 Hopkins, Thomas R. BUREAU OF INDIAN AFFAIRS SUMMER
PROGRAM. UNIVERSITY OF ALASKA, 24 JUNE TO 2 AUGUST
1963. Juneau: Bureau of Indian Affairs, September 1963. 58 p.

This work describes in detail a six-week college orientation program geared to aid Alaskan native students in
overcoming the cultural differences between their world
view and that which would be expected of them in college.

492 Hourihan, John J., and Chapin, Dexter. "Multicultural Education in a Pluralistic Society: Group v. Individual." ANTHRO-
POLOGY AND EDUCATION QUARTERLY 7 (November 1976):
23-26.

This work advocates the training of culturally pluralistic
individuals.

493 Jayagopal, R. "Problem Solving Abilities and Psychomotor Skills
of Navajo Indians, Spanish Americans and Anglos in Junior High
School. Ph.D. dissertation, University of New Mexico, 1970.
182 p.

494 Jensen, Arthur R. "Learning Abilities in Mexican American and
Anglo American Children." CALIFORNIA JOURNAL OF EDU-
CATIONAL RESEARCH 12 (1969): 147-59.

495 Johnson, Colleen L. "The Japanese American Family and Community in Honolulu: Generational Continuities in Ethnic Affila-
tion." Ph.D. dissertation, Syracuse University, 1972. 213 p.

496 Johnson, Granville B. [Jr.]. "The Relationship Existing Between Bilingualism and Racial Attitude." THE JOURNAL OF EDUCATIONAL
PSYCHOLOGY 42 (October 1951): 357-65.

497 Jonassen, Christen T. "Cultural Variables in the Ecology of an Ethnic Group." AMERICAN SOCIOLOGICAL REVIEW 14 (February 1949): 32-41.

This article traces of the movement of the Norwegian communities in New York City from the mid 1800s to the last known settlement in Bay Ridge.

498 Jones, Frank E., and Lambert, Wallace E. "Some Situational Influences on Attitudes Toward Immigrants." BRITISH JOURNAL OF SOCIOLOGY 18 (December 1967): 408-24.

This analysis of the attitudes of Canadian adults toward the immigrants reveals that variations in attitudes to immigrants are significantly related to certain dimensions of the interaction systems in which immigrants and natives participate.

499 Joseph, Stephen M., ed. THE ME NOBODY KNOWS: CHILDREN'S VOICES FROM THE GHETTO. New York: Avon Books, 1969. 139 p.

This work is a compilation of childrens' writings, ages seven to eighteen, mostly black and Puerto Rican, from ghetto areas in New York such as Bedford-Stuyvesant, Harlem, Jamaica, and the lower east and west sides.

500 Justin, Neal. "Mexican American Achievement Hindered by Culture Conflict." SOCIOLOGY AND SOCIAL RESEARCH 56 (1972): 271-79.

501 Kagan, Spencer, and Madsen, Millard C. "Rivalry in Anglo American and Mexican Children of Two Ages." JOURNAL OF PERSONALITY AND SOCIAL PSYCHOLOGY 24 (1972): 214-20.

502 Katz, J. "Bilingualism and Biculturalism in Canada." COMPARATIVE EDUCATION REVIEW 2 (1966): 113-18.

503 Kershner, J.K. "Ethnic Group Differences in Children's Ability to Reproduce Direction and Orientation." JOURNAL OF SOCIAL PSYCHOLOGY 88 (1972): 3-13.

504 Kimball, Solon T. "Cultural Influences Shaping the Role of the Child." In EDUCATION AND CULTURE: ANTHROPOLOGICAL APPROACHES. Edited by George D. Spindler, pp. 268-83. New York: Holt, Rinehart and Winston, 1963.

505 Kitano, Harry H.L. JAPANESE AMERICANS: THE EVOLUTION OF A SUBCULTURE. 2d ed. Englewood Cliffs, N.J.: Prentice-Hall, 1976. xvii, 231 p.

506 Kloss, Heinz. "Die deutschamerikanische Schule." JAHRBUCH FUR AMERIKASTUDIEN (Heidelberg) 2 (1962): 141-75.

507 Kollmorgen, Walter M., and Harrison, Robert W. "French-Speaking Farmers of Southern Louisiana." ECONOMIC GEOGRAPHY 22 (July 1946): 153-60.

This study of the agricultural problems and socioeconomic situation of the Cajun shows how cultural considerations have conditioned his economic adjustment.

508 Kuo, Eddie Chen-Yu. "Bilingual Socialization of Preschool Chinese Children in the Twin-Cities Area." Ph.D. dissertation, University of Minnesota, 1972. 192 p.

509 Lambert, Wallace E. "A Social Psychology of Bilingualism." THE JOURNAL OF SOCIAL ISSUES 23 (April 1967): 91-109.

This article describes distinctive behavior of the bilingual individual, the social influences that affect his behavior, and its consequences.

510 Lambert, Wallace E., and Taguchi, Y. "Ethnic Cleavage Among Young Children." JOURNAL OF ABNORMAL AND SOCIAL PSYCHOLOGY 53 (1956): 380-82.

511 Lampe, P.E. "The Acculturation of Mexican Americans in Public and Parochial Schools." SOCIOLOGICAL ANALYSIS 36 (Spring 1975): 211-46.

512 Layden, Russell Glenn. "The Relationship Between the Language of Instruction and the Development of Self-Concept, Classroom Climate and Achievement of Spanish-Speaking Puerto Rican Children." Ed.D. dissertation, University of Maryland, 1972. 191 p.

513 Leach, John Nathaniel. "Cultural Factors Affecting the Adjustment of Puerto Rican Children to Schooling in Hartford, Connecticut." Ph.D. dissertation, University of Connecticut, 1971. 109 p.

514 Lefley, Harriet P. "Effects of a Cultural Heritage Program on the Self-Concept of Miccosuxee Indian Children." JOURNAL OF EDUCATIONAL RESEARCH 67 (July-August 1974): 462-66.

515 Lesser, George S.; Fifer, Gordon; and Clark, Donald H. MENTAL
ABILITIES OF CHILDREN IN DIFFERENT SOCIAL AND CULTURAL
GROUPS. New York: Monograph of Society for Research in Child
Development, Serial no. 102, 1965. 102 p.

516 Levine, H. "Bilingualism, Its Effect on Emotional and Social
Development." JOURNAL OF SECONDARY EDUCATION 44
(1969): 69-73.

517 Lewis, Diane K. "The Multicultural Education Model and Minorities: Some Reservations." ANTHROPOLOGY AND EDUCATION
QUARTERLY 7 (1976): 32-37.

518 Lewis, E. Glyn. MULTILINGUALISM IN THE SOVIET UNION.
The Hague: Mouton, 1972. xx, 332 p.

This work is an examination of the major policies, sociolinguistic practices, and educational planning for bilingual education in the Soviet Union.

519 Lieberson, S[tanley]. "Bilingualism in Montreal: A Demographic
Analysis." AMERICAN JOURNAL OF SOCIOLOGY 71 (July
1965): 10-25.

520 Long, Barbara H., and Henderson, Edmund H. "Self-Social Concepts of Disadvantaged School Beginners." JOURNAL OF GENET-
IC PSYCHOLOGY 113 (1968): 41-51.

521 McCarthy, Jacqueline. "A Study of the Leisure Activities of
Taos Pueblo Indian Children." Ph.D. dissertation, North Texas
State University, 1970. 269 p.

522 McCauley, Margaret A. "A Study of Social Class and Assimilation in Relation to Puerto Rican Family Patterns." Ph.D. dissertation. Fordham University, 1972. 214 p.

523 McKay, Ralph Yarnelle. "A Comparative Study of the Character
Representation of California's Dominant Minority Groups in the
Officially Adopted California Reading Textbooks of the 1950's,
1960's, and 1970's." Ed.D. dissertation, University of the Pacific, 1971. 272 p.

524 McNickle, D'Arcy. "The Sociocultural Setting of Indian Life."
AMERICAN JOURNAL OF PSYCHIATRY 125 (August 1968): 219-
23.

525 Madsen, Millard C., and Shapira, A. "Cooperative and Competitive Behavior of Urban Afro American, Anglo American, Mexican American and Mexican Village Children." DEVELOPMENTAL PSYCHOLOGY 3 (1970): 16-20.

526 Martinez, Gilbert T[homas]., and Edwards, J.C. THE MEXICAN AMERICAN: HIS LIFE ACROSS FOUR CENTURIES. Boston: Houghton, Mifflin, 1973. 184 p.

527 Meacham, Merlin J. "Enhancing Environments for Children with Cultural Linguistic Differences." LANGUAGE, SPEECH AND HEARING SERVICES IN SCHOOLS 6 (July 1975): 156-60.

528 Meier, Matthew S., and Rivera, Feliciano. THE CHICANOS: A HISTORY OF MEXICAN AMERICANS. New York: Hill and Wang, 1972. 302 p.

529 Melody, Sister Laura. "Mexican American Mothers' Teaching Style and Their Children's Need for Structure." Ph.D. dissertation, University of Illinois, 1975. 133 p.

530 Menarini, Alberto. "Sull'italo-americano degli Stati Uniti." [On Italian-American of the United States]. In AI MARGINI DELLA LINGUA. By Alberto Menarni, pp. 145-208. Florence, Italy: Sansoni Editore, 1947.

   Reviewed by Robert A. Hall, Jr. in LANGUAGE 24
   (April-June 1948): 239-41. It deals with the transformation which Italian has undergone in this country,
   particularly in respect to vocabulary, and the influence
   of Italo-American speech on Italian dialects.

531 Mencher, Joan. "Child Rearing and Family Organization Among Puerto Ricans in Eastville: El Barrio de Nueva York." Ph.D. dissertation, Columbia University, 1958. 186 p.

532 Meyerstein, Ruth G. "Selected Problems of Bilingualism Among Immigrant Slovaks." Ph.D. dissertation, University of Michigan, 1959. 208 p.

   This thesis applies principles of modern linguistic science and bilingualism to the description of some speech
   features characteristic of Slovak immigrants in the United
   States.

533 Miller, Herbert Adolphus. THE SCHOOL AND THE IMMIGRANT. Cleveland, Ohio: National Foundation, 1961. Reprint. New York: Arno Press, 1975. 211 p.

This study is a brief summary of the effectiveness of
public school educational policy in adapting immigrants
to American culture. While concentrating upon the experience in one city, Cleveland, the findings and evaluation of this program can be applied to the efforts of
other pluralistic urban centers.

534 Moore, Joan W. MEXICAN AMERICANS. 2d ed. Englewood
Cliffs, N.J.: Prentice-Hall, 1976. xiv, 173 p.

535 Moquin, Wayne, and Van Doren, Charles, eds. A DOCUMEN-
TARY HISTORY OF THE MEXICAN AMERICANS. New York:
Praeger, 1971. 399 p.

536 Morrison, Karlene Elizabeth. "An Examination of Self-Concept
as It Relates to the Selected School Behaviors of Puerto Rican,
Black and White Senior High School Students in Camden, New
Jersey: An Inter-Disciplinary Study in Education, Sociology, and
Psychology." Ed.D. dissertation, Rutgers University, 1974. 268 p.

537 Nahirny, Vladimir C., and Fishman, Joshua A. "American Immigrant Groups: Ethnic Identification and the Problem of Generations." SOCIOLOGICAL REVIEW 13 (November 1965): 311-26.

538 Nava, Alfonso Rodriguez. "A Political History of Bilingual Language Policy in the Americas." Ph.D. dissertation, Claremont
Graduate School, 1977. 191 p.

The struggle for a consistent bilingual policy in the
Americas continues. In the early North American colo-
nies, maintenance of the mother tongue was encouraged.
The movement's low point was in the 1920s in the
United States. In the Spanish colonies, bilingual educa-
tion was an effective instrument of colonization.

539 Nava, Julian. "Cultural Barriers and Factors that Affect Learning by Spanish-Speaking Children." In MEXICAN AMERICANS
IN THE UNITED STATES: A READER, edited by John H. Burma,
pp. 125-34. Cambridge, Mass.: Schenkman, 1970.

540 Nava, Julian. THE MEXICAN AMERICAN IN AMERICAN HIS-
TORY. New York: American Book Co., 1973. 183 p.

541 _____, ed. MEXICAN AMERICANS: PAST, PRESENT, AND
FUTURE. New York: American Book Co., 1969. 120 p.

542 _____. MEXICAN AMERICANS: A BRIEF LOOK AT THEIR HISTORY. New York: Anti-Defamation League of B'nai B'rith, 1970. 56 p.

543 Naylor, Gordon Hardy. "Learning Styles at Six Years in Two Ethnic Groups in a Disadvantaged Area." Ph.D. dissertation, University of Southern California, 1971. 226 p.

544 Negron de Montilla, Aida. "The Public School System and the Americanization Process in Puerto Rico from 1900 to 1930." Ph.D. dissertation, New York University, 1970. 117 p.

545 Osborn, L[ynn].R. "Rhetoric, Repetition, Silence: Traditional Requisites of Indian Communication." JOURNAL OF AMERICAN INDIAN EDUCATION 12 (1973): 15-21.

546 Parenton, Vernon J. "Socio-Psychological Integration in a Rural French Speaking Section of Louisiana." SOUTHWESTERN SOCIAL SCIENCE QUARTERLY 30 (December 1949): 188-95.

   This article is a description of the social adaptation of the Acadians of Bayou Lafourche.

547 Pelletier, Wilfred. "Childhood in an Indian Village." NORTHIAN 7 (1970): 20-23.

548 Penalosa, Fernando. "The Changing Mexican American in Southern California." SOCIOLOGICAL AND SOCIAL RESEARCH 51 (1967): 405-17.

549 Penna Firme, Thereza. "Effects of Social Reinforcement on Self-Esteem of Mexican American Children." Ph.D. dissertation, Stanford University, 1969. 317 p.

550 Prago, Albert. STRANGERS IN THEIR OWN LAND: A HISTORY OF MEXICAN AMERICANS. New York: Four Winds Press, 1973. 226 p.

551 Proshansky, Harold M. "The Development of Intergroup Attitudes." In REVIEW OF CHILD DEVELOPMENT RESEARCH. Edited by L. and M. Hoffman, pp. 311-71. New York: Russell Sage Foundation, 1966.

552 Read, Allen Walker. "Bilingualism in the Middle Colonies, 1725-1775." AMERICAN SPEECH 21 (April 1937): 93-99.

This article discusses the "melting pot" in the colonial era. The author uses material drawn from newspaper advertisements for runaway slaves and indentured servants to build a picture of the linguistic conditions of the time in Pennsylvania and New York.

553 Reboussin, R., and Goldstein, J.W. "Achievement Motivation in Navajo and White Students." AMERICAN ANTHROPOLOGIST 68 (1966): 740-44.

554 Rodriguez, Valerio Sierra. "Mexican American Pupils' Self-Concept in Public Elementary Schools." Ph.D. dissertation, United States International University, 1974. 91 p.

555 Rosenblatt, J. "Cognitive Impulsivity in Mexican American and Anglo American Children." Ph.D. dissertation, University of Arizona, 1968. 312 p.

556 Rosenthal, Alan G. "Pre-School Experience and Adjustment of Puerto Rican Children." Ph.D. dissertation, New York University, 1955. 204 p.

557 Santos, Ida. "Cultural Differences Between Anglos and Chicanos." INTEGRATED EDUCATION 13 (November-December 1975): 21-23.

This work concerns the perceptions that Anglo teachers, children, and parents, and Chicano children and parents have of each other. The study included twelve Anglo teachers and ten Chicano and Anglo parents, with ten Chicano and Anglo students.

558 Schutzengel, Tirzah Gertrud. "The Effects of Bilingualism on Concept Formation: A Comparative Study of Monolingual and Bilingual Elementary School Students." Ed.D. dissertation, Clark University, 1974. 227 p.

559 Shasteen, Amos Eugene. "Value Orientations of Anglo and Spanish American High School Sophomores." Ed.D. dissertation, University of New Mexico, 1967. 165 p.

560 Simirenko, A. SOCIO-ECONOMIC VARIABLES IN THE ACCULTURATION PROCESS: A PILOT STUDY OF TWO WASHO INDIAN COMMUNITIES. Reno: University of Nevada, 1966. 272 p.

561 Smith, R. Lynn, and Parenton, Vernon J. "Acculturation Among the Louisiana French." AMERICAN JOURNAL OF SOCIOLOGY 44 (November 1938): 355-64.

This article examines how and why the white elements in the "extremely herterogeneous" mass of European settlers have been absorbed in particular into the French Acadian culture of South Louisiana.

562 Soares, Anthony T. and Louise M. "Self-Perceptions of Culturally Disadvantaged Children." AMERICAN EDUCATIONAL RESEARCH JOURNAL 6 (1969): 31-45.

563 Sosa, Alonzo Hernandez. "Bilingual Bicultural Education in Texas Elementary Public Schools, 1930-1975." Ed.D. dissertation, East Texas State University, 1975. 114 p.

During the 1930s and 1940s, Mexican-American children were in an alien world. Compensatory education began to play a role in the 1950s. In the 1960s, came the movement favoring bilingual bicultural education. In Texas, bilingual programs, reading, and vocabulary-building skills were given top priority.

564 Sotomayor, M. "Language, Culture and Ethnicity in Developing Self-Concept." SOCIAL CASEWORK 58 (April 1977): 195-203.

565 Southern, Mara, and Plant, Walter T. "Differential Cognitive Development within and between Racial and Ethnic Groups of Disadvantaged Preschool and Kindergarten Children." JOURNAL OF GENETIC PSYCHOLOGY 119 (1971): 259-66.

566 Spellman, C.M. "The Shift from Color to Form Preference in Young Children of Different Ethnic Background." Ph.D. dissertation, University of Texas, 1968. 118 p.

567 Spoerl, Dorothy T[ilden]. "Bilinguality and Emotional Adjustment." THE JOURNAL OF ABNORMAL AND SOCIAL PSYCHOLOGY 38 (January 1943): 37-57.

This work suggests that, although at the college level bilingualism as such does not affect the student's expressive power, there is in his mental organization a residual effect of the emotional turmoil and mental effort which might have been present in the early days of his school career when English was not, for him, a facile medium of expression.

568 Stans, Patricia A. Hanusik. "Attitudes of Eleventh Grade Students in Selected Southern New Mexico Public High Schools Concerning Some Aspects of School Life." Ph.D. dissertation, New Mexico State University, 1975. 123 p.

569 Staples, R. "Mexican American Family: Its Modification over Time and Space." PHYLON 32 (1971): 179-92.

570 Stedman, James M., and McKenzie, Richard E. "Family Factors Related to Competence in Young Disadvantaged Mexican American Children." CHILD DEVELOPMENT 42 (1971): 1602-7.

571 Steele, R. "A Contrastive Approach to Civilisation Studies." BABEL, JOURNAL OF THE AUSTRALIAN FEDERATION OF MODERN LANGUAGE TEACHERS' ASSOCIATIONS 11 (April 1975): 23-26.

> Since the cultural context of language is always present, teachers should be knowledgeable about stereotyped perceptions of other cultures held by the learner. The teaching must therefore function at three levels: semilogical, anthropological, and sociological.

572 Steward, Margaret, and Steward, David. "The Observation of Anglo, Mexican, and Chinese American Mothers Teaching Their Young Sons." CHILD DEVELOPMENT 44 (1973): 329-37.

573 Supervielle, Alfredo Fernandez. "The Bilingual Bicultural Communities and the Teaching of Foreign Languages and Cultures in the United States." Ph.D. dissertation, Florida State University, 1973. 135 p.

574 Svenson, Frances. "Language as Ideology: The American Indian Case." AMERICAN INDIAN CULTURE AND RESEARCH JOURNAL 1 (1975): 29-35.

575 Tait, Joseph. SOME ASPECTS OF THE EFFECT OF THE DOMINANT AMERICAN CULTURE UPON CHILDREN OF ITALIAN-BORN PARENTS. Preface by Francesco Cordasco. Clifton, N.J.: Augustus M. Kelley, 1972. ix, 72 p.

> Originally a doctoral dissertation from the Teachers College at Columbia University in 1942, this study explores the character traits of Italian children and undertakes to determine in what direction and to what extent children of Italian-born parents were affected by different degrees of contact with the dominant American culture.

576 Taylor, M.E. "Investigation of Parent Factors Affecting Achievement of Mexican American Children." Ph.D. dissertation, University of Southern California, 1969. 187 p.

577 Theriot, Maria del Norte. "French in the Public Elementary
Schools of Louisiana." THE FRENCH REVIEW 13 (February 1940):
344-46.

> This article gives a description of the steps undertaken
> by a group of French teachers to start FLES programs in
> the public schools of Louisiana.

578 Tireman, L[loyd].S., and Watson, Mary. A COMMUNITY SCHOOL
IN A SPANISH-SPEAKING VILLAGE. New York: Arno Press,
1976. 189 p.

> Originally published in 1943 under the title of LA COM-
> MUNIDAD, this important study describes and evaluates
> the creation and operation of an experimental school in
> a small northern New Mexico Hispano town during the
> late 1930s and early 1940s.

579 Tomanio, Antonio J., and LaMacchia, Lucille B. THE ITALIAN
AMERICAN COMMUNITY IN BRIDGEPORT. University of Bridge-
port Area Studies, Student Monograph no. 5. Bridgeport, Conn.:
University of Bridgeport, Sociology Department, 1953. 44 p.

> This work studies the social institutions of Italian-Ameri-
> cans in Bridgeport, their acculturation to the community,
> and the extent to which they have preserved elements
> of their original Italian culture.

580 Topper, Martin D. The Daily Life of a Traditional Navajo
Household: An Ethnographic Study in Human Daily Activities.
Ph.D dissertation, Northwestern University, 1972. 202 p.

581 Treudley, Mary Bosworth. "Formal Organization and the Americanization Process, With Special Reference to the Greeks of
Boston." AMERICAN SOCIOLOGICAL REVIEW 14 (February
1949): 44-53.

582 Troen, Selwyn K. THE PUBLIC AND THE SCHOOLS: SHAPING
THE ST. LOUIS SYSTEM 1838-1920. Columbia: University of
Missouri Press, 1975. 248 p.

> Materials on German-American bilingual education in
> the St. Louis schools are included in this work. See
> review by David B. Tyack, HISTORY OF EDUCATION
> QUARTERLY 16 (Summer 1976): 195-201.

583 Ulin, Richard O[tis]. "Ethnicity and School Performance: Analysis of the Variables: Italo-Americans." CALIFORNIA JOURNAL OF EDUCATIONAL RESEARCH 19 (September 1968): 190-97.

584 U.S. Bureau of the Census. WE THE MEXICAN AMERICANS: NOSTROS LOS MEXICO AMERICANOS. Washington, D.C.: U.S. Government Printing Office, 1970. 16 p.

585 U.S. Civil Service Commission. EQUAL EMPLOYMENT OPPORTUNITY--IMPLEMENTING THE SPANISH-SPEAKING PROGRAM. Washington, D.C.: U.S. Government Printing Office, 1973. 8 p.

586 Urbiztondo, Ursula Soler. "Cross-Cultural Familial Relationships in American Novels and Plays Assigned in the Freshman Reading Program at the University of Puerto Rico from 1969-1970." Ph.D. dissertation, New York University, 1975. 248 p.

587 Verrette, Adrien. "La mutualité chez les Franco-Américains." LE CANADA FRANCAIS 28 (January 1941): 477-96.

588 Viatte, Auguste. "Les franco-américains de Nouvelle-Angleterre." RENAISSANCE 2 and 3 (1944-1945): 322-35.

589 Wagenheim, Kal. A SURVEY OF PUERTO RICANS ON THE UNITED STATES MAINLAND IN THE 1970'S. New York: Praeger, 1975. xv, 133 p.

Of special interest is chapter 2 "Education, Language, and Literacy," pp. 18-25.

590 Wagenheim, Kal, with Wagenheim, Olga. THE PUERTO RICANS: A DOCUMENTARY HISTORY. New York: Praeger, 1973. xii, 332 p.

591 Warner, W. Lloyd, and Srole, Leo. THE SOCIAL SYSTEMS OF AMERICAN ETHNIC GROUPS. New Haven, Conn.: Yale University Press, 1945. 318 p.

This work is a study of ethnic groups, including the Irish, French Canadians, Jews, Armenians, and Poles. See especially chapter 7, pp. 220-253, "Language and the School: (1) Generation Shift in Language Usage; (2) The Catholic Parochial Schools; (3) The Hebrew School; and (4) The Greek Schools."

592 Wasserman, S.A. "Values of Mexican American, Negro, and Anglo Blue-Collar and White-Collar Children." CHILD DEVELOPMENT 42 (1971): 1624-28.

593 Wax, Murray L. "American Indian Education as a Cultural Transaction." TEACHERS COLLEGE RECORD 64 (May 1963): 693-704.

594 _____. INDIAN AMERICANS: UNITY AND DIVERSITY. Englewood Cliffs, N.J.: Prentice-Hall, 1971. xviii, 236 p.

595 Webster, D.H. "On Cross Cultural Communication." Fairbanks,
Alaska: Summer Institute of Linguistics, n.d. Mimeographed. 11 p.

A helpful guide to the teacher of Eskimo and Athabaskans
in developing a presentation in English to parallel the
thought patterns of the student's native language. Webster presents insights into these languages, contrasting
them with English. Both parts of the paper emphasize
the value of a coordinate language system.

596 Weffer, Rafaela del Carmen Elizondo de. EFFECTS OF FIRST
LANGUAGE INSTRUCTION IN ACADEMIC AND PSYCHOLOGI-
CAL DEVELOPMENT OF BILINGUAL CHILDREN. Ph.D. disser-
tation, Illinois Institute of Technology. 88 p.

597 White, John Rennardh. "An Experiment with Time: A Proposal
for Positive Identity Reinforcement through Historical/Cultural
Education for Native Americans." INDIAN HISTORIAN 5 (Winter
1972): 31-40.

598 Whyte, William Foote. STREET CORNER SOCIETY: THE SOCIAL
STRUCTURE OF AN ITALIAN SLUM. 2d ed. Chicago: The
University of Chicago Press, 1955. 276 p.

This work is a study of the sociological phenomena of
the gang as found among first- and second-generation
Italian Americans.

599 Wipf, Joseph A. "Hutterite Life: The Role of the German
School." UNTERRICHTSPRAXIS 9 (February 1976): 30-36.

All the Hutterite children attended a German-language
school for ten and a half hours a week. They sought
to preserve a cultural heritage.

600 Witkin, H.A. "A Cognitive-Style Approach to Cross-Cultural
Research." INTERNATIONAL JOURNAL OF PSYCHOLOGY 2
(1967): 233-50.

601 Wolcott, Harry F. A KWAKIUTL VILLAGE AND ITS SCHOOL.
New York: Holt, Rinehart and Winston, 1967. 197 p.

602 Wood, Ralph C., ed. THE PENNSYLVANIA-GERMANS. Princeton, N.J.: Princeton University Press, 1942. 299 p.

This work contains a good article by Clyde S. Stine on
the educational situation at the time, "The Pennsylvania
Germans and the School," pp. 103-27.

IV. CURRICULUM, PROGRAMS, GUIDANCE, AND COUNSELING

603 Ada, Alma Flor, and Olave, Maria del Pilar de. "Desarrollo Linguistico y Vivencia Cultural a Traves de la Literatura Infantil. Language Development and Cultural Awareness through Children's Literature." JOURNAL OF THE NATIONAL ASSOCIATION FOR BILINGUAL EDUCATION 1 (May 1976): 65-71.

　　How to incorporate children's literature and oral litera-
　　ture into a language arts program is discussed in this
　　article.

604 Adkins, P.G., and Young, R.G. "Cultural Perceptions in the Treatment of Handicapped School Children of Mexican American Parentage." JOURNAL OF RESEARCH AND DEVELOPMENT EDUCATION 9 (Summer 1976): 83-90.

605 Ainsworth, C.L., and Alford, Gay. RESPONSIVE ENVIRONMENT FOR SPANISH AMERICAN CHILDREN. Evaluation Report, 1971-72. Lubbock, Tex.: Adobe Educational Services, 1972. 273 p.

606 Alano, Angeles C. "Collect, Adapt and Use Varied Reading Materials." READING TEACHER 30 (May 1977): 875-79.

　　This article offers suggestions on how reading materials
　　might be adapted to help bilingual and other teachers.

607 Alvarez, Juan M. "Comparison of Academic Aspirations and Achievement in Bilingual versus Monolingual Classrooms." Ph.D. dissertation, University of Texas, 1975. 164 p.

　　This dissertation is an analysis of variance employed to
　　study four hypotheses related to the students' academic
　　aspirations. In Spanish reading achievement, those in
　　the bilingual program scored just as high even though
　　half as much time was given because of bilingual teach-
　　ing.

608 American Institutes for Research in the Behavioral Sciences. THE
MICRO-SOCIAL PRESCHOOL LEARNING SYSTEM, VINELAND,
NEW JERSEY: CHILDHOOD EDUCATION. MODEL PROGRAMS.
Palo Alto, Calif.: American Institutes for Research, 1970. 32 p.

This booklet describes the Micro-Social Preschool Learning System. Of the population of 50,000, approxi-
mately 20 percent is Puerto Rican, 10 percent Appalachian white, 7 percent black. Includes a discussion of
the language and behavioral objectives of the program.

609 Amsden, Constance. A READING PROGRAM FOR MEXICAN
AMERICAN CHILDREN; FIRST INTERIM REPORT. Los Angeles:
California State College, 1966. 157 p.

This work discusses a preliminary developmental program
in beginning reading in English established in an East
Los Angeles school to develop oral language skills and
to reinforce traditional Mexican cultural values. The
emphasis is on parent participation, individual instruction, self-instruction, and cultural awareness.

610 Anderson, Vivienne. SUMMER '72 YOUTH FILM/MEDIA WORK-
SHOP. FINAL REPORT. Albany: New York State Education
Department, Division of Humanities and Arts, 1973. 10 p.

This report is an evaluation of the videotapes produced
by the film/media workshop, held in the South Bronx
area of New York City in the summer of 1972. The
workshop sought to broaden the communication skills and
improve the self concepts and aspirations of educationally and emotionally deprived black and Puerto Rican
youngsters.

611 Antonovsky, Aaron. "Aspirations, Class and Racial-Ethnic Mem-
bership." JOURNAL OF NEGRO EDUCATION 36 (Fall 1967):
385-93.

This article compares the academic aspirations of blacks,
Puerto Ricans, and whites.

612 Arizona State University. "Annual ASU Conference: 200 Years--
What Now? Where Now?" AMERICAN INDIAN EDUCATION
15 (May 1976): 12-13.

The 17th annual Indian Education Conference (Arizona
State University) discusses the following topics: "Indian
Elders Look at Education," "Involvement of District,
State and Federal Agencies in Indian Education," and
"Bilingual/Bicultural Education."

613 Arredondo, Joe. "Historical Development of a Bilingual Program in a Northern Urban Society." Ed.D. dissertation, Indiana University, 1974. 276 p.

This study of the bilingual program in the Gary school system, shows some results of the bilingual program were a more positive self-image, improvement in study habits, and a drop in absenteeism.

614 [Aspira, Inc.]. "Aspira Today, Accountability Tomorrow." PERSONNEL AND GUIDANCE JOURNAL 50 (October 1971): 109-16.

This interview highlights the need for better counseling for Puerto Rican youngsters.

615 Backner, Burton L. "Counseling Black Students: Any Place for Whitey?" JOURNAL OF HIGHER EDUCATION 41 (November 1970): 630-37.

Although most black and Puerto Rican students in SEEK (Search for Education, Elevation, and Knowledge), a special program, related well with their white counselors, the author believes black and Puerto Rican counselors would better apply their ethnic background.

616 Baird, Janet Rae. "Analysis of Mexican American Culture Taught in Kansas Migrant Programs." Ph.D. dissertation, University of Kansas, 1973. 156 p.

This dissertation examines published materials used by the Kansas Title I Migrant Programs in the summer of 1972. The Hall Matrix was used to provide a frame of reference for defining Mexican-American culture. If bicultural education is to become a reality, there has to be more emphasis on bilingual-bicultural materials.

617 Balasubramonian, K. and Frederickson, C. "Innovative Approaches to Multi-Cultural Programming." JOURNAL OF THE NATIONAL ASSOCIATION FOR BILINGUAL EDUCATION 1 (December 1976): 21-27.

This work discusses how a bilingual program works without an ethnocentric bias, but any such program must be set up so it meets the needs of a specific community and group of students.

618 Balinsky, Warren, and Peng, Samuel. "An Evaluation of Bilingual Education for Spanish Speaking Children." URBAN EDUCATION 9 (1974): 271-78.

619 Batalle, Ana, et al. THE PUERTO RICANS: A RESOURCE UNIT
FOR TEACHERS. New York: B'nai B'rith, Anti-Defamation
League, 1972. 65 p.

> The contents of this work aim to present the Puerto
> Rican on the continent as he really is--his background,
> his attributes, his problems, his goals--so we may better
> understand and respect him. Also included are a bibli-
> ography, an annotated list of relevant audiovisual mate-
> rial, and list of sources of information, resources for
> future investigation and study.

620 Bernbaum, Marcia. EARLY CHILDHOOD PROGRAMS FOR NON-
ENGLISH SPEAKING CHILDREN. Albany: State Education Department, 1972. 112 p.

621 Blackford, Betty. "A Study of a Guidance Program for Bilingual-
Latino Youth." Ed.D. dissertation, Wayne State University,
1975. 151 p.

> This work studies the sixty-one Latino students who were
> enrolled in an experimental Latino guidance program
> which focused on vocational maturity and self-concept.
> School performance did affect results in measuring vo-
> cational motivation.

622 Blanco, George M. "Teaching Spanish as a Standard Dialect in
Grades 7-12: A Rationale for a Fundamental-Skills Approach."
Ph.D. dissertation, University of Texas, 1971. 206 p.

623 Bondarin, Arley. ASSIMILATION THROUGH CULTURAL UNDER-
STANDING: HOBOKEN, NEW JERSEY. A REPORT. New York:
Center for Urban Education, Program Reference Service, 1969.
64 p.

> This Elementary and Secondary Education Act Title III
> project is aimed at assimilating foreign-born and Puerto
> Rican children in the Hoboken, New Jersey school sys-
> tem. Eight programs are described.

624 Bonilla, Eduardo Seda. "Cultural Pluralism and the Education of
Puerto Rican Youths." PHI DELTA KAPPAN 53 (January 1972):
294-96.

> The article states that if current efforts to create effec-
> tive ethnic studies fail, the opportunity to train men
> with inquisitive minds, humane values, and positive iden-
> tities may be lost forever.

625 Boudreaux, Elia. "Some Aims and Methods in Teaching French in the Elementary Schools in Louisiana: The Oakdale Elementary School Experiment." THE MODERN LANGUAGE JOURNAL 24 (March 1940): 427-30.

626 Bouton, Lawrence F. "Meeting Needs of Children with Diverse Linguistic and Ethnic Backgrounds." FOREIGN LANGUAGE ANNALS 8 (December 1975): 81-86.

This article discusses an elementary school program: foreign pupils were tutored in some languages and were taught the language arts. Native English speakers worked on a second language and studied different cultures.

627 Braun, Shirley. "Bilingual Education, Old and New Style, in a New York School District." THE BILINGUAL REVIEW. LA REVISTA BILINGUE 2 (September-December 1975): 238-47.

This article discusses a five-year bilingual education program started in 1971 in a multilingual, multicultural school district. Two or three bilingual para-professionals were used for each school. In one group, they needed special training. A second group had a TESL room staffed by one teacher and a bilingual para-professional. Another group had a "bilingual school" as a subschool. Regardless of "bilingual" model, learning English was not impeded, but more of the Spanish-dominant than English-dominant seemed on their way to genuine bilingualism.

628 Brown, Marie L.S. "The Effect of Ethnicity on Visual-Perceptual Skills Related to Reading Readiness." Ph.D. dissertation, University of Colorado, 1971. 173 p.

629 Burnham, Glenn M. "A Study of the Treatment of the Hispanic Heritage in Secondary American History Classes in Selected Colorado School Districts." Ed.D. dissertation, University of Colorado, 1969. 175 p.

630 Burns, Ruth Aline Ketchum. "Model for a Career Life-Planning Program for Mexican American College Students." Ph.D. dissertation, University of Oregon, 1973. 146 p.

631 Button, Christine Bennett. "The Development of Experimental Curriculum to Effect the Political Socialization of Anglo, Black, and Mexican American Adolescents." Ph.D. dissertation, University of Texas at Austin, 1972. 187 p.

632 Carrero, Milagros. PUERTO RICO AND THE PUERTO RICANS:
A TEACHING AND RESOURCE UNIT FOR UPPER LEVEL SPANISH
STUDENTS OR SOCIAL STUDIES CLASSES. Upper Marlboro,
Md.: Prince George's County Board of Education, 1973. 89 p.

> This unit has sections dealing with the present conditions
> of the Puerto Ricans, their culture, and historical per-
> spectives. The appendixes outline the following: (1)
> demands of the Puerto Ricans, (2) notable Puerto Ricans,
> (3) background information for the teacher, (4) legends,
> (5) Spanglish, (6) Puerto Rican dishes, and (7) sources
> for information and materials. Also provided is a bib-
> liography of additional sources of information for Puerto
> Rico and Puerto Ricans. Text is in English.

633 Carrow, Elizabeth. "Auditory Comprehension of English by Monolingual and Bilingual Preschool Children." JOURNAL OF
SPEECH AND HEARING RESEARCH 15 (1972): 407-12.

634 Castaneda, Alfredo, et al. NEW APPROACHES TO BILINGUAL,
BICULTURAL EDUCATION. Austin, Tex.: Dissemination and
Assessment Center for Bilingual Education, 1975. 127 p.

635 Chapa, Ricardo Romeo. "English Reading and the Mexican American Child in a Second Grade Bilingual Program." Ph.D. dissertation, Michigan State University, 1975. 120 p.

> Although data in this dissertation were not significant in
> English reading achievement, the program children scored
> higher in comprehension, vocabulary, and combined
> score than the traditional group. Children in the treat-
> ment group attained successful proficiency in Spanish
> reading while maintaining a high level of success in
> English reading.

636 Chicago Public Schools. COMPENSATORY EDUCATION IN
THE CHICAGO PUBLIC SCHOOLS: STUDY REPORT NO. FOUR.
Chicago: Board of Education, 1964. 171 p.

> The minority groups discussed in this work are blacks,
> Puerto Ricans, Mexican Americans, and Appalachian
> whites. The subject areas discussed include educational
> and socioeconomic background of families, analysis of
> educational implications, and programs provided by the
> schools. Compensatory education programs at the ele-
> mentary and high school levels are presented.

637 Cohen, Andrew D. "The Culver City Spanish Immersion Project."
MODERN LANGUAGE JOURNAL 58 (1974): 95-103.

638 Cohen, Andrew D., et al. THE REDWOOD CITY BILINGUAL
EDUCATION PROJECT, 1971-1974: SPANISH AND ENGLISH
PROFICIENCY, MATHEMATICS AND LANGUAGE USE OVER-
TIME. Working Papers on Bilingualism, no. 8. Toronto: On-
tario Institute for Studies in Education, 1976. 30 p.

> This work shows that at the end of six years of bilin-
> gual schooling, the comparison group was better than
> the bilingually-schooled children in English reading;
> the latter were stronger in Spanish reading.

639 Cohen, S. Alan. "Diagnosis and Treatment of Reading Difficulties
in Puerto Rican and Negro Communities." Paper presented to the
Fairleigh Dickinson University Reading Conference, Rutherford,
N.J., 5 December 1964. 7 p. Mimeographed.

> In discussing reading difficulties, the author refers to
> perceptual factors, psychosocial factors, and psychoedu-
> cational factors.

640 _____. STUDY OF PERCEPTUAL DYSFUNCTION IN SOCIALLY
DISADVANTAGED FIRST GRADERS. New York: Mobilization
for Youth, 1965. 38 p.

> This program for black, Puerto Rican, and Chinese dis-
> advantaged children showing perceptual dysfunction dis-
> cusses an outline of activities, progress of the pilot
> group, and methodological problems. Outline for the
> resultant manual is presented, including exercises and
> control.

641 Coleman, Joseph G., and Wheeler, Barbara A., eds. HUMAN
USES OF THE UNIVERSITY: PLANNING A CURRICULUM IN
URBAN AND ETHNIC AFFAIRS AT COLUMBIA UNIVERSITY.
Praeger Special Studies in United States Economic and Social
Development. New York: Columbia University, Urban Center,
1970. 329 p.

> The purposes of this project were: (1) to recommend
> directions for the university's future development, (2)
> to order these recommendations according to priority,
> (3) to outline structural arrangements and strategies to
> facilitate their implementation. The report includes dis-
> cussion of faculty and administration views, student
> views, black and Puerto Rican community opinions, and
> national college curriculum in this area, trends in urban
> studies and learning programs, evolving structure and
> curricula of Columbia University, and recommendations
> and conclusions.

642 Cooper, Robert L.; Fowles, Barbara L.; and Givner, Abraham.
"Listening Comprehension in a Bilingual Community." MODERN LAN-
GUAGE JOURNAL 53 (April 1969): 235-41.

> This work includes the following topics: "Bilingualism,"
> "English (Second Language)," "Language Research,"
> "Language Skills," "Listening Comprehension," "Mea-
> surement," "Puerto Ricans," "Sociolinguistics," "Spanish
> Speaking," "Tables (Data)."

643 Cooper, Terry Touff. "Del Pueblo: A School That's 'Custommade'
for Learning." TEACHER 93 (October 1975): 58, 59, 61.

> Described in this article is the model bilingual-bicul-
> tural program produced by the Del Pueblo Elementary
> School in Denver, Colorado.

644 Cordasco, Francesco. "Teaching the Puerto Rican Experience."
In TEACHING ETHNIC STUDIES: CONCEPTS AND STRATEGIES.
Edited by James A. Banks, pp. 226-53. Washington, D.C.:
Council for the Social Studies, 1973.

645 _____. THE PUERTO RICAN COMMUNITY OF NEWARK (N.J.):
AN EDUCATIONAL PROGRAM FOR ITS CHILDREN (SUMMER
1970). N.J., Newark City Board of Education, 1970. 60 p.

> The educational program for Puerto Rican children which
> this construct describes came about as a result of a
> school-administration awareness and the mounting frus-
> trations experienced by the Puerto Rican community.

646 _____. EDUCATION PROGRAMS FOR PUERTO RICAN STU-
DENTS. NEW JERSEY PUBLIC SCHOOLS. Jersey City, N.J.:
Jersey City Board of Education, 1971. 47 p.

> This report has a descriptive and evaluative delineation
> of those programs which have been (or are being) de-
> veloped for Puerto Rican students in the public schools
> of Jersey City.

647 Cordasco, Francesco, and Bernstein, George, eds. "Bilingual
Education in New Jersey." MONTCLAIR EDUCATION REVIEW
7 (Fall 1977): 1-108.

> This issue is an overview of bilingual education in
> New Jersey with notices of legislation, teacher training,
> and school district programs.

648 Creamer, R.C., et al. "Simulation: An Alternative Method for Bilingual Bicultural Education." CONTEMPORARY EDUCA-TION 48 (Winter 1977): 90-91.

The author states that games and simulations should be investigated as a technique for bicultural-bilingual education programs.

649 Del Buono, Xavier Antonio. "The Relationship of Bilingual Bicultural Instruction to the Achievement and Self-Concept of Seventh Grade Mexican American Students." Ph.D. dissertation, Michigan State University, 1971. 180 p.

This work shows that Mexican-American seventh-grade students in the bilingual-bicultural program did significantly better in school achievement and had a better self-concept than Mexican Americans in the regular program. The descriptive study had preexisting groups compared on their mean posttest scores, on achievement in social studies, reading, language, and academic self-concept.

650 Development Associates, Inc. READING FOR FUN: A STUDY OF MATERIALS FOR MEXICAN AND SPANISH AMERICAN, PUERTO RICAN, CUBAN AND OTHER LATIN AMERICAN CHIL-DREN. Washington D.C.: 1972. 84 p.

A survey of selected neighborhoods in eight cities was conducted to determine the relevance, availability, and utilization of leisure-time reading materials in both English and Spanish for Hispanic-American children. Spanish-speaking children, parents, teachers, librarians, educators and community workers were interviewed in each of the eight cities. Suggested reading materials are included in the appendix.

651 Dimitroff, Lillian. "Small Group Training for Spanish-Speaking Pupils." CHICAGO SCHOOLS JOURNAL 45 (November 1963): 15-22.

A Puerto Rican student teacher taught English to small groups of Spanish-speaking pupils, age ten to fourteen, in a Chicago public school. The criteria for evaluation, difficult sounds for Spanish speakers, and attitudinal changes are briefly discussed.

652 Dissemination Center for Bilingual Education. PROCEEDINGS. First Annual International Multilingual Multicultural Conference.

San Diego, 1-5 April 1973. Austin, Tex.: Dissemination Center for Bilingual Bicultural Education, 1973. 56 p.

653 Drake, Glendon F. "Integrity, Promise and Language Planning." LANGUAGE LEARNING 25 (December 1975): 267-79.

Described in this article is a three-track system of bilingual education: (1) foreign-language teaching at school if home language does not appear threatened, (2) a mother-tongue based bilingualism, or (3) the mother tongue, without bilingualism.

654 Dumont, Robert V., Jr. "Learning English and How to Be Silent: Studies in Sioux and Cherokee Classrooms." In FUNCTIONS OF LANGUAGE IN THE CLASSROOM, edited by C.B. Cazden et al., pp. 48-61. New York: Teachers College Press, 1972.

655 Dumont, Robert V., Jr., and Wax, Murray L. "Cherokee School Society and the Intercultural Classroom." HUMAN ORGANIZA-TION 28 (1969): 217-26.

656 Edelman, Martin. "The Contextualization of School Children's Bilingualism." MODERN LANGUAGE JOURNAL 53 (1969): 179-82.

657 Ehrlich, Alan G. CONTENT ANALYSIS SCHEDULE FOR BILIN-GUAL EDUCATION PROGRAMS: BUILDING BILINGUAL BRIDGES. New York: City University, Hunter College Bilingual Educational Applied Research Unit, 1972. 33 p.

This work presents information on the history, finding, and scope of the project. Included are sociolinguistic process variables such as the native and dominant languages of students and their interaction.

658 Engle, Patricia Lee. "Language Medium in Early School Years for Minority Language Groups." REVIEW OF EDUCATIONAL RE-SEARCH 45 (Spring 1975): 283-325.

One of the main questions discussed in this article is whether children can learn more quickly in their second language when they have already learned to read in their primary language, and whether their being taught in their first language will add to their understanding more than if they are taught only in their first language.

659 Erickson, Frederick. "The Politics of Speaking." NOTES FROM WORKSHOP CENTER FOR OPEN EDUCATION 3 (Winter 1974): 9-15.

The author contends that strategies are needed to see whether there is a "hidden" curriculum which keeps students
from using their first language, if first-language maintenance is considered one goal of bilingual-bicultural
programs.

660 Feeley, Dorothy M. ETHNIC GROUPS IN OUR WORLD TODAY.
GRADE 2. Stoneham, Mass.: Stoneham Public Schools, 1974.
29 p.

This unit has been designed for use in grade two in conjunction with the regular social studies curriculum. It
attempts to foster a better understanding of major ethnic
groups in the United States by presenting information
about their history, life-styles, culture, and so forth.

661 _____. EVERYBODY IS SOMEBODY. GRADE 3. Stoneham,
Mass.: Stoneham Public Schools, 1974. 35 p.

Each section on blacks, Puerto Ricans, American Chinese, and American Indians contains the following: (1)
background on their native country including history,
geography, culture and life-styles, economy, and government, (2) American heritage or background, (3) current views and problems, (4) contributions of the group
and specific individuals in politics, exploration, education, athletics, entertainment, humanities, business, and
science and technology, (5) suggested activities, (6)
student evaluation tips, (7) student and teacher references, (8) audiovisual aids such as filmstrips or music.

662 _____. LEARNING TO LIVE IN TODAY'S WORLD: GRADE 1.
Stoneham, Mass.: Stoneham Public Schools, 1974. 18 p.

This curriculum unit has been designed for use in grade
one in conjunction with the regular social studies curriculum. It attempts to foster a better understanding of
the major ethnic groups in the United States by presenting information about their history, life-styles, culture,
and so forth.

663 Feeley, Joan T. "Bilingual Instruction: Puerto Rico and the
Mainland." THE READING TEACHER 30 (April 1977): 741-44.

This article is a report on teaching children English in
two Puerto Rican schools. In the high school visited,
the texts were in English, although class discussion was
in Spanish. Asks for more attention being given to
deeper comprehension rather than the flawless reproduc-
tion of "standard" English.

664 Fennessey, James. AN EXPLORATORY STUDY OF NON-ENG-LISH SPEAKING HOMES AND ACADEMIC PERFORMANCE. Baltimore: Johns Hopkins University, Center for the Study of Social Organization of Schools, 1967. 49 p.

> The language-related difficulties of Puerto Rican children in New York public schools were studied by a re-analysis of data previously collected in a U.S. Office of Education (USOE) survey. This study sought to answer two questions: (1) what is the relationship between language spoken in the home and other aspects of ethnic background, and (2) what differences are present at several different grade levels in vocabulary test scores of Puerto Rican children from contrasting, home-language backgrounds?

665 Fiege-Kollman, Maria Laila. "Reading and Recall Among Bilingual and Dialect Speaking Children." Ph.D. dissertation, University of California, 1975. 237 p.

666 Figeroa, Roman. CONTENT ANALYSIS SCHEDULE FOR BILINGUAL EDUCATION PROGRAMS: BILINGUAL PROJECT FORWARD-ADELANTE. New York: City University of New York, Hunter College Bilingual Education Applied Research Unit, 1971. 73 p.

> A content analysis which presents information on the history, funding, and scope of the project. Included are sociolinguistic process variables such as the native and dominant languages of students and their interactions.

667 Figueroa, Roman, and Shore, Marietta Saravia. CONTENT ANALYSIS SCHEDULE FOR BILINGUAL EDUCATION PROGRAMS: LET'S BE AMIGOS. New York: City University, Hunter College Education Applied Research Unit, 1972. 99 p.

> This content analysis schedule for the "Let's Be Amigos" project of the school district of Philadelphia presents information on the history, funding, and scope of the project.

668 Findling, Joav. "Bilingual Need Affiliation and Future Orientation in Extragroup and Intragroup Domains." MODERN LANGUAGE JOURNAL 53 (April 1969): 227-31.

> The following are presented in this article: "Bilingualism," "Employment Opportunities," "English (Second Language)," "Identification (Psychological)," "Language

Research," "Language Usage," "Puerto Ricans," "Spanish Speaking," "Tables (Data)."

669 Flores, Reynaldo. "Opinions of Chicano Community Parents on Curriculum and Language Use in Bilingual Preschool Education. AZTLAN 4 (February 1973): 315-34.

670 Gaarder, A. Bruce. "Teaching the Bilingual Child: Research, Development and Policy." THE MODERN LANGUAGE JOURNAL 49 (March 1965): 165-75.

Use of mother tongue as language of instruction in beginning school is recommended in this article.

671 _____. "Organization of the Bilingual School." THE JOURNAL OF SOCIAL ISSUES 23 (April 1967): 110-20.

Directed toward sociologists and school administrators interested in bilingual education, this work emphasizes teacher training and full consideration of school organization and classroom practices.

672 _____. "Beyond Grammar and Beyond Drills." FL ANNALS 1 (December 1967): 109-18.

This article states that the teacher should be conscious of the points being displayed, but the learner's focus should concentrate on significant meaning. Sample drills are given in Spanish.

673 Gaarder, A. Bruce, and Richardson, Mabel W[ilson]. "Two Patterns of Bilingual Education in Dade County, Florida." In FOREIGN LANGUAGE LEARNING: RESEARCH AND DEVELOPMENT: AN ASSESSMENT. Edited by Thomas E. Bird, pp. 32-44. Reports of the Working Committees of the 1968 Northeast Conference on the Teaching of Foreign Languages. Menasha, Wis.: George Banta Co., 1968.

This article is a short description of the "Spanish for Spanish-Speakers Program" started in Dade County in 1961 and of the Coral Way Bilingual School Program begun in 1963.

674 Gallegos, Leovigildo Lopez. "A Comparison of Social Studies Curriculum Needs as Perceived by Urban Mexican American Parents, Students, and Teachers." Ed.D. dissertation, University of Houston, 1974. 162 p.

675 Garcia, Joseph Odocio. "Cost Analysis of Bilingual, Special and Vocational Public School Programs in New Mexico." Ph.D. dissertation, University of New Mexico, 1976. 227 p.

> The 1976 New Mexico State Legislature used this study's results to refine the equalization guarantee formula so educational programs could be funded to reflect as accurately as possible actual expenditures. Worksheets were developed by the writer to calculate per pupil expenditures, cost differentials, and cost indexes for the regular education program (grades 4 to 6) bilingual, special and vocational education programs.

676 Garza, Roberto Jesus. "Chicano Studies: A New Curriculum Dimension for Higher Education in the Southwest." Ed.D. dissertation, Oklahoma State University, 1975. 160 p.

677 Giles, W.H. "Mathematics in Bilingualism: A Pragmatic Approach." ISA BULLETIN: THE INTERNATIONAL SCHOOLS ASSOCIATION 55 (February 1969): 19-26.

> This article discusses the bilingual teaching of mathematics in the Toronto French School, where, although the students are basically English-mother-tongue, 75 to 80 percent of all instruction is carried on in French.

678 Gill, Joseph. "A Handbook for Teachers of Sioux-Indian Students." Ph.D. dissertation, University of South Dakota, 1971. 213 p.

679 Gledich, Nicholas M. "Field Study in a Bilingual School." LANGUAGE ARTS 53 (April 1976): 407.

680 Gonzalez, Augustin, and Luckett, JoLeigh. EXPERIMENTAL GROUP TREATMENT WITH PUERTO RICAN NEWCOMERS. New York: Puerto Rican Family Institute, 1960. 7 p.

> This work describes an experimental program of treatment for a group of Puerto Rican adolescents and their families, with emphasis on the significance of the shift from the extended family group (and social group) pattern in Puerto Rico to the break in this pattern in New York.

681 Gonzalez, Josue M. "A Developmental and Sociological Rationale for Culture-Based Curricula and Cultural Context Teaching in the Early Instruction of Mexican American Children. Ed.D dissertation, University of Massachusetts, 1974. 215 p.

Among alternative models discussed in this dissertation
were: (1) those emphasizing socioeconomic factors
which were strictly cultural, (2) the benign cultural
differences model, (3) a biculturation model also described as nonlinear, alternation and matrix models.

682 Gordon, Jeffrey Stuart. "Mixed Dominant Grouping and Bilin-
gual Materials in Mathematics and Science Classes in Two Puerto
Rican Junior High Schools." Ph.D. dissertation, University of
Illinois, 1976. 241 p.

This study is on two Bayamon (Puerto Rico) schools.
Most students were bilingual. The English dominant
students paired with Spanish dominant students did significantly better on the posttest than English dominant
paired with English dominant.

683 Grove, Cornelius Lee. CROSS-CULTURAL AND OTHER PROB-
LEMS AFFECTING THE EDUCATION OF IMMIGRANT PORTU-
GUESE STUDENTS IN A PROGRAM OF TRANSITIONAL BILIN-
GUAL EDUCATION: A DESCRIPTIVE CASE STUDY. New York:
Teachers College, Columbia University, 1977. 403 p.

This work is a descriptive case study of one secondary-
level program in a Massachusetts town. It is an em-
pathetic description of problems and feelings of all connected with the education of the secondary-level immigrant Portuguese students.

684 Guerra, Emilio L. THE CHALLENGE OF BILINGUALISM IN
EDUCATION IN THE CITY OF NEW YORK. New York: American Association of Teachers of Spanish and Portuguese, 1968.
8 p.

In this brief account the efforts made by New York City
public schools to establish special programs for non-
English-speaking students, especially Puerto Rican migrants, are discussed. The pioneer project using bilingual teachers to instruct "orientation classes" in East
Harlem's Benjamin Franklin High School is described.

685 Gutierrez, Arturo Luis. "The Implications of Early Childhood
Education." In PROCEEDINGS OF THE NATIONAL CONFER-
ENCE ON BILINGUAL EDUCATION, APRIL 14-15, 1972, pp.
282-87. Austin, Tex.: Dissemination Center for Bilingual Bicultural Education, 1972.

686 Hahn, Joyce, and Dunstan, Virginia. "The Child's Whole World:
A Bilingual Preschool that Includes Parent Training in the Home."
YOUNG CHILDREN 30 (May 1975): 281-88.

> This article is a description of a home-based parent-
> education component of a bilingual-bicultural preschool
> program. Parents help make important decisions con-
> cerning the nature of the program.

687 Hale, James Michael. "Effects of Image-Enhancement Indoctri-
nation on the Self-Concept, Occupational Aspiration Level, and
Scholastic Achievement of Mexican-American Model Neighborhood
Area Students." Ed.D. dissertation, East Texas State University.
97 p.

> Thirty students were randomly selected for this study.
> Image-enhancement indoctrination was a valid tool with
> which to maintain the self-concept of Mexican Ameri-
> can Model Neighborhood Area students.

688 Harris, M.B., and Stockton, S. "A Comparison of Bilingual and
Monolingual Physical Education Instruction." JOURNAL OF EDU-
CATIONAL RESEARCH 6 (1973): 53.

689 Harvey, Curtis. "General Descriptions of Bilingual Programs
That Meet Students' Needs." In PROCEEDINGS, pp. 252-64.
National Conference on Bilingual Education, 14-15 April, 1972.
Austin, Tex.: Dissemination Center for Bilingual Bicultural Edu-
cation, 1972.

690 Has, Peter Yuan. "An Analysis of Certain Learning Difficulties
of Chinese Students in New York City." Ph.D. dissertation,
New York University, 1955. 187 p.

691 Hawkridge, David G., et al. A STUDY OF SELECTED EXEM-
PLARY PROGRAMS FOR THE EDUCATION OF DISADVANTAGED
CHILDREN: PART II. FINAL REPORT. Palo Alto, Calif.:
American Institutes for Research in the Behavioral Sciences, 1968.
341 p.

> In part 2 of this final report each of twenty-one suc-
> cessful compensatory education programs, preschool
> through grade twelve is described in enough detail to
> permit a school district to make a preliminary decision
> about the desirability of attempting a local replication.
> Most of the programs are inner-city projects for blacks,
> Puerto Ricans, and Mexican Americans.

692 Hepner, Ethel Marion. "Self-Concepts, Values and Needs of Mexican American Under-Achievers." Ph.D. dissertation, University of Southern California, 1970. 260 p.

This work states that the value system of the American school tends to restrict the potential of the Mexican-American boy who does not achieve because of deviation strains from the school culture. Teachers and administrators must be trained differently. Mexican-American underachievers did not suffer from negative self-esteem.

693 Herold, William R. "A Comprehensive Bilingual Program in Evangeline County." REVUE DE LOUISIANE: LOUISIANA REVIEW 1 (Winter 1972): 128-34.

694 Herrmann, Elmira, Marjorie. "Culture in French Bilingual Curricula: An Analysis of Six Title VII Program Designs from New England and Louisiana. Ph.D. dissertation, University of Texas, 1975. 208 p.

This study analyzes the cultural content of all the French-English bilingual curricula (K through 3). All projects developed French instructional aids, reading material, and games appropriate for the students. The tendency of writers was to portray the culture idealistically, not realistically. There were science and physical education units developed, among others.

695 Hess, Richard T. CONTENT ANALYSIS SCHEDULE FOR BILINGUAL EDUCATION PROGRAMS: THE LORAIN CITY BILINGUAL EDUCATION PROGRAM. New York: City University, Hunter College Bilingual Education Applied Research Unit, 1972. 42 p.

Presented in this work is information on the history, funding, and scope of the project. Included are sociolinguistic process variables such as the native and dominant languages of students and their interaction.

696 Hess, Richard T., and Shore, Marietta Saravia. CONTENT ANALYSIS SCHEDULE FOR BILINGUAL EDUCATION PROGRAMS: BILINGUAL EDUCATION IN A CONSORTIUM. New York: City University, Hunter College Bilingual Education Applied Research Unit, 1972. 38 p.

This work presents information on the history, funding, and scope of the project. Inserts include information on staff development, scheduling, and instructional materials.

697 Hill, Faith. "Using the Reading of Navajo as a Bridge to English for Unschooled Adults (A Proposed Program)." Unpublished
paper. Summer 1968. 14 p.

> This paper presents the rationale and some possible
> means of implementing a program where the vernacular
> is used as a bridge to reading in a second language.

698 Hillerby, Robert Webster. "Teaching First Grade Math to Spanish Speaking Students." Ed.D. dissertation, University of California, Los Angeles, 1970. 117 p.

699 Hocker, Phillip Norton. "Two Stimulus Transposition as Demon-
strated by Spanish/English Speaking Children from Bilingual
(Spanish/English) and Monolingual (English) Instruction Classrooms."
Ph.D. dissertation, New Mexico State University, 1973. 79 p.

700 Hoffman, Virginia. ORAL ENGLISH AT ROUGH ROCK: A
NEW PROGRAM FOR NAVAHO CHILDREN. Rough Rock, Ariz.:
Navaho Curriculum Center, Rough Rock Demonstration School,
Dine, 1968. 58 p.

> An illustrated presentation of the language program at
> Rough Rock with its rationale and examples of their
> materials is discussed in this work.

701 Hollomon, John Wesley. "Problems of Assessing Bilingualism in
Children Entering School." Ph.D. dissertation. University of
New Mexico, 1973. 387 p.

> The research methods, instrumental techniques, and pro-
> cedures showed an adequate assessment of bilingual com-
> petence in communication. The study worked on com-
> petance in actual settings. A model was provided for
> studying a bilingual population in preparation for de-
> veloping bilingual curricula.

702 Horn, Thomas D. A STUDY OF THE EFFECTS OF INTENSIVE
ORAL-AURAL ENGLISH LANGUAGE INSTRUCTION, ORAL-
AURAL SPANISH LANGUAGE INSTRUCTION AND NON-ORAL-
AURAL INSTRUCTION ON READING READINESS IN GRADE
ONE. Cooperative Research Project no. 2648. Austin, Tex.:
University of Texas, 1966. 58 p.

> This work compared the effectiveness of three methods
> for developing reading readiness in Spanish-speaking
> first-grade children.

703 Huffman, Voncile B. "Beginning Reading Materials for Bilingual Children." Ph.D. dissertation, University of Denver, 1957. 59 p.

704 Irizarry, Maria Antonio. "A Proposed Model for a Bilingual Approach Mode of Instruction at the Two-Year College Level." (Spanish-English). Ed.D. dissertation, Columbia University, Teachers College, 1977. 146 p.

> This study examines bilingual programs and situations in seven New York City community colleges. The author asks for an interdisciplinary approach, that is, the articulation of a bilingual-bicultural curriculum with a framework of coordination and different departments.

705 Jacobson, Rodolfo. "The Dilemma of Bilingual Education Models: Duplication of Compartmentalization." NEW DIRECTIONS IN SECOND LANGUAGE LEARNING, TEACHING, AND BILINGUAL EDUCATION.. Edited by Marina K. Burt and Heidi C. Dulay, pp. 123-318. Washington, D.C.: TESOL, 1975.

> Jacobson sees the full bilingual program as domain-free and school-based, while the bilingual program is domain-sensitive and society-based. The focus of the first is to develop some balanced competency in individuals while the latter aims at producing a balanced society. He sees a full bilingual program as having many duplications because the teacher is expected to teach all content in both languages. He wants to make bilingual education not a program for the disadvantaged, but an experience in multicultural coexistence.

706 Jenkins, Mary. BILINGUAL EDUCATION IN NEW YORK CITY. New York: Board of Education, Office of Bilingual Education and Office of Personnel, 1971. 79 p.

707 John[-Steiner], Vera P., and Horner, Vivian M. EARLY CHILDHOOD BILINGUAL EDUCATION. New York: Yeshiva University, Early Childhood Bilingual Education Project, 1971. 209 p.

> Three major groups discussed here in connection with bilingual education programs are Puerto Ricans, Mexican Americans, and American Indians. Contents include sections on: (1) demographic information on minorities, (2) language groups, (3) program descriptions, (4) teacher recruitment, (5) curriculum materials, (6) testing and evaluation procedures, (7) research in bilingual education, and (8) models of bilingual education.

708 Johnson, B.H. NAVAHO EDUCATION AT ROUGH ROCK. Rough Rock, Ariz.: Dine, 1968. 212 p.

This work illustrates and details documentation of the first two years of the Rough Rock Demonstration School operated by the local community.

709 Johnson, Kenneth R. TEACHING CULTURALLY DISADVANTAGED PUPILS (GRADES K-12) UNIT IV: THE CULTURALLY DISADVAN- TAGED MEXICAN-AMERICAN, PUERTO RICAN, CAUCASIAN, AND AMERICAN INDIAN PUPIL. Chicago: Science Research Associates, 1967. 34 p.

The fourth in a series of teacher-education units on the disadvantaged pupil discusses Mexican Americans, Puerto Ricans, Appalachians and Southern white migrants, and American Indians. For a discussion of Puerto Ricans, the reader is referred to part 3: "The Culturally Dis- advantaged Puerto Rican Student," pp. 13-18.

710 Johnson, Vally Lou. "A Study to Determine the Levels in· Cur- riculum Areas Where Remedial Work is Needed Most in an Ele- mentary School for Spanish-Speaking Children Shown by Correla- tion of Mental Age and Educational Age." Ed.D. dissertation, University of Northern Colorado, 1971. 190 p.

711 Kagan, Spencer, and Madsen, Millard C. "Cooperation and Competition of Mexican American and Anglo American Children of Two Ages under Four Instructional Sets." DEVELOPMENTAL PSYCHOLOGY 5 (1971): 32-39.

712 Katsh, Abraham I. "Current Trends in the Study of Hebrew in Colleges and Universities." THE MODERN LANGUAGE JOUR- NAL 44 (February 1960): 64-67.

713 Keating, George Andrew. "A Comparison of Four Methods of Teaching Word Recognition to Bicultural, Bilingual Adults." Ed.D. dissertation, University of Northern Colorado, 1972. 101 p.

Four methods were used to teach bilingual-bicultural adults with limited reading skills in this work. There was no significant difference in mean score resulting from a combination of techniques.

714 King, Ann. "The 'Section Bilingue' Experiment at Haygrove School." AUDIO-VISUAL LANGUAGE JOURNAL 13 (Summer 1975): 87-89.

The article discusses two classes that were taught geography through the use of French for other subjects.
One class was selective in ability and the other represented different degrees of ability.

715 King, Paul E. BILINGUAL READINESS IN PRIMARY GRADES: AN EARLY CHILDHOOD DEMONSTRATION PROJECT. New York: Hunter College of the City University of New York, December 1966. 126 p.

716 Kleinfeld, Judith S. SOME INSTRUCTIONAL STRATEGIES FOR THE CROSS-CULTURAL CLASSROOM. Juneau: Alaska State Department of Education, 1971. 143 p.

717 Kloss, Heinz. "Deutscher Sprachunterricht im Grundschulalter in den Vereinigten Staaten." AUSLANDSKURIER 8 (August 1967): 22-24.

718 Knight, Lester N. LANGUAGE ARTS FOR THE EXCEPTIONAL: THE GIFTED AND THE LINGUISTICALLY DIFFERENT. Itasca, Ill.: F.E. Peacock, 1974. 157 p.

719 Kolers, Paul A. "Reading and Talking Bilingually." AMERICAN JOURNAL OF PSYCHOLOGY 79 (September 1966): 357-76.

This report describes an experiment in which French-English bilinguals were tested in several linguistic tasks, including how well bilinguals comprehend material in their native language and in the foreign language.

720 Kosinski, Leonard Vincent. "Bilingualism and Reading Development: A Study of the Effects of Polish American Bilingualism Upon Reading Achievement in Junior High School." Ph.D. dissertation, University of Wisconsin, 1963.

This work is a comparison of reading achievement among three groups of junior high students with Polish and English backgrounds.

721 Kostohryz, Vernon Ray. "Changes in Social Distance After the Inclusion of Spanish Instruction in a Fifth Grade Social Studies Unit." Ph.D. dissertation, North Texas State University, 1971. 115 p.

722 Kuzma, K.J., and Stern, C. "Effects of Three Preschool Intervention Programs in the Development of Autonomy in Mexican

American and Negro Children." JOURNAL OF SPECIAL EDU-
CATION 6 (1972): 197-205.

723 La Fontaine, Hernan, and Pagan, Muriel. "A Model for the
Implementation of the Elementary School Curriculum through Bilingual Education." 1969. Mimeographed. 10 p.

A theoretical model is presented to the staff of the Bilingual School (P.S. 25, Bronx, New York) for discussion, modification, and implementation beginning September 1968.

724 Lakin, David Schoonmaker. "Cross Age Tutoring with Mexican
American Pupils." Ed.D. dissertation, University of California,
Los Angeles, 1971. 100 p.

The purpose of this study was to see whether Mexican-
American fifth- and sixth-grade pupils would make significant gains in word recognition and oral reading skills
when used as tutors for Headstart children. Sixty Mexican Americans and sixty Anglo Americans were used.
Both tutoring groups were low in academic achievement.
The Mexican-American tutors improved significantly
through their tutoring.

725 Lambert, Wallace E., et al. "Cognitive and Attitudinal Consequences of Bilingual Schooling: The St. Lambert Project Through
Grade 5." JOURNAL OF EDUCATIONAL PSYCHOLOGY 65
(1973): 141-59.

726 Larson, Anna Marie Gustafson. "Instruction by Tutoring of Third
Grade, Bilingual, Inner-City Children in Meaning Vocabulary."
Ph.D. dissertation, University of Illinois, 1975. 178 p.

727 Leonard, James Thomas. "The Development of a Bilingual Program for Spanish-Speaking Elementary School Children in Lynn,
Massachusetts." Ed.D. dissertation, University of Massachusetts,
1973. 239 p.

728 Letang, Linus Leo. "A Study of the Nature of Elementary School
Guidance in the Public Schools of New Mexico." Ed.D. dissertation, University of New Mexico, 1970. 286 p.

729 Lopez, Annette Marie. "Using Puerto Rican Nonverbal Communication through Storytelling to Enhance English Language Comprehension of Spanish-Speaking Puerto Rican Children." Ed.D. dissertation, Temple University, 1975. 248 p.

730 Lopez, William. "New York: The South Bronx Project. Libraries and the Spanish Speaking." WILSON LIBRARY BULLETIN 44 (March 1970): 757-60.

This article discusses the New York Public Library's South Bronx Project, a federally funded demonstration program, designed to reach out into this urban poverty area of Spanish-speaking people and break through local barriers.

731 Lopez-Ferrer, Edgardo, et al. CONTENT ANALYSIS SCHEDULE FOR BILINGUAL EDUCATION PROGRAMS: BILINGUAL EDUCATION CENTER. New York: City University, Hunter College Bilingual Education Applied Research Unit, 1971. 62 p.

This work presents information on the history, funding, and scope of the project. Included are sociolinguistic process variables such as the native and dominant language of students and their interaction. Information is provided on staff selection and the linguistic background of project teachers.

732 Lopez-Santiago, Andres, and Shore, Marietta Saravia. CONTENT ANALYSIS SCHEDULE FOR BILINGUAL EDUCATION PROGRAM: THE BILINGUAL SCHOOL, P.S. 25. New York: City University, Hunter College Bilingual Education Applied Research Unit, 1971. 41 p.

This work presents information on the history, funding, and scope of the project. Included are sociolinguistic process variables such as the native and dominant languages of students and their interaction.

733 Lucas, Isidro. "Puertorriquenos En Chicago: El Problema Educativo Del Dropout." RICAN 1 (May 1975): 5-18.

734 McCanne, Roy. A STUDY OF APPROACHES TO FIRST-GRADE ENGLISH READING INSTRUCTION FOR CHILDREN FROM SPANISH-SPEAKING HOMES. Denver: Colorado State Department of Education, 1966. 270 p.

This work is a comparison made among three approaches to developing English arts skills, particularly in basal, second-language, and language-experimental reading.

735 McColgan, Michael Daniel. "Individual Role in Educational Change and a Framework for Its Analysis, with Particular Reference to the Establishment of a Bilingual Sub-School in an Urban School System." Ed.D. dissertation. Teachers College, Columbia University, 1972. 521 p.

This work discusses the data analyzed in terms of role theory, with the focus on the program manager set in the context of a new subsystem entering the extant organizational structure. Concepts of description, prescription, sanctioning, and dissensus were employed.

737 Magana, Concepion L. "Some Thoughts for Improving the Effectiveness of Bilingual Programs." HISPANIA 55 (March 1972): 109-10.

737 Mahan, James Mark, and Criger, Mary Kathryn. "Culturally Oriented Instruction for Native American Students." INTEGRATED EDUCATION 15 (March-April 1977): 9-13.

This article states that ready-made programs are not adequate in this context. Teachers must have the courage to become culture-learners since Indian children do not want attention drawn to themselves.

738 Mallory, Gloria Elaine Grifflin. "Sociolinguistic Considerations for Bilingual Education in an Albuquerque Community Undergoing Language Shift." Ph.D. dissertation, University of New Mexico, 1971. 115 p.

The goal of the study was to determine whether the Bilingual Learning Environment Research Project had affected sociolinguistic performance in six selected first graders compared with others in their family. A version of the matched guise techniques was used for the children.

739 Mannino, F.V., and Shore, M.F. "Perceptions of Social Supports by Spanish-Speaking Youth with Implications for Program Development." JOURNAL OF SCHOOL HEALTH 46 (October 1976): 471-74.

740 Marjama, Pat. "Success in a Bilingual First Grade." HISPANIA 58 (May 1975): 330-32.

This article discusses a successful program for Puerto Rican children in Rochester, New York, which gave special emphasis to reading instruction.

741 Marsh, Linda Kessler. "Self-Esteem, Achievement Responsibility, and Reading Achievement of Lower Class Black, White and Hispanic Seventh-Grade Boys." Ph.D. dissertation, New York University, 1975. 225 p.

742 Martinelli, James. "Bilingual Slide-Tape Library Orientation."
AUDIO VISUAL INSTRUCTION 21 (January 1976): 55-56.

This slide-tape library orientation was translated so that
it might be used by bilingual students.

743 Mendenhall, Betty Joan. "Developing Self-Acceptance and Reading Achievement Among Second-Grade Chicano Children." Ph.D.
dissertation, University of Colorado, 1973. 145 p.

744 Miami, Florida. PLANNING FOR NON-ENGLISH SPEAKING
PUPILS. Miami: Dade County Public Schools, 1963. 34 p.

This work presents the necessary guidelines for the development of an adequate bilingual program, including
a summary of the guiding principles underlying the program, the details of the administration, and techniques
used in teaching.

745 Montgomery, Linda. "A Carnival of Bilingual Learning." AMERI-
CAN EDUCATION 10 (August-September 1974): 34-37.

"Carrascolendas," originally launched as a TV program
for Mexican-American youngsters, will be directed
toward all children. The program incorporates region-
alisms, and frequently referes to Cuban, Puerto Rican,
and Mexican-American customs.

746 Moore, G. Alexander. URBAN SCHOOL DAYS: SELECTED
DAYS IN URBAN ELEMENTARY SCHOOL LIFE. New York:
Teachers and Resources for Urban Education, Hunter College,
1964. 274 p.

This work is a guide for prospective urban elementary
school teachers, with little or no knowledge of urban
schools, minority groups, or ghetto life. Classes in
three schools were observed; daily routines, conversa-
tions, and incidents were recorded. Interpretive discussions follow the observations.

747 Mousley, Woodrow V. "The Effect of Learning to Read with an
Initial Teaching Alphabet and Traditional Orthography on the
Spelling Achievement of Bilingual and Monolingual Children."
Ph.D. dissertation, University of California, Berkeley, 1971.
88 p.

748 Moyer, Dorothy Clauser. "The Growth and Development of
Children's Books about Mexico and Mexican Americans." Ed.D.
dissertation, Lehigh University, 1974. 380 p.

749 Nedler, Shari Evans. "Curriculum Development for Preschool
Spanish-Speaking Children of the Southwest: A Study of the
Translation of a Developmental Process into Classroom Practice."
Ph.D. dissertation, 1972. 329 p.

750 New York City. Board of Education. RESOURCE UNITS FOR
CLASSES WITH PUERTO RICAN PUPILS IN THE FIRST GRADE.
New York: Board of Education, 1955. 154 p.

This guide on curriculum and activities includes suggestions for creating a learning and assimilatory environment with the primary objective being the acquisition of
English. Themes include school work and play, home
and family life, and spring. References are (books,
films) included.

751 _____. RESOURCE UNITS FOR CLASSES WITH PUERTO RICAN
PUPILS IN THE FOURTH GRADE. New York: Board of Education, 1955. 151 p.

A guide on curriculum and activities suggesting a learning and orientating environment with a primary purpose,
the learning of English, which is a project sponsored by
the New York City Board of Education. Themes revolve
around life in New York City. References are included.

752 _____. RESOURCE UNITS FOR CLASSES WITH PUERTO RICAN
PUPILS IN THE FIFTH GRADE. New York: Board of Education,
1956. 184 p.

This guide on curriculum and activities is based on the
New York City social studies curriculum and intended
for recent Puerto Rican migrant children and those in
a transitional stage in the learning of English. Areas
include colonists, the South, Middle West, and West.
Reference materials are cited.

753 _____. WHO ARE THE PUERTO RICAN PUPILS IN THE NEW
YORK CITY PUBLIC SCHOOLS? New York: Board of Education,
1956. 103 p.

This work investigates the following sociological and educational concerns: (1) the family, (2) educational background, (3) ability to understand spoken English and to
read English, (4) ability to do basic arithmetical computations, and (5) performance on nonverbal intelligence
tests.

754 _____. RESOURCE UNITS FOR CLASSES WITH PUERTO RICAN PUPILS IN THE SECOND GRADE. New York: Board of Education, 1956. 131 p.

This guide on curriculum and activities includes suggestions for creating a learning and assimilatory environment with the purpose of stimulating children to learn English. Themes include school, neighborhood and other places, and people who work for us. References are listed.

755 _____. RESOURCE UNITS IN THE TEACHING OF OCCUPATIONS: AN EXPERIMENT IN GUIDANCE OF PUERTO RICAN TEENAGERS. New York: Board of Education, 1956. 157 p.

This work is a vocational guide for Puerto Rican students likely to leave school in ninth or tenth grade without mainland standards of communication ability in English. Topics include self-evaluation, methods of choosing work, Puerto Rican workers in the United States, legal considerations, vocational testing and vocational schools.

756 _____. THE FUTURE IS NOW: THE PUERTO RICAN STUDY, THE EDUCATION AND ADJUSTMENT OF PUERTO RICANS IN NEW YORK CITY. New York: Board of Education, 1957. 34 p.

This work is based on the comprehensive report entitled THE PUERTO RICAN STUDY--A REPORT ON THE EDUCATION AND ADJUSTMENT OF PUERTO RICANS PUPILS IN THE PUBLIC SCHOOLS OF THE CITY OF NEW YORK (1958). The latter describes four years of intensive research and experimentation in the development of method and materials for teaching non-English-speaking pupils.

757 _____. A GUIDE TO THE TEACHING OF SCIENCE, FOR USE WITH PUERTO RICAN PUPILS IN THE SECONDARY SCHOOL. New York: Board of Education, 1957. 172 p.

This guide on a science curriculum and activities is for secondary school Puerto Rican students with varying grasps of the English language and United States culture. Topics include safety, health, and everyday experiences with technology and biology.

758 _____. RESOURCE UNITS FOR CLASSES WITH PUERTO RICAN PUPILS: SECONDARY SCHOOL ORIENTATION STAGE. New York: Board of Education, 1957. 127 p.

This guide on curriculum and activities is based on New York City's social studies curriculum and intended for secondary school students in the early stages of learning English. Topics include new school and friends, new surroundings, and New York City and State. Reference materials are listed.

759 _____. TEACHING ENGLISH TO PUERTO RICAN PUPILS IN GRADES 5 AND 6. New York: Board of Education, 1957. 283 p.

760 _____. RESOURCE UNITS FOR CLASSES WITH PUERTO RICAN PUPILS IN THE SIXTH GRADE. New York: Board of Education, 1957. 195 p.

This guide on curriculum and activities is based on the New York City social studies curriculum and intended for recent Puerto Rican migrant children and those in a transitional stage of learning English. Topics include the modern U.S. links with the other Americas and other nations. Reference materials are cited.

761 _____. RESOURCE UNITS FOR CLASSES WITH PUERTO RICAN PUPILS: SECONDARY SCHOOL EXTENDED-ORIENTATION STAGE. New York: Board of Education, 1957. 164 p.

This guide on curriculum and activities is based on the New York City social sciences curriculum and intended for Puerto Rican migrant students insufficiently oriented to U.S. life and insufficiently proficient in English. Topics include traveling, housing, and industry. References are cited.

762 _____. RESOURCE UNITS FOR CLASSES WITH PUERTO RICAN PUPILS: SECONDARY SCHOOL TRANSITION STAGE. New York: Board of Education, 1957. 132 p.

This guide on curriculum and activities is based on the New York City social studies curriculum for the eighth grade and intended for classes including Puerto Rican students relatively oriented to life in the United States but with insufficient mastery of English. Topics include American people throughout the continent, democracy, and American standard of living. Reference materials are cited.

763 _____. TEACHING ENGLISH TO PUERTO RICAN PUPILS IN GRADES 3 and 4. New York: Board of Education, 1957. 219 p.

764 _____. RESOURCE UNITS FOR CLASSES WITH PUERTO RICAN
PUPILS IN THE THIRD GRADE. New York: Board of Education,
1957. 124 p.

This guide on curriculum and activities includes suggestions for creating a learning and orienting environment
with the purpose of stimulating the learning of English.
Such themes as going places and getting things, and
living and working in the community are approached.
References are cited.

765 _____. REPORT OF WORKSHOPS OF THE FOURTH ANNUAL
CONFERENCE ON PUERTO RICAN EDUCATION. IT'S TIME
FOR NEW DECISIONS ON POLICIES, PROGRAMS, PRACTICES
FOR EDUCATING NEW YORK PUPILS OF PUERTO RICAN ORI-
GIN. New York: Board of Education, 1963. 50 p.

This conference, the participants desiring to revise mainland practices in light of island changes, addressed itself to eight areas for discussion and recommendation:
guidance, community relations, language, school administration, family life, teacher training, the arts, vocational education. Underlying most discussions were the
issues of language and adjustment vs. cultural identity.

766 _____. TEACHING ENGLISH TO PUERTO RICAN PUPILS IN
GRADES 1 AND 2. New York: Board of Education, 1963.
195 p.

767 _____. THE OPEN ENROLLMENT PROGRAM IN THE NEW
YORK CITY PUBLIC SCHOOLS: PROGRESS REPORT, SEPTEM-
BER 1960–SEPTEMBER 1963. New York: Board of Education,
1963. 46 p.

This work summarizes the steps taken in organizing the
program in September 1960 and in its development
through September 1963. Includes the recommendations
of the commissioner on integration, which dealt with
educational standards and curriculum, guidance, educational stimulation and placement, physical plant and
maintenance, teachers' assignments and personnel, zoning and community relations, and information. Sample
application forms, questionnaires, letters, and statistical
data are included in an appendix.

768 _____. PUERTO RICAN PROFILES. New York: Board of Education, 1964. 101 p.

This curriculum bulletin is devoted to articles and book
chapters taken from primary sources dealing with both

island and mainland Puerto Rican society. The Puerto
Rican in New York City is discussed in relation to
problems of adjustment, housing, employment, neighborhood, and school.

769 _____. PUERTO RICAN PROFILES, RESOURCE MATERIALS FOR
TEACHERS. New York: Board of Education, 1964. 96 p.

The large influx of Puerto Rican residents into New York
City has been most deeply felt in the school system.
Gathered here is information about Puerto Rican life,
both in Puerto Rico and New York to help facilitate
better student-teacher relationships.

770 _____. PUERTO RICAN STUDIES: RELATED LEARNING MA-
TERIALS AND ACTIVITIES IN SOCIAL STUDIES FOR KINDER-
GARTEN, GRADE 1 AND GRADE 2. Curriculum Bulletin no.
6, 1972-73 Series. New York: Board of Education, Bureau of
Curriculum Development, 1973. 246 p.

Intended as a supplement to the social studies program
in the kindergarten through the second grade, this bulletin suggests teaching materials and activities in Puerto
Rican studies to provide young children with knowledge
of the history, customs, values, and contributions of
the Puerto Rican people.

771 New York City. Board of Education. Bilingual Resource Center.
DESCRIPTION OF BILINGUAL PROGRAMS FUNDED BY TITLE VII,
ESEA. New York: Board of Education, 1973. 24 p.

This pamphlet presents a description of 23 bilingual programs funded by Title VII, ESEA, in New York City.
Information includes a description and list of objectives
for each program and the number of participants when
applicable.

772 _____. BILINGUAL ERIC REPRINTS. New York: Board of
Education, 1973. 38 p.

Titles of the articles are the following: (1) "Bilingualism in Puerto Rico: A History of Frustration," by John
C. Fisher, (2) "Paraprofessionals: Their Role in ESOL
and Bilingual Education," by Hernan LaFontaine, and
(3) "Second Language Learning in Bilingual Communities," by Sylvia Rothfarb.

773 _____. DESCRIPTION OF BILINGUAL PROGRAMS FUNDED BY
TITLE I, ESEA. New York: Board of Education, 1973. 21 p.

This booklet presents a description of 16 bilingual programs funded by Title I, ESEA, in New York City.
Information includes a description and list of objectives
for each program.

774 _____. DESCRIPTION OF BILINGUAL PROGRAMS FUNDED BY
TITLE III, ESEA. New York: Board of Education, 1973. 4 p.

This booklet presents descriptions of three bilingual programs funded by Title III, ESEA: The East Harlem Pre-
School, the Bilingual Elementary School Program, and
the Bilingual Resource Center. Program objectives are
included.

775 New York City. Board of Education. Division of General Education,
Albany. PROGRAMS PROVIDING BILINGUAL EDUCATION: TITLE
VII-ESEA (ELEMENTARY AND SECONDARY EDUCATION ACT):
QUESTIONS AND ANSWERS, PARTICIPATING SCHOOLS, CONTACT
PERSONS. New York: Board of Education, 1968. 27 p.

This booklet is designed to acquaint the reader with
some of the most basic provisions of ESEA, Title VII
and to provide some idea of how these funds are being
used in New York State. The first part provides a
general survey of ESEA, Title VII in New York State.

776 New York City. Board of Education. Office of Bilingual Education.
BUILDING BRIDGES TO BETTER BILINGUAL EDUCATION. New
York: Board of Education, 1973. 15 p.

The primary aim of the program is to promote the linguistic and academic progress of those Title I eligible
Spanish-speaking children whose achievement levels are
below the grade level of the district and city as a
whole. For this purpose it has initiated a teacher-
preparation program specifically designed to meet their
instructional needs.

777 New York State Education Department. Albany. PROGRAMS,
SERVICES, MATERIALS OF THE NEW YORK STATE EDUCATION
DEPARTMENT FOR BLACK AND PUERTO RICAN STUDIES. 1969.
59 p.

This booklet provides a brief descriptive listing of programs and services, and materials and resources for
black and Puerto Rican studies available at present, to
be available in 1970-71, and in the planning stages.
The services described are those of research, advising,
consulting, funding, and support.

778 New York University. Center for Field Research and School Ser-
vices. AN EVALUATION OF THE EXTENDED KINDERGARTEN
PROGRAM. New York: New York University, Center for Field
Research and School Services, 1969. 90 p.

> An all-day kindergarten program was established in
> September 1968 for three classes of black and Puerto
> Rican children at P.S. 101 in the East Harlem area of
> New York City. The objective of the program was to
> identify and develop the learning styles of the children
> through a wide variety of school experiences and ex-
> posure to multimedia educational approaches with heavy
> emphasis on cognitive skills along with language devel-
> opment, and mathematical and social concepts.

779 Nine-Curt, Carmen Judith. "Non-Verbal Communication in the
Classroom: A Frill or a Must." In NEW DIRECTIONS IN
SECOND LANGUAGE LEARNING, TEACHING AND BILINGUAL
EDUCATION. Edited by Marina K. Burt and Heidi C. Dulay,
pp. 171-78. Washington, D.C.: TESOL, 1975.

> This article focuses on important observations that have
> been made about movement (kinesics), space (proxemics),
> and how you order your activity (temporality) and touch-
> ing (haptics).

780 Noreen, Sister, D.C. "A Bilingual Curriculum for Spanish-
Americans: A Regional Problem With Nation-Wide Implications." CATHOLIC SCHOOL JOURNAL 66 (January 1966):
25-26.

781 Office of Education. Division of Compensatory Education, Washington, D.C. A TITLE I ESEA CASE STUDY: SPANISH ENG-
LISH DEVELOPMENTAL PROGRAM. Buffalo, N.Y.: 1972. 34 p.

> This pamphlet describes the Spanish English Developmen-
> tal Program, one component of Buffalo's overall Title I
> program. Begun in January 1970 with funds from New
> York's Urban Education Act, the program seeks to pro-
> vide bilingual instruction for nearly sixteen hundred stu-
> dents of Spanish origin.

782 Ohannessian, Sirapi. PLANNING CONFERENCE FOR A BILIN-
GUAL KINDERGARTEN PROGRAM FOR NAVAJO CHILDREN:
CONCLUSIONS AND RECOMMENDATIONS, 11-12 October
1968. Washington, D.C.: Center for Applied Linguistics, 1969.
16 p.

783 Older, Edith. RECALL AND PRINTED-WORD RECOGNITION OF RECENTLY-TAUGHT EMOTIONALLY CHARGED WORDS AS COMPARED TO RECENTLY-TAUGHT NEUTRAL WORDS. New York: Columbia University, Teachers College, 1971. 16 p.

> This work discusses ten third-grade Puerto Rican children in New York City, representative of students with reading difficulties from low-income families that were taught emotionally charged or neutral words. The author concluded that the content of reading materials and the methods for teaching them should be revised so that reading deals with events, ideas, and feelings which are emotionally significant to the child. Tables and references are included.

784 Ortega, Manuel Geoffrey Rivera. "A Content Analysis of the Mexican American in Elementary Basal Readers." Ph.D. dissertation, University of Oregon, 1974. 297 p.

785 Osborn, Lynn R. "The Teaching of Indian and Non-Indian Communication: A Curricular Innovation." JOURNAL OF AMERICAN INDIAN INNOVATION 12 (May 1974): 20-26.

786 Ott, Elizabeth H[aynes]. "Organizing Content for the Bilingual Child." In ON TEACHING ENGLISH TO SPEAKERS OF OTHER LANGUAGES. Edited by Carol J. Kreidler, pp. 55-59. Champaign, Ill.: National Council of Teachers of English, 1966.

> This article is a description of a curriculum designed to meet the particular needs of the non-English-speaking child.

787 Painter, Nathan Edward. "The Effect of an Instructional Technique in the Modification of Vocabulary Growth of Deprived Bilingual Children." Ed.D. dissertation, Arizona State University, 1965. 237 p.

788 Parra, José Antonio. "Bilingual Programming for Latinos: The Media's Missing Link?" PUBLIC TELECOMMUNICATIONS REVIEW 4 (July-August 1976): 14-18.

789 Pollack, Erwin, and Menacker, Julius. SPANISH-SPEAKING STUDENTS AND GUIDANCE. Boston: Houghton, Mifflin, 1971. 86 p.

> This work states that the primary source of the failures of Puerto Rican migrant children in mainland schools stems from misunderstanding of the subtleties of manners

and customs to which these children are accustomed in
island schools. This same misunderstanding also accounts
for failures to involve parents. Chapters 3, 5, 6, and
7 describe some of these subtle customs and offer specific concrete suggestions for guidance personnel working
with Puerto Rican migrant students.

790 Poulsen, Marie Kanne. "Automatic Patterning of Grammatical
Structures and Auditory and Visual Stimuli as Related to Reading
in Disadvantaged Mexican American Children." Ph.D. dissertation, University of Southern California, 1971. 121 p.

791 Puerto Rican Congress of New Jersey. EVALUATION ECHOES:
A TEACHERS GUIDE FOR SELECTING BILINGUAL EDUCATION
MATERIALS. Trenton, N.J.: Puerto Rican Congress of New
Jersey, 1976. 111 p.

792 Quintanilla, Guadalupe Campos. "The Little School of the 400
and Its Impact on Education for the Spanish Dominant Bilingual
Children of Texas." Ed.D. dissertation, University of Houston,
1976. 177 p.

The purpose of the "Little School of the 400" was to
teach Spanish-speaking children four hundred basic words
in English and to prepare them to cope with the public
schools' first grade curriculum. Parents, relatives, and
friends were encouraged to participate in teaching the
children.

793 Raisner, Arnold. "New Horizons for the Student of Spanish-
Speaking Background." HIGH POINTS 48 (February 1966):
19-23.

This is an experimental program of eighteen classes de-
vised to teach science in Spanish to junior high school
pupils in New York.

794 Raisner, Arnold; Bolger, Philip [Albert]; and Sanguinetti, Carmen.
SCIENCE INSTRUCTION IN SPANISH FOR PUPILS OF SPANISH-
SPEAKING BACKGROUND: AN EXPERIMENT IN BILINGUAL-
ISM. Washington, D.C.: U.S. Government Printing Office,
1967. 180 p.

This work discusses an experiment in bilingual schooling
to improve self-image.

795 Regan, Timothy, ed. BILINGUAL/BICULTURAL EDUCATION IN
THE COMMUNITY COLLEGE. ADVANCED INSTITUTIONAL DE-

VELOPMENT PROGRAM (AIDP) TWO-YEAR COLLEGE CONSOR-
TIUM. Washington, D.C.: McManis Associates, 1976. 32 p.

This work discusses the extent to which bilingual-bicultural programs are available in the United States, how
linguistic theory might be applied to bilingual-bicultural
programs and a description of the program at El Paso
Community College.

796 Reyes, Vinicio H. "Self-Concept and the Bicultural Child."
JOURNAL OF THE NATIONAL ASSOCIATION FOR BILINGUAL
EDUCATION 1 (December 1976): 57-59.

A bilingual-bicultural program must have a curriculum
which gives attention to both imparting necessary knowledge and developing a healthy self-concept.

797 Rippee, Billy Dean. "An Investigation of Anglo American and
Spanish-American Students' Expectations of the Counseling Relationship." Ed.D. dissertation, New Mexico State University,
1967. 105 p.

798 Ritzenthaler, Jeanette A. "New Approaches in Migrant Education in New Jersey." Ed.D. dissertation, Rutgers University,
State University of New Jersey, 1971. 252 p.

799 Rivera, Feliciano, and Cordova, Hector L. "Curriculum and
Materials for Bilingual, Bicultural Education." NATIONAL ELE-
MENTARY PRINCIPAL 50 (November 1970): 56-61.

800 Rivera, Hugo H. "Ascertaining Language and Computational
Curriculum Needs for Economically Disadvantaged Mexican Ameri-
can Elementary Students." Ph.D. dissertation, Arizona State
University, 1971. 93 p.

801 Rivera, Marie. "Culture Conflicts Among Puerto Rican College
Students." NEW YORK STATE PERSONNEL AND GUIDANCE
JOURNAL 8 (1973): 19-24.

This article states that there is a crucial need to provide counseling services which meet the specific needs
of Puerto Rican students. In order to understand the
reality of the Puerto Rican community, many factors
must be examined. Decisive among these are language
and culture.

802 Rodgers, David. AN INVENTORY OF EDUCATIONAL IMPROVE-
MENT EFFORTS IN THE NEW YORK CITY SCHOOLS. New
York: Teachers College, Columbia University, 1977. 283 p.

> The book includes an overview of bilingual programs
> and discusses funding with notices of Title VII programs,
> for example, decentralized district programs and cen-
> tralized high school programs.

803 Rodriguez, Armando. "The Necessity for Bilingual Education.
Libraries and the Spanish-Speaking." WILSON LIBRARY BULLE-
TIN 44 (March 1970): 724-30.

> This article is an overview of the education of the
> Spanish-speaking in the United States, covering the
> historical and current situation.

804 Rodriguez M[ungia]., Juan C. SUPERVISION OF BILINGUAL
PROGRAMS. New York Times Bilingual Bicultural Education in
the United States Series. New York: Arno Press, 1978. 194 p.

> The enactment of a Transitional Bilingual Education Act
> by the Commonwealth of Massachusetts was the nation's
> first such state mandatory law. In this study, an eval-
> uation of the first year of (1972-73) implementation of
> the Massachusetts statute was made with special atten-
> tion to supervision at the state level. In addition, the
> study assessed the opinions of parents of Spanish-speaking
> children participating in transitional bilingual education
> programs, and evaluated the objectives of the state's
> Transitional Bilingual Education Bureau which was re-
> sponsible for the implementation of the Transitional Bi-
> lingual Education Act. The evaluations (along with
> recommendations) were made with reference to needs in
> Massachusetts, and with reference to the analysis of
> national trends in the social and educational status of
> Spanish-speaking people in the United States.

805 Rojas, Pauline M. "Instructional Materials and Aids to Facilitate
Teaching a Bilingual Child." THE MODERN LANGUAGE JOUR-
NAL 49 (April 1965): 237-39.

806 Rosales, J.A. "Bilingual Education: The Need for an Alternative Instructional Approach." COLORADO JOURNAL OF EDU-
CATIONAL RESEARCH 15 (Winter 1976): 7-13.

> This article considers bilingual education as related to
> Spanish-surnamed students of the Southwest.

807 Rosen, Carl L., and Ortego, Phillip D. "Resources: Teaching Spanish-Speaking Children." THE READING TEACHER 25 (1971): 11-13.

808 Rosier, Paul, and Farella, Marilyn. "Bilingual Education at Rock Point--Some Early Results." TESOL QUARTERLY 10 (December 1976): 379-88.

This article describes a bilingual education program at Rock Point, Arizona, where English and Navaho are used. The conclusion reached on the basis of tests is that reading in one's mother tongue first leads to better reading skills.

809 Rustin, Stanley L., and Del Toro, Maria. "The Two Worlds of the Puerto Rican College Student." NEW YORK STATE PERSONNEL GUIDANCE JOURNAL 8 (1973): 25-29.

Experience in counseling Puerto Rican college students reveals conflicts between traditional Puerto Rican values and middle-class American values, personal identity confusion, and sexual role conflicts. This paper reviews the means a group of Puerto Rican students used to resolve such conflicts while attending an urban college.

810 Salazar, Arturo. "The Need for Bilingual Vocational Education Programs in Secondary Schools as Perceived by Bilingual and Vocational Program Directors, Vocational Counselors, Secondary School Counselors, and Industry Representatives in Texas." Ph.D. dissertation, Texas A and M University, 1976. 332 p.

The data for this work came from opinionnaires sent in by 636 respondents. Significant differences were found among the five groups regarding nineteen of twenty-eight perception statements, seven of fifteen attitude scale bipolar adjectives relating to the need for vocational bilingual programs.

811 San Diego City Schools. California. MATERIÆLES EN MARCHA PARA EL ESFUERZO BILINGUE [BICULTURAL MATERIALS ON THE MARCH FOR THE PROMOTION OF BILINGUALISM]. San Diego: 1973. 24 p.

This newsletter, intended to promote the cause of bilingual-bicultural education, contains articles on "Chicano Federation and Bilingual-Bicultural Education," "Have I Got a Math Series for You!," "Puerto Rican Social Studies Perspective," and "Multilingual Assessment Pro-

gram Builds Better Testing Mousetrap." The first article
appears in Spanish and English.

812 Santiago, Jorge, et al. ESTUDIO CULTURAL DE PUERTO RICO
[A cultural study of Puerto Rico]. Austin, Tex.: Education Service Center Region 13, 1973. 90 p.

This book, in Spanish, presents resource materials for
teaching the cultural heritage of the Puerto Rican student. It includes biographical sketches of outstanding
figures in Puerto Rican history from colonial times to
the twentieth century, descriptions of national festivities
and holidays, as well as poetry representative of Puerto
Rican literature.

813 Schmidt, L., and Gallessich, J. "Adjustment of Anglo-American
and Mexican-American Pupils in Self-Contained and Team-Teach-
ing Classrooms." JOURNAL OF EDUCATIONAL PSYCHOLOGY
62 (1971): 328-32.

814 Schrade, Arlene Ovidia. "Children's Responses Toward Spanish
Cultures Through the Integration of FLES, Language Arts and
Social Studies." Ph.D. dissertation, Ohio State University,
1972. 223 p.

815 Schwartzberg, Herbert. "The Effect of a Program of Choral
Speaking on the Silent Reading Achievement of Sixth-Grade Bi-
lingual Puerto Rican Children in the New York City Elementary
Schools." Ed.D. dissertation, New York University, 1963. 193 p.

816 THE SELECTOR'S GUIDE FOR BILINGUAL EDUCATION MATE-
RIALS: SPANISH 'BRANCH' PROGRAMS. New York: Educational Products Information Exchange Institute, 1976. 152 p.

817 THE SELECTOR'S GUIDE FOR BILINGUAL EDUCATION MATE-
RIALS: SPANISH LANGUAGE ARTS. New York: Educational
Products Information Exchange Institute, 1976. 131 p.

Under contract to the National Institute of Education,
the EPIE convened 36 cooperating bilingual experts to
analyze some twelve hundred elementary and secondary
school Spanish bilingual materials and some materials in
four Asian languages. See entries 816 and 818.

818 THE SELECTOR'S GUIDE FOR BILINGUAL EDUCATION MATE-
RIALS: THE STATUS OF PROGRAMS IN CHINESE, JAPANESE,

KOREAN AND VIETNAMESE. New York: Educational Products Information Exchange Institute, 1978. 70 p.

819 Sheldon, William D. "Teaching Reading to the Disadvantaged: Progress and Promise." Paper read at the conference of the International Reading Association, Anaheim, California, 6-9 May 1970. 19 p. Mimeographed.

Discusses the teaching of reading to black and Puerto Rican children in New York City.

820 Shiraishik Reyko, Ruth. "Effects of a Bilingual Bicultural Career Guidance Project on the Occupational Aspirations of Puerto Rican Adolescents." Ed.D. dissertation, Boston University, 1975. 186 p.

The findings of this study show the importance of developing particular learning experiences for bilingual-bicultural youngsters. Some were helped by the project which involved career role models and counselors who were both bilingual and bicultural. Results for the experimental group were examined after three test situations. The increased occupational aspiration was still present at posttest.

821 Spence, Raquel, and Rodriguez, Felicita, comps. MUCHO GUSTO EN CONOCERTE. [Happy to meet you]. Harrisburg, Pa.: State Department of Education, Bureau of General and Academic Education, 1972. 11 p.

This pamphlet answers questions concerning the Puerto Rican student in the Anglo school situation. Problems arising from cultural and linguistic differences are explored and suggestions to help teachers appraise and modify their own expectations concerning the child and his native culture are offered.

822 Stabb, Martin S., et al. CONFERENCE REPORT ON "ACQUI SE HABLA ESPANOL": A CONFERENCE ON THE ROLE OF EDUCATIONAL INSTITUTIONS IN SOLVING PROBLEMS RELATED TO THE IDENTITY, STATUS AND FUTURE OF SPANISH-SPEAKING PEOPLES OF THE UNITED STATES. University Park: Pennsylvania State University, Latin American Studies Committee, 1972. 48 p.

This conference sought to bring to the attention of a broad audience of educators the problems facing Spanish speakers of this country. Conclusions drawn were that much more had to be done to aid the Spanish-speaking person, especially in the field of bilingual education.

Appendixes, which amount to almost half the report,
provide a roster of participants, a list of Puerto Rican
studies programs in the Delaware Valley, a statewide
design for bilingual education, and a selected bibliography.

823 Steen, Margaret Trotter. "The Effects of Immediate and Delayed
Reinforcement on the Achievement Behavior of Mexican American
Children of Low Socioeconomic Status." Ed.D. dissertation,
Stanford University, 1966. 70 p.

824 Stodola, Robert Edmund. "Improvement of Communicative Skills
for Mexican American Pupils in Secondary School." Ph.D. dissertation, United States International University, 1971. 100 p.

825 Sutherland, Kenton. "Community Colleges: Attracting Spanish-
Speaking Students." CHANGE 7 (September 1975): 51-52.

Cañada College (California) began to meet the needs of
Spanish-speaking students when it created a program
that had courses taught either bilingually or in Spanish.

826 Talley, Kathryn Stephenson. "The Effects of a Program of Special Language Instruction on the Reading and Intellectual Levels
of Bilingual Children." Ph.D. dissertation, University of New
Mexico, 1965. 215 p.

827 Tannenbaum, Abraham J. AN EARLY INTERVENTION PROGRAM
THAT FAILED. New York: Columbia University, Teachers College,
1966. 14 p.

The objective of this program was to test whether reading clinic services administered at the beginning of the
child's elementary school experience made any difference
in his early reading performance. The population consisted of twenty-four pairs of children matched on age,
sex, ethnicity (almost all were lower-class Puerto Ricans
and blacks), and the Bender-Gestalt test.

828 _____. MOBILIZATION FOR YOUTH IN NEW YORK CITY.
New York: Mobilization for Youth, 1973. 16 p.

This work is a description of the Mobilization for Youth
Program, which centers around a discussion of five areas
of services: (1) curriculum planning and development,
(2) teacher education, (3) early educational intervention,
(4) correction and remediation, and (5) pupil personnel
services.

829 Texas Education Agency. PRESCHOOL INSTRUCTIONAL PRO-
GRAM FOR NON-ENGLISH SPEAKING CHILDREN. Bulletin
no. 642. Austin: Texas Education Agency, 1964. 132 p.

830 Theiss, Frances Case. "Bilingual Education: A Care Package
for Elementary School Principals." NATIONAL ELEMENTARY
PRINCIPAL 56 (July-August 1977): 58-64.

Guidelines are presented in this article on how to deal
with community and staff, for choosing an appropriate
reading program, and for beginning a "kick-off" learning center.

831 Topping, Donald M. "A Bilingual Education Program for Micro-
nesia." LINGUISTIC REPORTER 17 (May-June 1975): 5-6.

This article discusses the University of Hawaii's bilingual education program for Micronesian students. It
has created grammars and dictionaries.

832 Tovar, Federico Ribes. EL LIBRO PUERTORRIQUENO DE NUEVA
YORK. New York: Plus Ultra Educational Publishers, 1970.
496 p.

For information regarding education of Puerto Ricans in
New York, the reader is referred to section 2, "Analysis of the Educational Process in New York," pp. 61-93.

833 Trevino, Bertha Alicia Gamez. "An Analysis of the Effectiveness
of a Bilingual Program in the Teaching of Mathematics in the
Primary Grades." Ph.D. dissertation, University of Texas, 1969.
126 p.

834 U.S. Congress. Senate Select Committee on Equal Educational
Opportunity. EQUAL EDUCATION OPPORTUNITY: HEARINGS
BEFORE THE SELECT COMMITTEE ON EQUAL EDUCATIONAL
OPPORTUNITY OF THE UNITED STATES SENATE. 91st Cong.,
2d sess. on Equal Educational Opportunity. See parts 3E, 4, 5,
6, 7, and 8. Washington, D.C.: U.S. Government Printing
Office, 1971. 1,789 p.

Part 8 focuses on the problems of "equal educational
opportunity for Puerto Rican children." The public education system of Puerto Rico is contrasted with the urban
schools serving mainland Puerto Rican students.

835 Vasquez, Jo Ann. "Will Bilingual Curricula Solve the Problem
of the Low-Achieving Mexican American Students?" THE BILIN-

GUAL REVIEW. LA REVISTA BILINGUE 1 (September–December 1974): 236–42.

This article maintains that a bilingual curriculum alone is insufficient to solve the problems of the low-achieving Mexican-American student. Most essential are the teachers who are able to handle new concepts and skills.

836 Vasquez, Librado Keno. "An Experimental Pilot Bilingual Model School for Transient Mexican American Students." Ph.D. dissertation, University of Oregon, 1969. 212 p.

The model school is open to all transient and stable Mexican American students (K through 12). The study contains a plan for a future experimental pilot bilingual model school for Mexican Americans. The school has a five-week instructional period.

837 Veidt, Frederick P. "German-English Bilingual Education: The Cincinnati Innovation." UNTERRICHTSPRAXIS 9 (February 1976): 45–50.

A bilingual alternative school program established in 1974, took 200 monolingual first and second graders into a level of reading and math equal to or greater than that offered the regular pupils.

838 Wall, Muriel, comp. AUDIO VISUAL AIDS TO ENRICH THE CURRICULUM FOR THE PUERTO RICAN CHILD IN THE ELEMENTARY GRADES. 2 parts. New York: City University, Hunter College, 1971. 33 p.

An annotated list of more than sixty records and tapes for use in the curriculum, as well as lists of distributors of sheet music, records, tapes, films, and filmstrips is included in this book.

839 Wampler, H. "A Case Study of 12 Spanish-Speaking Primary Children Concerning School Achievement and Socialization." Ph.D. dissertation, Pennsylvania State University, 1972. 190 p.

840 Warriner, Helen P. THE EFFECTIVENESS OF THE USE OF FOREIGN LANGUAGES IN TEACHING ACADEMIC SUBJECTS: A RESEARCH CONTRIBUTION TO EDUCATION PLANNING. Richmond: Division of Educational Research, State Department of Education, 1968. 40 p.

This work is a report of an experiment in which a language foreign to the students was used as a medium of instruction.

841 Weinberg, George. "School in Transition." JOURNAL OF
EDUCATIONAL SOCIOLOGY 25 (November 1951): 140-45.

842 Williams, Frederick, and Van Wart, Geraldine. CARRASCOL-
LENDAS: BILINGUAL EDUCATION THROUGH TELEVISION.
New York: Praeger, 1974. 147 p.

843 Wilson, Robert D. "A Bilingual Academic Program for the Early
Grades of the Schools of the Bureau of Indian Affairs in the
Navajo Area." 1968. Mimeographed. 8 p.

   This article defines the implementation and guidelines
   for the project.

844 Witherspoon, Gary. "Navajo Curriculum Center." JOURNAL
OF AMERICAN INDIAN EDUCATION 7 (May 1968): 36-41.

845 Wolff, Max, and Stein, Annie. FACTORS INFLUENCING THE
RECRUITMENT OF CHILDREN INTO THE HEAD START PROGRAM,
SUMMER 1965: A CASE STUDY OF SIX CENTERS IN NEW
YORK CITY. New York: Puerto Rican Forum, 1966. 30 p.

   Through a home interview questionnaire, data were
   gathered on 244 families, black and Puerto Rican, one-
   half Headstart and the other half non-Headstart participants in order to complete this study. Comparisons were
   made between blacks and Puerto Ricans and conclusions
   drawn as to which mothers more often than not sent their
   children to Headstart programs.

846 York, P.A., and Barnett, S.E. "Bilingual/Bicultural Health Education for Migrant Workers." HEALTH EDUCATION 8 (Septem-
ber-October 1977): 4-6.

847 Young, John. "Essential Considerations in Compiling Asian Bilingual Curriculum Development Materials." JOURNAL OF THE
CHINESE LANGUAGE TEACHERS ASSOCIATION 11 (February
1976): 11-25.

   This article states that Asian bilingual programs have
   not received the support they need. Thus far, Asian
   bilingual teaching materials have not been compiled
   according to necessary systematic models.

848 Zamora, Jesus Ernesto. "A Status Survey of Texas' Bilingual-
Bicultural Education Programs." Ph.D. dissertation, University
of Texas, 1977. 402 p.

This survey shows that the number of programs has increased, but the number of methods is still quite limited.
Efficient and effective BBE programs embrace the five
basic organizational components of management, instruction, parental-community involvement, staff development,
and materials development and acquisition. Few operating programs have all components.

849 Zevin, Patricia Ernenwein. "An Interdisciplinary Approach to
Bilingual Bicultural Education: The Palomar College Model."
Ph.D. dissertation, United States International University, 1977.
158 p.

This model was unique in several ways. There were
language and culture in dual-language community bilingual centers for adults and their children. There was
also bilingual bicultural paraprofessional and teacher
trainee preparation at community college level.

850 Zirkel, Perry Alan. PUERTO RICAN PARENTS AND MAINLAND
SCHOOLS, HARTFORD, CONNECTICUT. Hartford, Conn.:
Hartford Model Cities, 1971. 98 p.

This study resulted from an institute, the purpose of
which was to focus on facilitating the relationship between the home and school environment of Puerto Rican
pupils in Hartford as a possible model for other mainland school systems.

851 Zirkel, Parry Alan, and Castejon, Sandra de. "'La Escuelita'--
Bilingual School." SCHOOL MANAGEMENT 18 (October 1974):
16-17, 19, 27.

In Hartford, Connecticut, the Ann Street Bilingual Community School provides specialized services to over
three hundred Spanish-speaking students from preschoolers
to parents. This article describes the school and its
program.

V. ENGLISH AS A SECOND LANGUAGE

852 Allen, Harold B. A SURVEY OF THE TEACHING OF ENGLISH
TO NON-ENGLISH SPEAKERS IN THE UNITED STATES. Champaign, Ill.: National Council of Teachers of English, 1966.
158 p.

This report is based on 810 questionnaires sent to administrators in colleges, schools, and other agencies regarding the teaching of English as a second language.
Describes the teacher, teaching situation, aids and materials as well as problems and needs in this area. See
entry no. 105.

853 _____. TEACHING ENGLISH AS A SECOND LANGUAGE.
New York: McGraw-Hill, 1972. 278 p.

854 Anderson, Virginia, and Hoffman, Paul. "Teaching English to
Puerto Rican Pupils." HIGH POINTS 46 (March 1964): 51-54.

The authors point out that, in teaching English to Puerto
Rican pupils, teachers should also be aware of the traditions and customs of Puerto Rico.

855 Belfrom, Celia C. "ESL Programs for Puerto Rican Pupils in New
York City Schools." FLORIDA FL REPORTER 7 (Fall 1969): 18-19.

This article includes the following chapters: "Curriculum Development," "English (Second Language)," "Experimental Programs," "Instructional Staff," "Language
Programs," "Material Development," "Puerto Ricans,"
"Teacher Education."

856 Blatchford, Charles H., comp. TESOL [TEACHING ENGLISH TO
SPEAKERS OF OTHER LANGUAGES] TRAINING PROGRAM DI-
RECTORY, 1974-1976. Washington, D.C.: TESOL, 1975. 92 p.

857 Burt, Marina K., and Dulay, Heidi C., eds. NEW DIRECTIONS IN SECOND LANGUAGE LEARNING, TEACHING AND BILINGUAL EDUCATION. Washington, D.C.: TESOL, 1975. 135 p.

858 Cohen, A[ndrew].[D.], and Laosa, L.M. "Second Language Instruction: Some Research Considerations." JOURNAL OF CURRICULUM STUDIES 8 (1976): 149–65.

859 Croft, Kenneth. TESOL [TEACHING ENGLISH TO SPEAKERS OF OTHER LANGUAGES], 1967–68: A SURVEY. Washington, D.C.: TESOL, 1970. 33 p.

860 Dulay, Heidi C., and Pepe, Helene. THE INFLUENCE OF A SOCIAL SETTING ON SECOND LANGUAGE LEARNING. Washington, D.C.: TESOL, 1970. 32 p.

An educational experiment concerning second language acquisition is described in this report. It is hypothesized that low ethnocentrism, positive attitudes toward the other group, and an integrative orientation toward language comprise high motivation, with the opposite criteria controlling low motivation.

861 Finocchiaro, Mary. TEACHING ENGLISH AS A SECOND LANGUAGE. Rev. ed. New York: Harper and Row, 1969. xvi, 478 p.

862 _____. EDUCATION OF PUERTO RICANS ON THE MAINLAND: OVERCOMING THE COMMUNICATION BARRIER. San Juan, P.R.: Department of Education, 1970. 14 p.

The complexity of the problems concerning the teaching of English to Puerto Ricans in the United States has rarely been fully appreciated. The author discusses some factors involved.

863 Fox, Robert P., ed. ESSAYS ON TEACHING ENGLISH AS A SECOND LANGUAGE AND AS A SECOND DIALECT. Urbana, Ill.: National Council of Teachers of English, 1973. 116 p.

864 Frankfort, Nancy. "The English as a Second Language Component of Selected Bilingual Programs in a New York City Community School District. A Descriptive Study." Ed.D. dissertation, New York University, 1975. 223 p.

865 Gonzalez-Mena, Janet. "English as a Second Language for Preschool Children." YOUNG CHILDREN 32 (November 1976):
14-19.

   Children are motivated to learn a second language
   through their relationship with other children. This de-
   mands a total development program.

866 Green, Kathleen. "Values Clarification Theory in ESL and Bilingual Education." TESOL QUARTERLY 9 (June 1975): 155-64.

   Techniques used for values clarification might be helpful
   for those working with college-level English as a foreign
   language and in elementary school bilingual programs.

867 Hickman, John M. "Barreras linguisticas y socioculturales a la
communicacion." [Linguistic and sociocultural barriers to com-
munication]. AMERICA INDIGENA 29 (January 1969): 129-41.

   Presents cardinal rules for teachers of a second language
   to take into account as they fulfill their function as
   "cultural change agents" in order that the student
   become truly bicultural.

868 Holmes, Graham; Benham, William J.; and Stepp, Walter M.
"Rationale of Navajo Area's English-as-a-Second Language Program." June 1966. Mimeographed. 16 p.

   This important background paper, traces the history of
   government- and religion-sponsored education developments among the Navahos. It contains materials and
   philosophy as well as appendixes.

869 Hunter, Diane Marie. "The Cultural Communication Factor in
ABE-TESOL Programs." Ph.D. dissertation, Georgetown University, 1975. 141 p.

870 Jacobson, Rodolfo, ed. STUDIES IN ENGLISH TO SPEAKERS OF
OTHER LANGUAGES AND STANDARD ENGLISH TO SPEAKERS
OF A NONSTANDARD DIALECT. New York: New York State
English Council, 1971. 185 p.

871 King, John B. THE MOST POWERFUL WEAPON IN OUR WAR
ON POVERTY: TEACHING ENGLISH AS A SECOND LAN-
GUAGE TO ENVIRONMENTALLY HANDICAPPED PUPILS AND
AS A THIRD LANGUAGE TO PUPILS OF FOREIGN LANGUAGE
BACKGROUND. New York: Board of Education, Annual Con-

ference on Teaching English to Speakers of Other Languages, 1966. 16 p.

The speaker emphasizes that a comparative examination of children of Puerto Rican, southern black, and suburban middle class backgrounds should be made, highlighting the differentials in educational orientation and the special language development problems of the first two groups of students.

872 Kreidler, Carol J., ed. ON TEACHING ENGLISH TO SPEAKERS OF OTHER LANGUAGES: Series 2, Papers read at the TESOL Conference, San Diego, California, 12-13 March 1965. Champaign, Ill.: National Council of Teachers of English, 1966. 304 p.

This work is a set of articles on TESOL as a professional field, reports on special programs, some key concepts and current concerns, and the preparation and use of materials and aids.

873 Lambert, Wallace E. "Developmental Aspects of Second-Language Acquisition." JOURNAL OF PSYCHOLOGY 43 (February 1956): 83-104.

This article discusses some of the variables in the linguistic behavior of those who are at different levels of development in the French language.

874 Lambert, Wallace E.; Gardner, R.C.; Olton, R.; and Tunstall, K. "A Study of the Attitudes and Motivation in Second-Language Learning." In READINGS IN THE SOCIOLOGY OF LANGUAGE. Edited by Joshua A. Fishman, pp. 473-91. The Hague: Mouton, 1968.

875 Legarreta[-Marcaida], Dorothy. "Language Choice in Bilingual Classrooms." TESOL QUARTERLY 11 (March 1977): 9-16.

This article states that English is used more than 70 percent of the time in concurrent translation classes. The language is employed principally in correcting and directing children. There is more balance between English and Spanish in alternate day classes.

876 Lewis, E. Glyn. FOREIGN AND SECOND LANGUAGE TEACHING IN THE USSR. ETIC Occasional Papers, no. 1. London: British Council English-Teaching Information Center, 1962. 16 p.

This report of foreign-language teaching and bilingualism in the Soviet educational system, includes comments on type of schools, language policy, and attitudes toward foreign-language teaching, teacher training, methodology, audiovisual aids, and bilingual education in the USSR.

877 Lozano, Anthony Girard. "The Role of ESL in Bilingual Education: Objectives and Implementation." FOREIGN LANGUAGE ANNALS 8 (December 1975): 317-20.

The long-range objectives of ESL in bilingual and bicultural programs would include the following: (1) writing competent prose, (2) reading English at an acceptable level, (3) competence in grammatical analysis, (4) competence in the skills of verbal persuasion, (5) competence in the skills of a coordinate bilingual, (6) a functional understanding of both cultures, and (7) the varied use of language.

878 McFadden, John. "A Bicultural Approach to ESL for Adults: A Paulo Freire Model of the Basic Learning Group." CALIFORNIA JOURNAL OF EDUCATIONAL RESEARCH 25 (November 1974): 289-93.

A five-point model of Freire's "Learning Group" is discussed in this article. The model is related to the needs of bicultural adult education.

879 Manning, John C., and Brengelman, Frederick. TEACHING ENGLISH AS A SECOND LANGUAGE TO KINDERGARTEN PUPILS WHOSE NATIVE LANGUAGE IS SPANISH. Fresno, Calif.: Fresno State College, 1965. 131 p.

880 Nedler, Shari E[vans]. "Explorations in Teaching English as a Second Language." YOUNG CHILDREN 30 (September 1975): 480-88.

Different approaches in approaching bilingual education are reviewed, including the naturalistic, the phonetic, and the programmed.

881 New York City. Board of Education. TEACHING ENGLISH TO PUERTO RICAN PUPILS IN THE SECONDARY SCHOOL. New York: 1960. 165 p.

Curriculum guide.

882 _____. EDUCATING STUDENTS FOR WHOM ENGLISH IS A SECOND LANGUAGE: PROGRAMS, ACTIVITIES AND SERVICES FOR GRADES PRE-K-12. New York: 1965. 105 p.

This guide grew out of a recognized need to bring together in one volume detailed information on all current educational programs related to the teaching of English as a second language. It is the product of the cooperative effort of all the school levels and many bureaus of the New York City Board of Education. Included also is information on the services of libraries, guidance centers, textbooks, and supplies.

883 Newton, Anne, comp. THE ART OF TESOL. 2 vols. Rowley, Mass.: Newbury House, 1978.

The work includes a broad range of articles, largely drawn from THE ENGLISH TEACHING FORUM on TESOL (Teaching English to Speakers of Other Languages) methodology, and techniques.

884 Ohannessian, Sirapi. THE STUDY OF THE PROBLEMS OF TEACHING ENGLISH TO AMERICAN INDIANS: REPORT AND RECOMMENDATIONS. Washington, D.C.: Center for Applied Linguistics, July 1967. 40 p.

885 Osgood, Charles E., and Ervin[-Tripp], Susan M. "Second Language Learning and Bilingualism." Supplement to THE JOURNAL OF ABNORMAL AND SOCIAL PSYCHOLOGY. Vol. 40, part 2 (October 1954). PSYCHOLINGUISTICS: A SURVEY OF THEORY AND RESEARCH PROBLEMS; REPORT OF THE 1953 SUMMER SEMINAR SPONSORED BY THE COMMITTEE ON LINGUISTICS AND PSYCHOLOGY OF THE SOCIAL SCIENCE RESEARCH COUNCIL, pp. 138-46. Edited by Charles E. Osgood and Thomas A. Sebeok. Baltimore, Md.: Waverly Press, 1954.

This article is a technical treatment of the psychological aspects of the acquisition and utilization of two linguistic codes. Distinction made between compound and coordinate language systems.

886 Peña, Albar [Antonio]. "Cooperation between Bilingual Education and TESOL: Our Children's Legacy." In NEW DIRECTIONS IN SECOND LANGUAGE LEARNING, TEACHING AND BILINGUAL EDUCATION. Edited by Marina K. Burt and Heidi C. Dulay, pp. 15-17. Washington, D.C.: TESOL, 1975.

Peña, the first president of the National Association for Bilingual Education, asks for dialogue between the organizations espousing bilingual education and those advocating English as a second language. He sees the two groups as basically serving the same population.

887 Powers, Francie, and Hetzler, Marjorie. SUCCESSFUL METHODS OF TEACHING ENGLISH TO BILINGUAL CHILDREN IN SEATTLE PUBLIC SCHOOLS. Project in Research in Universities. Pamphlet no. 76. Washington, D.C.: U.S. Government Printing Office, 1937. 17 p.

888 Ramirez, Inez Ruiz. "The Effect of English as a Second Language Instruction on Oral English Proficiency, Self-Concept, and Scholastic Achievement of Kindergarten-Age Mexican-American Students." Ed.D. dissertation, East Texas State University, 1973. 138 p.

889 Rexach, Maria G. "Improving Teacher Education for the Teaching of English as a Second Language in Puerto Rico." Ed.D. dissertation, New York University, 1960. 252 p.

890 Robinett, Betty Wallace, ed. ON TEACHING ENGLISH TO SPEAKERS OF OTHER LANGUAGES. Series 3. Papers read at the TESOL Conference, New York City, 17-19 March 1966. Washington, D.C.: Teachers of English to Speakers of Other Languages, 1967. 189 p.

This work contains articles on the teaching of English as a second language in Eastern Europe, Japan, and France; reports on special programs such as language policy in the primary schools of Kenya, education of the Spanish-speaking child in Florida, ESL for Alaska natives, ESL for pupils of FL background, especially Chinese and Arabic, and the training of ESL teachers.

891 Rojas, Pauline M. "The Miami Experience in Bilingual Education." In ON TEACHING ENGLISH TO SPEAKERS OF OTHER LANGUAGES. Series 2. Edited by Carol J. Kreidler, pp. 43-45. Champaign, Ill.: National Council of Teachers of English, 1966.

A brief description of the Dade County Public Schools' Spanish-English bilingual programs, their administrative policy, their curriculum, and the Ford Foundation Project is included in this article.

892 Saville-Troike, Muriel [R.]. "Basing Practice on What We Know About Children's Language." In her CLASSROOM PRACTICES IN ESL AND BILINGUAL EDUCATION, pp. 137-46. Washington, D.C.: Teachers of English to Speakers of Other Languages, 1973.

893 _____, ed. CLASSROOM PRACTICES IN ESL AND BILINGUAL EDUCATION. Washington, D.C.: TESOL, 1973. 84 p.

894 [Teaching English to Speakers of Other Languages]. "Survival English Does the Job." MANPOWER 2 (December 1970): 8-12.

In this program English is taught as a second language, so that Puerto Ricans can meet the necessary language requirements for career development while maintaining their cultural integrity.

895 _____. PROGRAM OF THE SEVENTH ANNUAL TESOL CONVENTION, 9-13 May 1973. San Juan, P.R. Washington, D.C.: 1973. 102 p.

Includes abstracts of papers presented at the convention.

896 _____. PROGRAM OF THE EIGHTH ANNUAL TESOL CONVENTION, 5-10 March 1974. Denver, Colo. Washington, D.C.: 1974. 139 p.

This work contains the abstracts of papers presented at the convention as well as art from the Southwest.

897 _____. PROGRAM OF THE NINTH ANNUAL TESOL CONVENTION, 4-9 March 1975, Los Angeles. Washington, D.C.: 1975. 183 p.

This work contains ninety-six abstracts of papers presented at the convention.

VI. TEACHER EDUCATION, STAFF TRAINING,
AND ADMINISTRATION

898 Ainsworth, C.L., ed. TEACHERS AND COUNSELORS FOR
MEXICAN AMERICAN CHILDREN. Austin, Tex.: Southwest
Educational Development Corporation, 1969. 137 p.

This is a report on a feasibility study conducted at
Texas Technological College. The areas of research
described and interpreted include characteristics of
Mexican Americans (including migrants), sociological
implications of their culture, the role of linguistics,
the guidance needs of Mexican-American youth, and
competency patterns of teachers who work with youths
of other cultures.

899 Arnez, Nancy L. PARTNERS IN URBAN EDUCATION: TEACH-
ING THE INNER-CITY CHILD. Morristown, N.J.: Silver
Burdett, 1973. 58 p.

This handbook is organized into six sections dealing
with: (1) a description of the inner city child, (2)
curriculum implementation and classroom interrelations,
(3) extraclassroom concerns, such as working with the
community, homework assignments, and so forth, (4)
working with parents, paraprofessionals and community
residents, (5) using and choosing resources for the classroom, and (6) a bibliography of books, films, and so
forth.

900 Axelrod, Joseph. THE EDUCATION OF THE MODERN FOREIGN
LANGUAGE TEACHER FOR AMERICAN SCHOOLS: AN ANALY-
SIS OF ENDS AND MEANS FOR TEACHER-PREPARATION PRO-
GRAMS IN MODERN FOREIGN LANGUAGES BASED ON A
STUDY OF NDEA FOREIGN LANGUAGE INSTITUTES. New
York: Modern Language Association of America, 1966. 55 p.

901 Baca de McNicholas, Patricia. "Responsive Bilingual-Bicultural Instructional Strategies: A Prospectus." CHILDHOOD EDUCATION 53 (November 1976): 111-15.

This article states that bilingual teachers need specialized training in the areas of culture, language, and different styles of learning. There is a discussion of recent research on Mexican-American children, including how they communicate with others.

902 Baker, Gwendolyn C. "The Effects of Training in Multiethnic Education on Preservice Teachers' Perceptions of Ethnic Groups." Ph.D. dissertation, University of Michigan, 1972. 183 p.

903 Ballesteros, Octavio Antonio. "The Effectiveness of Public School Education for Mexican-American Students as Perceived by Principals of Elementary Schools of Predominantly Mexican-American Enrollment." Ed.D. dissertation, East Texas State University, 1974. 209 p.

904 Baratta, Anthony Nicholas. "Changes in Professional Attitudes in a Group of Latin Americans Participating in a Bilingual Education Program." Ed.D. dissertation, Pennsylvania State University, 1960. 173 p.

905 Bolger, Philip Albert. "The Effect of Teacher Spanish Language Fluency upon Student Achievement in a Bilingual Science Program." Ph.D. dissertation, St. John's University, 1967. 147 p.

This study was done in selected New York City junior high schools. The bilingual science program obtained better results when the teachers were fluent Spanish-speaking science teachers. Omitting control of student bilingual dominance could affect results of such a study.

906 Bordie, John. "Cultural Sensitivity Training for the Teacher of Spanish-Speaking Children." TESOL QUARTERLY 4 (December 1970): 337-42.

907 Brault, Gerard J. "The Special NDEA Institute at Bowdoin College for French Teachers of Canadian Descent." PUBLICATIONS OF THE MODERN LANGUAGE SOCIETY OF AMERICA 77 (September 1962): 1-5.

This article describes the essentials of the institute program and curriculum, as well as its effect on the participants.

908 Burger, Henry G. ETHNO-PEDAGOGY: A MANUAL IN
CULTURAL SENSITIVITY, WITH TECHNIQUES FOR IMPROVING
CROSS-CULTURAL TEACHING BY FITTING ETHNIC PATTERNS.
Albuquerque, N. Mex.: Southwestern Cooperative Educational Lab-
oratory, June 1968. 193 p.

> Based on a review of around fifteen hundred publica-
> tions, inspection of some three dozen southwestern
> ethnic schools, projects, and laboratory activities, this
> manual offers a systematic, theoretical, and practical
> approach to the school as a major institution of culture.
> Attempts to present the basic information that the
> teacher-leader must know for an interethnic classroom.

909 [California. State Commission for Teacher Preparation and Licens-
ing.] COMMISSION FOR TEACHER PREPARATION AND LICEN-
SING: A REPORT OF BILINGUAL/CROSS-CULTURAL EDUCA-
TIONAL CREDENTIALING REQUIREMENTS. Sacramento: 1975.
38 p.

> The documentation is based on the performance of minor-
> ity-language peoples. The report recommends that the
> commission determine the standards for giving credentials,
> and calls for the effective establishment of a career
> ladder.

910 Caragonne, Bobbie Kathryn Smith. "Bilingual/Bidialectal Teacher
Educational Materials: Attitudes Toward Non-Standard Spanish."
Ph.D. dissertation, The University of Texas at Austin, 1976.
255 p.

> The development of modules is discussed, with their
> actual production explained in narrative form. The work
> highlights the need for teacher education materials for
> Spanish-English bilingual and bicultural programs, and
> gives attention to the variety of dialects that must be
> taken into account.

911 Carrillo, Frederico Martinez. "The Development of a Rationale
and Model Program to Prepare Teachers for the Bilingual-Bicultural Secondary School Programs." Ph.D. dissertation, University
of New Mexico, 1974. 213 p.

> This study is divided into four phases: (1) an examina-
> tion of Mexican-American students' needs, (2) bilingual
> and bicultural education as a possible solution, (3)
> skills and competencies needed by people in such pro-
> grams, and (4) a model for an undergraduate bilingual
> and bicultural program.

912 Carter, Thomas P. PREPARING TEACHERS FOR MEXICAN AMERI-
CAN CHILDREN. Las Cruces, N. Mex.: ERIC Clearinghouse
on Rural Education and Small Schools; Washington, D.C.: ERIC
Clearinghouse on Teacher Education, February 1969. 15 p.

This work stresses the need for "a new breed of educators—one equipped to make objective appraisals of problems, and to take rational and appropriate steps to encourage their elimination."

913 Casso, Henry J. BILINGUAL/BICULTURAL EDUCATION AND
TEACHER TRAINING. Washington, D.C.: National Education
Association, 1976. 96 p.

Included in this work are: (1) "The Renaissance in
Bilingual Bicultural Education," (2) "The Controversy
in Bilingual Bicultural Education: Melting Pot vs. Cultural Pluralism," (3) "Implications for Bilingual Bicultural Teacher Training," (4) "A Review of ERIC Publications," as well as a number of appendixes on fellowship
programs, grant awards, Lau centers, Civil Rights Hearings, preparation and certification of teachers, and a
bibliography.

914 Castillo, Max Spencer. "A Study of Competency Behaviors for
Elementary Teachers in Bilingual Environments." Ed.D. dissertation, University of Houston, 1975. 302 p.

915 Center for Applied Linguistics. GUIDELINES FOR THE PREPARA-
TION AND CERTIFICATION OF TEACHERS OF BILINGUAL/
BICULTURAL EDUCATION. Arlington, Va.: Center for Applied
Linguistics, 1974. 6 p.

This work is a planning and evaluation document for
teacher certification requirements and programs.

916 _____. INFORMATION FOR ADMINISTRATORS AND TEACHERS.
Bilingual/Bicultural Series, no. 1. Indochinese Refugee Education
Guides. Arlington, Va.: Center for Applied Linguistics, 1976.
10 p.

917 Cordasco, Francesco, and Bucchioni, Eugene. "An Institute for
Preparing Teachers of Puerto Rican Students." SCHOOL AND
SOCIETY 100 (Summer 1972): 308-9.

The authors propose a staff development institute for
elementary and secondary school teachers of Puerto Rican
students, which will be concerned with the development
of knowledge of Puerto Rican culture and specific professional skills.

918 _____. THE PUERTO RICAN COMMUNITY AND ITS CHILD-
REN ON THE MAINLAND: A SOURCE BOOK FOR TEACHERS,
SOCIAL WORKERS AND OTHER PROFESSIONALS. Metuchen,
N.J.: Scarecrow Press, 1972. xiii, 465 p.

This work deals with the following areas concerning
Puerto Ricans, both in Puerto Rico and on the mainland:
culture, the family, conflict and acculturation, and
North American schools. Recommendations by the
PUERTO RICAN STUDY are made for the program in
New York City schools.

919 Cordasco, Francesco, and Castellanos, Diego. "Teaching the
Puerto Rican Experience." In TEACHING ETHNIC STUDIES:
CONCEPTS AND STRATEGIES. Edited by James Banks, pp.
227-53. Washington, D.C.: National Council for Social Studies,
1973.

This essay is a description of what bilingual education
is (should be). Begins by contrasting the educational
experiences of first- and second-generation Puerto Rican
students (the latter being exposed to bilingual education
in the schools). Also discusses bilingual education in
the schools.

920 Court, Ian. "Inservice Training Problems in Introducing a Foreign
Based Science Curriculum into Puerto Rico." Ph.D. dissertation,
University of Illinois, 1972. 97 p.

921 D'Amours, Ernest R. "Le College de l'Assomption de Worcester:
son origine et son evolution." [The Assumption College of Worcester: its origin and evolution]. LE CANADO-AMERICAIN 2
(1960-1961): 10-17.

The origin and evolution of Franco-American Assumption
College in Worcester, Massachusetts, is discussed in this
article.

922 De los Santos, Gilberto. "Analysis of Strategies Used by Com-
munity Junior Colleges to Serve the Educational and Cultural
Needs of Their Mexican-American Students." Ph.D. dissertation,
University of Texas, 1972. 272 p.

923 _____. "El Paso's Organizational Development Model." COM-
MUNITY AND JUNIOR COLLEGE JOURNAL 46 (October 1976):
14-15.

A study of El Paso Community College, Texas. The
college has worked hard at increasing awareness in its

community and has developed a bilingual staff with a knowledge of management objectives.

924 Encinias, Miguel. "Hispanic Bilingual-Bicultural Education in New Mexico: A Study of Teacher Preparation." Ph.D. dissertation, University of New Mexico, 1976. 271 p.

The recent history of bilingual and bicultural education is examined. Proficiency in Spanish and knowledge of Hispanic culture are considered. The curriculum is dominated by methodology and excludes almost totally Western liberal education. The author presents a teacher education model with recommendations on how to implement it.

925 Escobedo, Theresa Herrera. "The Impact of a Mexican-American Cultural Awareness Model on the Attitudes of Prospective Teachers." Ed.D. dissertation, Texas Technical University, 1974. 163 p.

926 Estupinian, Rafael H. "Individualization of Instruction and the Bilingual Bicultural Teacher in the Education of the Mexican American." THRUST FOR EDUCATION LEADERSHIP 4 (January 1975): 26-28, 31.

927 Gamez, Gloria Irma. "Questioning Behaviors of First-Grade Bilingual Teachers During Reading Instruction: English versus Spanish." Ph.D. dissertation, University of Texas, 1976. 173 p.

Twenty-six first-grade bilingual teachers with varying degrees of experience were taped as they taught two lessons in Spanish and English. No significant differences were found between the number of English and Spanish low-cognitive (memory level) or the numbers of high-cognitive (abstract level) questions asked during reading instruction.

928 Garcia, Augustine [B.]. "A Study of the Relationship Between Teacher Perceptions and Bicultural/Bilingual Affective Interaction in the Classroom." Ph.D. dissertation, University of New Mexico, 1972. 196 p.

Twenty-one teachers in an inservice training program were selected in Albuquerque, New Mexico, along with their students. The Teacher Perception Questionnaire was used. The study was based on Comb's model, which maintains that all teaching behavior is the result of teacher perceptions of the students, the teaching situation, and the teacher's self-adequacy. The study's

recommendation is that teacher inservice training in bilingual and bicultural education be placed on the development of accurate teacher perceptions.

929 Garcia, Tony, Jr. "The Role of the Principal Who Supervises a
Bilingual Education Program within His School in Regard to Planning, Program Operation, Inservice Training, Community Development and Evaluation." Ed.D. dissertation, University of Houston,
1974. 152 p.

930 Godwin, Douglas. "The Bilingual Teacher Aide: Classroom
Asset." ELEMENTARY SCHOOL JOURNAL 77 (March 1977):
265-67.

The five functions of the bilingual paraprofessional discussed in the article are advocate, supporter, model,
supervisor, and informational resource.

931 Handschin, Charles Hart. THE TEACHING OF MODERN LAN-
GUAGES IN THE UNITED STATES. United States Bureau of
Education, Bulletin no. 3. Washington, D.C.: U.S. Govern-
ment Printing Office, 1913. 154 p.

932 Hassett, J.J. "Bilingual Teaching for Newly Arrived Immigrant
Children." CLEARING HOUSE 50 (May 1977): 409-12.

933 Hernandez, Leodoro. "A Textbook for Bilingual Teachers." Ed.D.
dissertation, University of Northern Colorado, 1976. 320 p.

Chapter 1 offers an explanation of bilingual education.
Chapter 2 is a history of the Chicano, while chapter 3
works on the Chicano language. Chapter 4 is an exploration of Chicano identity, and chapter 5 contains
tools for school personnel.

934 Hilliard, Asa G. "Cross-Cultural Teaching." JOURNAL OF
TEACHER EDUCATION 18 (Spring 1967): 32-35.

935 Hunter, William A., ed. MULTICULTURAL EDUCATION
THROUGH COMPETENCY-BASED TEACHER EDUCATION. Washington, D.C.: American Association of Colleges for Teacher Education, 1977. 272 p.

936 Jaramillo, Mari-Luci. "Ongoing Teacher Preparation." TODAY'S
EDUCATION 64 (January-February 1975): 74-77.

The article offers a brief description of some innovative programs for preparing bilingual teachers in schools of education and inservice programs.

937 Juarez, Paul Hill. "The Views of Public School Board Trustees and School Superintendents on Selected Issues in the Area of Bilingual Bicultural Education." Ph.D. dissertation, United States International University, 1975. 292 p.

The purpose of this study was to learn the views of school board trustees and administrators at superintendency level on selected bilingual education issues in California. Trustees did not favor expanding bilingual education programs in their districts with local funds. Administrators at superintendency level saw evaluation as the weakest component of such programs.

938 Klassen, Frank H., and Gollnick, Donna M., eds. PLURALISM AND THE AMERICAN TEACHER: ISSUES AND CASE STUDIES. Washington, D.C.: Published by the Ethnic Heritage Center for Teacher Education of the American Association of Colleges for Teacher Education, 1977. 252 p.

This work includes papers from the 1976 Leadership Training Institute on Multicultural Education in Teacher Education, sponsored by the American Association of Colleges for Teacher Education. There are descriptions of programs in university settings, clarifications of the concepts of multicultural education, and guidelines for developing curricula.

939 Laosa, L.M. "Toward a Research Model of Multicultural Competency-Based Teacher Education." In MULTICULTURAL EDUCATION THROUGH COMPETENCY-BASED TEACHER EDUCATION. Edited by William A. Hunter, pp. 135-45. Washington, D.C.: American Association of Colleges for Teacher Education, 1977.

940 Light, Richard. "Preparing Educators for Bilingual Education: Needs and a Response." THE BILINGUAL REVIEW. LA REVISTA BILINGUE 2 (September-December 1975): 331-38.

This is a preliminary report on some work of the bilingual education project (1970-73) of the State University of New York at Albany. Funded by the Federal Government, it had a bilingual staff, an advisory group with lay persons, an interdisciplinary program, and field-centered experiences.

941 Longres, John. PERSPECTIVES FROM THE PUERTO RICAN FAC-
ULTY TRAINING PROJECT. New York: Council on Social
Work Education, 1976. 68 p.

   A group of twenty-five Puerto Rican social work professionals met under the guidance of leading social work
   faculty with the objective of preparing themselves for
   full participating as social work faculty.

942 Lopez, Thomas Francisco. "Perceptions and Expectations of Bilingual Bicultural Educational Program Directors, Their Staff and
Superordinates Regarding Leader Behavior of Directors of Bilingual-
Bicultural Programs. Ed.D. dissertation, Wayne State University,
1974. 137 p.

   One hundred fifty-four teachers, and twelve directors
   and superordinates answered the questionnaire on this
   study. There seems to be a difference between the
   Chicano and Anglo value system regarding leader behavior. The Chicanos give less attention to initiating
   structure.

943 McCrossan, Linda V. "Bilingual/Bicultural Education for the
Spanish-Speaking Students in Massachusetts. An Analysis of
Perceived Dimensions of an Ideal Bicultural Teachers." Ed.D.
dissertation, University of Massachusetts, 1975. 246 p.

   A systematic set of procedures were designed to simplify
   vague goals in this study. Categories were given to
   Hispanic and non-Hispanic teachers. The former stressed
   "sensitivity to students" and understanding the child's
   culture, while the latter were more concerned with dis-
   cipline.

944 Mahan, J[ames].M[ark]., and Smith, M.F. "Adults in Latino
Communities Strengthen the Education of Pre-Service Teachers."
ADULT LEADERSHIP 25 (Summer 1976): 5-6.

945 Manuel, Herschel T. "Recruiting and Training Teachers for
Spanish-Speaking Children in the Southwest." SCHOOL AND
SOCIETY 96 (30 March 1968): 211-14.

946 Migdail, Sherry Resnick. "An Analysis of Current Select Teacher
Training Programs in Bilingual/Bicultural Education and the De-
velopment of New Teacher Training Designs." Ed.D. dissertation,
American University, 1976. 290 p.

   The author drew data from a grographic sample of ten
   school districts funded under Title VII (1965 and 1967)

and as amended in 1974. Data also came from nine
universities. The population in the Southeast was least
supported by university training programs. The Northeast Puerto Rican population was the most ambivalent.
A coordinated multidimensional model for training is
proposed and training programs suggested for both languages.

947 Morales, Frank Joseph. "A Descriptive Study of Bilingual Teacher
Aides and Their Utilization in Elementary Spanish-English Bilingual Classrooms." Ph.D. dissertation, University of New Mexico,
1978. 210 p.

The data collected in this dissertation pointed to gen-
eralizations, some of which were as follows: the bilingual and bicultural skills of aides were not being used
fully, career programs are not available for aides, pre-
service and inservice programs were not available for
most of them.

948 Ney, James [W.]. "Predator or Pedagogue?: The Teacher of the
Bilingual Child." ENGLISH RECORD 21 (April 1971): 12-18.

This article states that there should be an increase in
bidimensional bilingual schools and classes, and an understanding that students who know "playground English"
cannot necessarily deal effectively with classroom English.

949 Ohannessian, Sirapi. THE STUDY OF THE PROBLEMS OF
TEACHING ENGLISH TO AMERICAN INDIANS: REPORT AND
RECOMMENDATIONS. Washington, D.C.: Center for Applied
Linguistics, July 1967. 40 p.

A group of specialists in field related to these problems
assessed the learning and teaching of English in several
specified areas in elementary and secondary schools
sponsored by the B.I.A. and in selected public schools
having American Indian students. The main problem
areas dealt with administration, teachers, student performance, and instructional materials.

950 Oliveira, Arnulfo Luis. "A Comparison of the Verbal Teaching
Behaviors of Junior High School Mexican-American and Anglo-
American Teachers of Social Studies and Mathematics with Classes
of Predominantly Spanish-Speaking Children." Ph.D. dissertation,
University of Texas, 1970. 117 p.

Forty secondary teachers participated in this study.
Among the findings were the following: Pupils responded

more when they had Mexican-American teachers; Anglo-American teachers used more informing statements; pupils asked more substantive questions in mathematics classes than in social studies classes.

951 Palmer, Judith Walker. "Competency-Based Bilingual Teacher Training: A Sample Program." HISPANIA 58 (December 1975): 905-9.

This article discusses a program developed by the departments of education and Spanish at Dominican College.

952 Perez, Bertha G. "A Process Model of Inservice Education for Teachers of Mexican American Students." Ed.D. dissertation, University of Massachusetts, 1974. 133 p.

The process model comes from a review of selected literature and from an analysis of five inservice programs in San Antonio, Texas. The model outlines recommended strategies. The curriculum section outlines six areas including analysis of teacher behavior, sociocultural foundations, and Spanish for teachers.

953 Ramirez, Frank. "Marketability of Bilingual/Bicultural Teachers in 1974 in the Los Angeles Unified School District." Ph.D. dissertation, Claremont Graduate School, 1976. 98 p.

The district's main recruitment thrust was to see minority teachers, particularly those with Spanish surnames. All the contracts given bilingual, Spanish-speaking teachers were on the elementary level in 1973-74 and 1974-75. Despite the general teacher surplus, there should be a continuing need for bilingual teachers.

954 Rivera, Carmen E[lena]. "Administration, Supervision, and Implementation of a Bilingual Bicultural Curriculum." In PROCEEDINGS, pp. 105-20. National Conference on Bilingual Education, 14-15 April 1972. Austin, Tex.: Dissemination Center for Bilingual Bicultural Education, 1972.

955 Simmons, James LeRoy. "The Development and Evaluation of Materials and Procedures for the Training of Teachers of Migrant Students in Guidance and Counseling Functions." Ph.D. dissertation, Florida State University, 1975. 179 p.

956 Smothergill, N.L.; Olson, F.; and Moore, S.G. "The Effects of Manipulation of Teacher Communication Style in the Preschool." CHILD DEVELOPMENT 42 (1971): 1229-39.

957 Southwest Council of Foreign Language Teachers. REPORTS:
BILINGUALISM. Edited by Charles Stubing. Third Annual Conference, 4-5 November 1966. El Paso, Tex.: 1966. 62 p.

> This important booklet contains useful information on
> the feasibility of bilingual schooling and reports on the
> programs, methods, and materials from the viewpoint of
> the administrator and counselor. Analyzes the problems
> of recruitment and preparation of bilingual teachers.

958 Stone, James C., and DeNevi, Donald P., eds. TEACHING
MULTI-CULTURAL POPULATIONS: FIVE HERITAGES. New
York: Van Nostrand Reinhold Co., 1971. 497 p.

> This work is an attempt to help fill the tremendous gap
> that presently exists between teachers' will to become
> more skillful with multicultural student populations and
> the as yet short supply of the quality materials they
> need in order to do so. In general, each cultural heri-
> tage is explored according to a scheme beginning with
> a broad cultural-historical view of the group, extend-
> ing to a familial focus, and ending with the child. An
> extensive appendix of further resources is included at the
> end of the volume.

959 TEACHER EDUCATION PROGRAMS FOR BILINGUAL EDUCATION
IN U.S. COLLEGES AND UNIVERSITIES, 1975-1976. Austin,
Tex.: Dissemination and Assessment Center for Bilingual Educa-
tion, 1975. 49 p.

960 [Teacher Training]. "Training Teachers for Bilingual Education."
HISPANIA 56 (1973): 762-66.

961 [Temple University]. The NDEA National Institute for Advanced
Study in Teaching Disadvantaged Youth. POSITION PAPERS
FROM LANGUAGE EDUCATION FOR THE DISADVANTAGED.
Report, no. 3, June 1968. Washington, D.C.: American Asso-
ciation of Colleges for Teacher Education. 16 p.

> The contents are as follows for this work: Harold B.
> Allen, "What English Teachers Should Know About Their
> Language," pp. 2-4; William Labov, "The Non-Standard
> Vernacular of the Negro Community: Some Practical
> Suggestions," pp. 4-7; H.A. Gleason, Jr., "The Gram-
> mars of English," pp. 7-11; Carl A. Lefevre, "Values
> in the Teaching of English and the Language Arts," pp.
> 11-16.

962 Terry, Dewayne. "Orientation and Inservice Education for Teachers of Mexican American Pupils." Ph.D. dissertation, University of California, Los Angeles, 1972. 245 p.

963 Thompson, Thomas A. "American Indian Teacher Training: The Teacher Corps Model." JOURNAL OF TEACHER EDUCATION 26 (Summer 1975): 123-34.

This article states that, by and large, American Indian youth are educated by non-Indians who are upper middle class. There are a number of culturally pluralistic programs with a Teacher Corps orientation in Alaska, Arizona, North and South Dakota, and Montana. The programs have a bilingual and bicultural direction.

964 Townsend, Darryl Raymond. "A Comparison of the Classroom Interaction Patterns of Bilingual Early Childhood Teachers." Ph.D. dissertation, University of Texas, 1974. 177 p.

965 Troy, Bernard Alan. "A Paradigm for the Implementation of Accountability Measures in Bilingual Education." Ph.D. dissertation, University of Southern California, 1974. 232 p.

966 Walsh, Sister Marie Andre. THE DEVELOPMENT OF A RATIONALE FOR A PROGRAM TO PREPARE TEACHERS FOR SPANISH-SPEAKING CHILDREN IN THE BILINGUAL-BICULTURAL ELEMENTARY SCHOOL. San Francisco: R and E Research Associates, 1976. 91 p.

This study is divided into four parts. The first presents a profile of the depressed educational achievement of Mexican Americans in the total Southwest and Texas. The second studies the process of program development. The third works on a program rationale, while the fourth indicates needed directions in research.

967 Whitmore, Don R. "Partners for Bilingual Education." BULLETIN OF THE ASSOCIATION OF DEPARTMENTS OF FOREIGN LANGUAGES 7 (November 1975): 17-19.

The author discusses how linguists, sociologists, and other professionals might help in the training of bilingual-bicultural teachers.

968 Wonder, John P. "The Bilingual Mexican-American as a Potential Teacher of Spanish." HISPANIA 48 (March 1965): 97-99.

969 Wylie, Richard E., and de McNicholas, Patricia Baca. "Responsive Bilingual-Bicultural Instructional Strategies: A Prospectus." CHILDHOOD EDUCATION 53 (November-December 1976): 111-15.

This article is a review of some bilingual–bicultural teaching strategies, including the training of bilingual–bicultural specialists.

970 Zamora, Gloria Lu Jean Rodriguez. "Staff Development for Bilingual/Bicultural Programs--A Philosophical Base." In PROCEEDINGS, pp. 299-303. National Conference on Bilingual Education, 14-15 April 1972. Austin, Tex.: Dissemination Center for Bilingual Bicultural Education, 1972.

971 _____. "A Comparison of the Nonverbal Communication Patterns of Bilingual Early Childhood Teachers." Ph.D. dissertation, University of Texas, 1974. 230 p.

972 Zintz, Miles V. WHAT CLASSROOM TEACHERS SHOULD KNOW ABOUT BILINGUAL EDUCATION. Albuquerque, N. Mex.: College of Education, University of New Mexico, March 1969. 57 p.

VII. LEGISLATION: FEDERAL AND STATE ROLES

973 Alexander, David J., and Nava, Alfonso [Rodriguez]. A PUBLIC
POLICY ANALYSIS OF BILINGUAL EDUCATION IN CALIFORNIA.
San Francisco: R and E Research Associates, 1976. x, 70 p.

974 Beck, Nicholas Patrick. "The Other Children: Minority Education in California Public Schools from Statehood to 1890." Ed.D.
dissertation, University of California Los Angeles, 1975. 216 p.

975 Behnke, Martin Kyle. "Resources and Suggested Organizational
Procedures for Courses in Mexican and Mexican-American Music."
Ph.D. dissertation, University of Colorado, 1975. 224 p.

976 Beloz, George. "The Vocational Education Amendments of 1968
and 1974: Postsecondary Disadvantaged-Bilingual Vocational Education Programs for the Spanish-Surnamed, Spanish-Speaking Students in the United States." Ph.D. dissertation, Southern Illinois
University, 1976. 139 p.

   Among the findings are the following: (1) seventeen
   states have established PD BVE (Post-Secondary Disadvantaged-Bilingual Vocational Education) programs and
   plan to continue them, (2) thirteen states had not yet
   established any but planned to, and (3) twenty-one
   states did not plan on establishing any. The author
   believes that the level of instruction should rise and
   efforts be made to reduce the apprehension concerning
   the value of such programs.

977 Belzer, Bruce. "Bilingual Education and State Legislatures."
THE EDUCATIONAL FORUM 40 (May 1976): 537-41.

978 Benavides, Ezequiel. "Una Crisis para la Educacion Bilingue en
Nuevo Mejico. A Crisis for Bilingual Education in New Mexico."
LA CONFLUENCIA 1 (December 1976): 23-27.

The bilingual situation in New Mexico is reviewed briefly by the author. The federal government's financial support can only be forthcoming if New Mexico unified its objectives and efforts.

979 Bethke, Brian. "The Illinois Bilingual Education Mandate: Serving the Needs of Limited-English Speaking Students." ILLINOIS CAREER EDUCATION JOURNAL 33 (February 1975): 10-11.

980 BILINGUAL-BICULTURAL EDUCATION: A HANDBOOK FOR ATTORNEYS AND COMMUNITY WORKERS. Cambridge, Mass.: Center for Law and Education, 1975. 67 p.

This work is a brief description of the Massachusetts Transitional Bilingual Education Act of 1971 (Mass. Gen. Laws, ch. 71A) and other statutes.

981 Cebollero, Pedro Angel. A SCHOOL LANGUAGE POLICY FOR PUERTO RICO. San Juan, P.R.: Imp. Baldrich, 1945. 133 p.

This work is adapted from an Ed.D. dissertation, Teachers College, Columbia University, 1938.

982 Chachkin, Norman J. "The Law and Foreign Languages." BULLETIN OF THE ASSOCIATION OF DEPARTMENTS OF FOREIGN LANGUAGES 6 (May 1975): 28-32.

A survey is presented in this article of the early history and the legal status of foreign-language education in the United States as well as the background to the Lau v. Nichols decision.

983 Chen, May Ying. "Lau vs. Nichols: Landmark in Bilingual Education." BRIDGE 3 (February 1975): 3-6.

The article includes reflections by an Asian teacher and social worker who has seen the problems faced by school children.

984 Colorado Commission on Spanish-Surnamed Citizens. REPORT TO THE COLORADO GENERAL ASSEMBLY: THE STATUS OF SPANISH-SURNAMED CITIZENS IN COLORADO. Denver: State of Colorado, January 1967. 125 p.

This report contains statistical, sociological, and psychological data; and makes recommendations in the areas of education, income, poverty, health, housing, and consumer problems.

985 Fernandez, Rafael. "El Nuevo Aspecto de la Educacion Bilingue."
JOURNAL OF THE NATIONAL ASSOCIATION FOR BILINGUAL
EDUCATION 1 (May 1976): 61-64.

Legal issues surrounding bilingual education are discussed
in this article. Bilingual educators are asked to be
more alert to the need to fight for positive legal provisions, and to encourage more community involvement.

986 Foster, William P. "Bilingual Education: An Educational and
Legal Survey." JOURNAL OF LAW AND EDUCATION 5 (April
1976): 149-71.

987 Freda, Robert Anthony. "The Role of the New Jersey Coalition
for Bilingual Education in the Enactment of the New Jersey Bilingual Education Law." Ed.D. dissertation, Rutgers University,
1976. 278 p.

The main portion of the study is devoted to the coalition's politics. The coalition's guidelines are intended
to serve as a tentative model of community intervention
in the arena of educational politics. The study also
provides an overview of New Jersey demographic developments, and of documents related to bilingual and
bicultural education.

988 Geffert, Hannan N., et al. THE CURRENT STATUS OF U.S.
BILINGUAL EDUCATION LEGISLATION. Bilingual Education
Series, no. 4. Washington, D.C.: Center for Applied Linguis-
tics, 1975. 126 p.

This work examines the federal, state, and other "American flag" legislation relating to bilingual education in
effect as of April 1975.

989 Gordy, Margaret. "The Massachusetts Story." TODAY'S EDU-
CATION 64 (January-February 1975): 79-80.

This article discusses the Massachusetts Coalition for Bilingual Education, which worked for the passage of crucial state legislation.

990 Hall, Beverly. "Bilingual and Bicultural Schools." NOTES
FROM WORKSHOP CENTER FOR OPEN EDUCATION 6 (Spring
1977): 28-36.

This article is an evaluation of the implementation of
Colorado's Bilingual-Bicultural Education Act which was
passed in 1975.

991 Hermenet, Argelina [Maria] Buitrago. "Education: A Humanistic
Manpower Development Approach to Bilingual-Bicultural Education."
LA LUZ: NATIONAL REVIEW OF LA RAZA 2 (May 1975): 44-
45.

> The author reviews the Massachusetts Bilingual Education
> of 1971.

992 Hiller, Richard [J.], and Teitelbaum, Herbert. "A Court-Ordered
Bilingual Program in Perspective: ASPIRA of New York vs.
Board of Education of the City of New York." JOURNAL OF
THE NATIONAL ASSOCIATION FOR BILINGUAL EDUCATION
1 (December 1976): 67-71.

> The ASPIRA suit aimed to get for Puerto Rican and other
> Hispanic public school students who have English-lan-
> guage difficulties their rights under federal laws.

993 Hopkins, Thomas R. "Educational Provisions for the Alaskan
Native Since 1876." M.Ed. dissertation, University of Texas,
1959. 117 p.

> The author provides an overview of the development of
> the Alaskan native and of schools in this area, an analysis
> of curriculum problems, and the administrative structure of
> Alaskan native education under the Bureau of Indian
> Affairs.

994 Illivicky, M. "Bilingual Education: Politics or Process?" NA-
TIONAL ASSOCIATION OF SECONDARY SCHOOL PRINCIPALS
BULLETIN 60 (December 1976): 56-59.

995 Kloss, Heinz. "Experts from the National Minority Laws of the
United States of America." Translated from the German by Ulrich
Hans R. Mammitzch. Occasional papers of Research Translations,
Institute of Advanced Projects, Fast-West Center, Honolulu,
Hawaii. Mimeographed. 72 p.

> The author concludes that non-English-speaking ethnic
> groups in the United States were Anglicized not because
> of nationality laws which were unfavorable toward their
> languages but in spite of nationality laws favorable to
> them.

996 Krear, Serafina Elizabeth. "A Proposed Framework Derived from
an Analysis of 1969-1970 Title VII Bilingual Education Proposals
in California." Ph.D. dissertation, University of California,
Berkeley, 1971. 99 p.

997 Macaulay, R.K.S. "Lingualism: The Real Implications of Lau vs. Nichols." CLAREMONT READING CONFERENCE YEARBOOK 41 (1977): 86-93.

998 Michael, Bernard. "Language Policy in Puerto Rican Education." Ph.D. dissertation, Columbia University, 1960. 80 p.

999 Montoya, Joseph M. "Bilingual-Bicultural Education: Making Equal Educational Opportunity Available to National Origin Minority Students." GEORGETOWN LAW JOURNAL 61 (March 1973): 991-1007.

1000 Rice, Roger. "Recent Legal Developments in Bilingual/Bicultural Education." INEQUALITY IN EDUCATION 19 (February 1975): 51-53.

This article is a summary of the status of bilingual and bicultural education litigation which followed the crucial Lau v. Nichols decision of 1974.

1001 Sanchez, Gilbert. "An Analysis of the Bilingual Education Act, 1967-1968." Ph.D. dissertation, University of Massachusetts, 1973. 274 p.

The author gathers data from the literature, from governmental documents, and from in-depth interviews with some of those involved with the passage of the act.

1002 Schneider, Susan Gilbert. "The 1974 Bilingual Education Amendments: Revolution, Reaction or Reform." Ph.D. dissertation, University of Maryland, 1976. 519 p.

This study concerns itself with such topics as: the history and legislative background of bilingual and bicultural education, the developing positions of the U.S. House and Senate, and the position of the federal administration. Lau v. Nichols substantially influenced the positions of the legislative bodies.

1003 _____. REVOLUTION, REACTION OR REFORM: THE 1974 BILINGUAL EDUCATION ACT. New York: L.A. Publishing Co., 1976. 238 p.

An analysis is given of the historical context, the legislative developments, and people involved in the realization of the historic act.

1004 Sinowitz, Betty E. "The Court Speaks Out." TODAY'S EDUCA-
TION 64 (January-February 1975): 63-84.

This is a brief discussion of court decisions affecting implementation of bilingual and bicultural programs.

1005 Teitelbaum, Herbert, and Hiller, Richard J. "Bilingual Education:
The Legal Mandate." HARVARD EDUCATIONAL REVIEW 47 (May
1977): 138-70.

An overview of the Lau v. Nichols decision of the U.S.
Supreme Court and subsequent cases is discussed, with a
notice of obstacles to overcome and options for remedy-
ing discrimination against linguistic minority students.

1006 University of Southwestern Louisiana. "The Role of Education
and Government in the Regional Preservation of French: A
Colloquy." Lafayette, La.: 1968. 28 p.

This is a collection of papers discussing the problem of
French-language maintenance in Louisiana.

1007 Van Geel, Tyll. "Law, Politics, and the Right to Be Taught
English." SCHOOL REVIEW 83 (1975): 245-72.

1008 Waugh, D., and Koon, B. "Breakthrough for Bilingual Education:
Lau v. Nichols and the San Francisco School System." CIVIL
RIGHTS DIGEST 6 (Summer 1974): 18-26.

1009 "Why Some Kids Have a Right to Bilingual Education." COM-
PACT 9 (August 1975): 16-19.

This article analyzes the legal principles and court decisions which bear upon the responsibilities of states in
the matter of bilingual education.

1010 Zirkel, Perry [Alan]. "The Legal Vicissitudes of Bilingual Education." PHI DELTA KAPPAN 58 (January 1977): 409-11.

VIII. LINGUISTICS, LANGUAGE, AND MULTILINGUALISM

1011 Aarons, Alfred C.; Gordon, Barbara Y.; and Stewart, William A.[C.],
      eds. "Linguistic-Cultural Differences and American Education."
      FLORIDA FL REPORTER 7 (Spring-Summer 1969): 1-175.

1012 Agheyisi, Rebecca, and Fishman, Joshua A. "Language Attitude
      Studies: A Brief Survey of Methodological Approaches." ANTHRO-
      POLOGICAL LINGUISTICS 12 (1970): 137-57.

1013 Alatis, James E., ed. BILINGUALISM AND LANGUAGE CON-
      TACT: ANTHROPOLOGICAL, LINGUISTIC, PSYCHOLOGICAL,
      AND SOCIOLOGICAL ASPECTS. Monograph Series on Languages
      and Linguistics, no. 23. Washington, D.C.: Georgetown Uni-
      versity Press, 1970. vii, 314 p.

1014 American Council of Learned Societies. CONFERENCE ON NON-
      ENGLISH SPEECH IN THE UNITED STATES, ANN ARBOR, MICHI-
      GAN, 2-3 AUGUST 1940. Bulletin no. 34, March 1942. 89 p.

          The papers read were as follows: (1) Hans Kurath,
          "Pennsylvania Germans," (2) R.M.S. Heffner, "German
          Settlements in Wisconsin," (3) Hayward Keniston, "The
          Spanish in the United States," (4) Walter von Wartburg,
          "An Atlas of Louisiana French," Panel discussions were
          as follows: (1) Alfred Senn, "Swiss Dialects in America,"
          (2) Einar Haugen, "Scandinavian," (3) George L. Trager,
          "The Slavic-Speaking Groups," (4) T. Mayarro Tomas,
          "The Linguistic Atlas of Spain and the Spanish in the
          Americas," and (5) Ernest F. Haden, "French-Speaking
          Areas in Canada."

1015 Arnold, Richard D., and Taylor, Thomasine H[ughes]. "Mexican-
      Americans and Language Learning." CHILDHOOD EDUCATION
      46 (1969): 149-54.

1016 Barbeau, Marius. "Louisiana French." CANADIAN GEOGRAPH-
ICAL JOURNAL 54 (January 1957): 2-11.

This article is a brief discussion of the Acadian settlements, their origins, customs, and language.

1017 Barker, George C. "Social Functions of Language in a Mexican
American Community." ACTA AMERICANA 5 (1947): 185-202.

1018 Berney, Tomi D[eutsch]., and Cooper, Robert L. "Semantic Independence and Degree of Bilingualism in Two Communities." MO-
DERN LANGUAGE JOURNAL 53 (March 1969): 182-85.

This article includes the following topics: "Bilingual-
ism," "English (Second Language)," "Language Research,"
"Language Usage," "Psycholinguistics," "Puerto Ricans,"
"Spanish Speaking," "Verbal Operant Conditioning,"
"Word Recognition."

1019 Berney, Tomi D[eutsch].; Cooper, Robert L.; and Fishman, Joshua A.
"Semantic Independence and Degree of Bilingualism in Two Puerto
Rican Communities." REVISTA INTERAMERICANA DE PSICOLOGIA
2 (1968): 289-94.

This is a study of semantic independence and relative
proficiency as related to independent dimensions of the
bilingual's language systems.

1020 Biondi, Lawrence. THE ITALIAN AMERICAN CHILD: HIS SO-
CIOLINGUISTIC ACCULTURATION. Washington, D.C.: Georgetown University Press, 1975. viii, 160 p.

This work discusses the investigation of the manner in
which monolingual and bilingual children of the Boston
North End Italian American community speak English
and the manner in which they learn the rules for social
interaction in an acculturating community.

1021 Boas, Frank. "The Classification of American Languages."
AMERICAN ANTHROPOLOGIST 22 (1920): 367-76.

1022 Botha, Elize. "The Effect of Language on Values Expressed by
Bilinguals." THE JOURNAL OF SOCIAL PSYCHOLOGY 80
(1970): 143-45.

1023 Brannon, J.B. "A Comparison of Syntactic Structures in the
Speech of Three and Four Year Old Children." LANGUAGE
AND SPEECH 11 (1968): 171-81.

1024 Brault, Gerard J. "New England French Vocabulaty." THE FRENCH REVIEW 35 (December 1961): 163-75.

This article illustrates the lexical strengths and weaknesses of the French spoken by Franco Americans.

1025 Brisk, M.E. "The Spanish Syntax of the Pre-School Spanish American: The Case of New Mexican Five-Year-Old Children." Ph.D. dissertation, University of New Mexico, 1972. 246 p.

1026 Brizuela, Constance Sweet. "Semantic Differential Responses of Bilinguals in Argentina, Costa Rica, and the United States." Ph.D. dissertation, University of Wyoming, 1975. 78 p.

1027 Broussard, James F. LOUISIANA CREOLE DIALECT. Baton Rouge, La.: Louisiana State University Press, 1942. 134 p.

This is a study of Louisiana Creole phonetics, grammer, idioms, folklore, proverbs, medical prescriptions, poetry, tales, and a glossary.

1028 Brown, Roger. A FIRST LANGUAGE: THE EARLY STAGES. Cambridge, Mass.: Harvard University Press, 1973. 213 p.

1029 Brown, Roger, and Bellugi, Ursula. "Three Processes in the Child's Acquisition of Syntax." LANGUAGE AND LEARNING, a special issue of HARVARD EDUCATIONAL REVIEW 34 (1964): 133-51.

1030 Buffington, Albert F., and Barba, Preston A. A PENNSYLVANIA GERMAN GRAMMAR. Allentown, Pa.: Schlechter, 1954. 187 p.

1031 Carrow, Elizabeth. "Comprehension of English and Spanish by Pre-School Mexican-American Children." MODERN LANGUAGE JOURNAL 55 (1971): 299-306.

1032 Carrow, Mary Arthur, Sister. "The Development of Auditory Comprehension of Language Structure in Children." JOURNAL OF SPEECH AND HEARING DISORDERS 33 (1968): 105-8.

1033 Cazden, Courtney B. "Subcultural Differences in Child Language." MERRILL-PALMER QUARTERLY 12 (1966): 185-219.

1034 _____. "The Situation: A Neglected Source of Social Class Differences in Language Use." JOURNAL OF SOCIAL ISSUES 26 (1970): 35-59.

1035 _____. "The Hunt for the Independent Variables." In LAN-
GUAGE ACQUISITION MODELS AND METHODS. Edited by
Renira Huxley and Elizabeth Ingram, pp. 41-49. New York:
Academic Press, 1971.

1036 Cazden, Courtney B.; John[-Steiner], Vera [P.]; and Hymes,
Dell, eds. FUNCTIONS OF LANGUAGE IN THE CLASSROOM.
New York: Teachers College Press, 1972. 240 p.

1037 Cebollero, Pedro Angel. LA POLITICA LINGUISTICO-ESCOLAR
DE PUERTO RICO. San Juan, P.R.: Impr. Baldrich, 1945.
145 p.

This work contains a brief history of the language problem in Puerto Rico with a review of the studies related
to this problem, and an analysis of the social necessity of
English.

1038 [Center for Applied Linguistics]. RECOMMENDATIONS FOR
LANGUAGE POLICY IN INDIAN EDUCATION. Arlington, Va.:
Center for Applied Linguistics, 1973. 152 p.

1039 Chafe, Wallace L. "Estimates Regarding the Present Speakers of
North American Indian Languages." INTERNATIONAL JOURNAL
OF AMERICAN LINGUISTICS 28 (1962): 162-71.

1040 Chomsky, Carol. THE ACQUISITION OF SYNTAX IN CHIL-
DREN FROM FIVE TO TEN. Cambridge, Mass.: The M.I.T.
Press, 1969. 221 p.

1041 Christopherson, Paul. SECOND-LANGUAGE LEARNING: MYTH
AND REALITY. London: Penguin Books, 1973. 146 p.

1042 Cohen, Andrew D. A SOCIOLINGUISTIC APPROACH TO BILIN-
GUAL EDUCATION. Rowley, Mass.: Newbury House, 1975.
230 p.

1043 Cohen, R.; Fraenkel, G.; and Brewer, J. "Implications for
'Culture Conflict' from a Semantic Feature Analysis of the Lexicon of the Hard Core Poor." LINGUISTICS 44 (1968): 11-21.

1044 Conwell, Marylin J.; and Juillaud, Alphonse. LOUISIANA
FRENCH GRAMMAR. Vol. 1: PHONOLOGY, MORPHOLOGY,
AND SYNTAX. Janua Linguarum, Series Practica, no. 1. The
Hague: Mouton, 1963. 207 p.

This is a technical study of the three French dialects
of Louisiana, with an introduction giving a picture of
the history and education of the Acadians, and a long
and up-to-date bibliography on dialectal description and
Louisiana French.

1045 Cooper, R[obert].L. "Two Contextualized Measures of Degree of
Bilingualism." MODERN LANGUAGE JOURNAL 53 (March
1969): 172-78.

1046 Cordasco, Francesco, ed. THE ITALIAN COMMUNITY AND
ITS LANGUAGE IN THE UNITED STATES. THE ANNUAL RE-
PORTS OF THE ITALIAN TEACHERS ASSOCIATION. Totowa,
N.J.: Rowman and Littlefield, 1975. xvi, 472 p.

The reports cover the period from 1921-38. See review essay by Joseph G. Fucilla, ITALIAN AMERICANA
2 (1975): 101-7.

1047 Cornejo, Ricardo. "Bilingualism: Study of the Lexicon of the
Five-Year-Old Spanish-Speaking Children of Texas." Ph.D.
dissertation, University of Texas at Austin, 1969. 231 p.

1048 _____. "The Acquisition of Lexicon in the Speech of Bilingual
Children." In BILINGUALISM IN THE SOUTH WEST. Edited by
Paul Turner, pp. 67-93. Tucson: University of Arizona Press,
1973.

1049 Correa-Zoli, Yole. "Lexical and Morphological Aspects of
American Italian in San Francisco." Ph.D. dissertation, Stanford
University, 1970. 175 p.

1050 Covello, Leonard. "Language Usage in Italian Families." AT-
LANTICA 16 (October 1934): 327-29; ATLANTICA 16 (November 1934): 369-71, 396.

1051 Dawidowicz, Lucy S. "Yiddish: Past, Present and Perfect."
COMMENTARY 33 (May 1962): 375-85.

The essay is an account of the Yiddish language in
the world and its importance in the United States.

1052 Delacorte, Albert P. SOME RECOMMENDATIONS FOR A PRE-
VENTIVE PHONETICS PROGRAM FOR SPANISH-SPEAKING STU-
DENTS. New York: Mobilization for Youth, 1968. 55 p.

This work offers a method utilizing phonetics for teachers
to use in teaching Spanish-speaking students to speak
and understand English.

1053 Delgado, Jose. "Los Acronimos En El Habla de Puerto Rico." LANGUAGE SCIENCES 30 (April 1974): 19-20.

> This article includes the following: "Abbreviations," "Spanish," "Language Usage," "Language Patterns," "Trend Analysis," "Business," "Communications," "English," "Determiners (Language)."

1054 DiPietro, Robert J. "Language as a Marker of Italian Ethnicity." STUDI EMIGRAZIONE - ETUDES MIGRATIONS 8 (June 1976): 202-17.

> Five stages of ethnicity in Italian Americans through the use of language-related data is identified in this article.

1055 Donofrio, R.M. SITUATIONS AND LANGUAGE: A SOCIO-LINGUISTIC INVESTIGATION. FINAL REPORT. Washington, D.C.: National Center for Research and Development, 1972. 124 p.

1056 Dorrance, Ward Allison. "The Survival of French in the Old District of Sainte-Genevieve." THE UNIVERSITY OF MISSOURI STUDIES: A QUARTERLY OF RESEARCH 10 (April 1935): 1-134.

> This is an extensive study of the Creole French Dialect of Missouri, with an analysis of the historical and social background of the French peasants living in the district, followed by an extensive glossary and some characteristic aspects of their folklore.

1057 Dozier, Edward P. "Two Examples of Linguistic Acculturation: The Yaqui of Sonora and Arizona and the Tewa of New Mexico." LANGUAGE 32 (1965): 146-57.

> "These two contrasting acculturative situations, in both linguistic and non-linguistic aspects, appear to be due to the contact situation, one permissive [Yaqui has exhaustive borrowing from Spanish] and the other forced [the Tewa have resisted acculturation]."

1058 Drach, Kerry, et al. THE STRUCTURE OF LINGUISTIC INPUT TO CHILDREN. Berkeley and Los Angeles: University of California, 1969. 121 p.

1059 Dulay, Heidi C. "Goofing: An Indicator of Children's Second Language Learning Strategies." LANGUAGE LEARNING 22 (1972): 235-52.

1060 Dulong, Gaston. BIBLIOGRAPHIE LINGUISTIQUE DU CANADA FRANÇAIS. Quebec: Les Presses de l'Université Laval, 1966. 166 p.

1061 Eikel, Fred, Jr. "New Braunfels German." AMERICAN SPEECH 41 (February 1966): 5-16; 41 (December 1966): 254-60; 42 (May 1967): 83-104.

Part 1 of this article gives a brief history of German settlements in Texas, part 2 deals with the phonology of the New Braunfels dialect, and part 3 is concerned with its morphology and syntax.

1062 Engle, Patricia L[ee]. THE USE OF VERNACULAR LANGUAGES IN EDUCATION. LANGUAGE MEDIUM IN EARLY SCHOOL YEARS FOR MINORITY LANGUAGE GROUPS. Bilingual Education Series, No. 3. Washington, D.C.: Center for Applied Linguistics, 1975.

1063 Ervin-Tripp, Susan [M.]. "Semantic Shift in Bilingualism." AMERICAN JOURNAL OF PSYCHOLOGY 74 (June 1961): 233-41.

Semantic shift was examined in this work in the color-naming of Navaho bilinguals in comparison with two monolingual groups.

1064 _____. LANGUAGE ACQUISITION AND COMMUNICATIVE CHOICE. Stanford, Calif.: Stanford University Press, 1973. 230 p.

1065 Evans, J.S. "Word-Pair Discrimination and Imitation Abilities of Preschool Economically-Disadvantaged Native-Spanish-Speaking Children." Ph.D. dissertation, the University of Texas, 1971. 227 p.

1066 Evans, J.S., and Bangs, T.E. "Effects of Preschool Language Training on Later Academic Achievement." JOURNAL OF LEARNING DISABILITIES 5 (1972): 585-92.

1067 Fantini, Alvino Edward. "Language Acquisition of a Bilingual Child. A Sociolinguistic Perspective (to Age Five)." Ph.D. dissertation, University of Texas, 1974. 322 p.

1068 Fedder, Ruth, and Gabaldon, Jacqueline. NO LONGER DEPRIVED: THE USE OF MINORITY CULTURES AND LANGUAGES IN THE EDUCATION OF DISADVANTAGED CHILDREN AND THEIR TEACHERS. New York: Teachers College Press, 1970. 218 p.

1069 Feldman, Carol, and Shen, M. "Some Language-Related Cognitive Advantages of Bilingual Five-Year-Olds." JOURNAL OF GENETIC PSYCHOLOGY 118 (1971): 235-44.

1070 Ferguson, Charles A. "Diglossia." WORD 15 (August 1959): 325-40.

> This article presents the linguistic aspects of a situation where "two varieties of a language exist side by side throughout the speech community, with each having a different role to play."

1071 Fertig, Sheldon, and Fishman, Joshua A. "Some Measures of the Interaction Between Language, Domain and Semantic Dimension in Bilinguals." MODERN LANGUAGE JOURNAL 53 (April 1969): 244-49.

> This article includes the following: "Bilingualism," "Diglossia," "English (Second Language)," "Language Research," "Language Usage," "Puerto Ricans," "Rating Scales," "Semantics," "Spanish," "Tables (Data)."

1072 Fishman, Joshua A. "Language Maintenance and Language Shift as a Field of Inquiry: A Definition of the Field and Suggestions for Its Further Development." LINGUISTICS 9 (1964): 32-70.

> The author analyzes habitual language use at more than one point in time or space under conditions of intergroup contact.

1073 _____. "Varieties of Ethnicity and Varieties of Language Consciousness." In REPORT OF THE SIXTEENTH ANNUAL ROUND TABLE MEETINGS ON LINGUISTICS AND LANGUAGE STUDIES. Edited by Charles W. Kreidler, pp. 59-79. Monograph Series in Language and Linguistics, no. 18. Washington, D.C.: Georgetown University Press, 1971.

> This article studies "parallelism between social complexity and complexity of linguistic situations."

1074 _____. "Who Speaks What Language to Whom and When?" LA LINGUISTIQUE 2 (1965): 67-88.

> The author presents the concept of "domains of language choice" in an "attempt to provide socio-cultural organization and socio-cultural context for consideration of variance in language choice in multilingual settings."

1075 _____. "Yiddish in America: Socio-Linguistic Description and Analysis." INTERNATIONAL JOURNAL OF AMERICAN LINGUISTICS 31 (April 1965): 1-94.

This is a systematic study examining all facets of Yiddish language maintenance in the United States. Appendix: "The Hebrew Language in the United States," pp. 77-85.

1076 _____. "The Implications of Bilingualism for Language Teaching and Language Learning." In TRENDS IN LANGUAGE TEACHING. Edited by Albert Valdman, pp. 121-32. New York: McGraw-Hill, 1966.

1077 _____. AN INVESTIGATION INTO THE MEASUREMENT AND DESCRIPTION OF LANGUAGE DOMINANCE IN BILINGUALS. New York: Yeshiva University, 1967. 15 p.

The author seeks to construct, refine, and apply interdisciplinary instruments and procedures for the measurement and description of relatively stable and widespread intragroup bilingualism.

1078 _____. "Socio-linguistics and the Language Problems of the Developing Countries." INTERNATIONAL SOCIAL SCIENCE JOURNAL 20 (1968): 211-25.

The author analyzes the social and linguistic components of the problems of developing nations, and suggests some sociolinguistic research methods.

1079 _____. "Sociolinguistic Perspective on the Study of Bilingualism." LINGUISTICS, AN INTERNATIONAL REVIEW 32 (May 1968): 21-49.

1080 _____. "A Sociolinguistic Census of a Bilingual Neighborhood." AMERICAN JOURNAL OF SOCIOLOGY 75 (1969): 323-39.

1081 _____. SOCIOLINGUISTICS: A BRIEF INTRODUCTION. Rowley, Mass.: Newbury House, 1971. 180 p.

1082 _____. LANGUAGE AND NATIONALISM. Rowley, Mass.: Newbury House, 1973. 260 p.

1083 _____, ed. READINGS IN THE SOCIOLOGY OF LANGUAGE. The Hague: Mouton, 1968. 808 p.

This work contains seven readings related to small-group interaction, social strata and sectors, sociocultural organization, multilingualism, maintenance and shift, and social contexts.

1084 Fishman, Joshua A., and Cooper, Robert L. "Alternative Measures of Bilingualism." JOURNAL OF VERBAL LEARNING AND VERBAL BEHAVIOR 8 (April 1969): 276-82.

 This report is based upon work designed to study simultaneously the psychological, linguistic, and sociological aspects of bilingual behavior.

1085 Fishman, Joshua A., and Lovas, John [C.]. "Bilingual Education in a Socio-linguistic Perspective." TESOL QUARTERLY 4 (September 1970): 215-22.

1086 Fishman, Joshua A.; Ferguson, Charles A.; and Das Cupta, Jyotirindra, eds. LANGUAGE PROBLEMS OF DEVELOPING NATIONS. New York: John Wiley and Sons, 1968. 521 p.

 The authors provide "examples of the diverse societal and national functions of language varieties . . . of the changes in these functions as the roles and statuses of their speakers change, and . . . of the changes in the language varieties per se that accompany their changed uses and users."

1087 Fonfrias, Ernesto Juan. "Las Vicisitudes del Espanol de Puerto Rico." YELMO 14 (October-November 1973): 44-49.

 This paper was presented at a symposium on the preservation of the Spanish language in the United States, 7-10 August 1973, Mexico City.

1088 Francescato, G. "Theoretical and Practical Aspects of Child Bilingualism." LINGUA STILE 4 (1969): 31-38.

1089 Fucilla, Joseph G. THE TEACHING OF ITALIAN IN THE UNITED STATES. New Brunswick, N.J.: Rutgers University Press, 1967. Reprint. New York: Arno Press/New York Times, 1975. 299 p.

 This work is a general survey. For the decline of Italian language instruction in the United States, see Herbert H. Golden, "The Teaching of Italian: The 1962 Balance Sheet," ITALICA (1962): 275-88. See also, Howard R. Marraro, "Doctoral Dissertations in Italian Accepted by Romance Language Departments in American Universities, 1876-1950," BULLETIN OF BIBLIOGRAPHY 20 (January-April 1951): 94-99; and Mario E. Cosenza, THE STUDY OF ITALIAN IN THE UNITED STATES (1924).

1090 Gallois, C., and Markel, N.N. "Turn-Taking: Social Personal- ity and Conversational Style." JOURNAL OF PERSONALITY AND SOCIAL PSYCHOLOGY 31 (June 1975): 1134-40.

1091 Gehrke, William H. "The Transition from the German to the English Language in North Carolina." NORTH CAROLINA HISTORICAL REVIEW 12 (1935): 1-19.

1092 Gievins, J.W., Neville, A.R., and Davidson, R.E. "Acquisi- tion of Morphological Rules and Usage as a Function of Social Experience." PSYCHOLOGY OF THE SCHOOL 7 (1970): 217- 21.

1093 Gilbert, Glenn G. "The German Dialect Spoken in Kandall and Gillespie Counties, Texas." Ph.D. dissertation, Harvard University, 1963. 276 p.

1094 Gisolfi, Anthony M. "Italo-American: What it Has Borrowed from American English and What It Is Contributing to the Ameri- can Language." COMMONWEAL 30 (21 July 1939): 311-18.

The author traces the general lines of the evolution of the dialect of Italian immigrants in America.

1095 Golazeski, Clare T. LANGUAGE INTERFERENCE AND VISUAL PERCEPTION FOR NATIVE AND PUERTO RICAN SPEAKERS OF ENGLISH IN SECOND GRADE. New Brunswick, N.J.: Rutgers, State University, Graduate School of Education, 1971. 65 p.

The author seeks to determine whether language inter- ference would have a significant effect on visual per- ception and whether the effect would be marked for boys more than for girls.

1096 Gonzales, James Lee. "The Effects of Maternal Stimulation on Early Language Development of Mexican-American Children." Ph.D. dissertation, University of New Mexico, 1972. 237 p.

1097 Gonzalez, Gustavo. "A Linguistic Profile of the Spanish-Speaking First-Grader in Corpus Christi." M.A. dissertation, University of Texas, 1968. 98 p.

1098 _____. "The Acquisition of Spanish Grammar by Native Span- ish Speakers." Ph.D. dissertation, University of Texas, 1970. 212 p.

1099 _____. "The Acquisition of Questions in Texas Spanish: Age
2-Age 5." Arlington, Va.: Center for Applied Linguistics,
1973. 33 p.

1100 Gordon, Susan B. "The Relationship Between the English Lan-
guage Abilities and Home Language Experiences of First Grade
Children, from Three Ethnic Groups, of Varying Socioeconomic
Status and Varying Degrees of Bilingualism." Ph.D. dissertation,
University of New Mexico, 1969. 238 p.

1101 Greenfield, L[awrence]. "Situational Measures of Normative
Language Views in Relation to Person, Place and Topic among
Puerto Ricans." ANTHROPOS 65 (1970): 602-18.

1102 Gumperz, John J. LANGUAGE IN SOCIAL GROUPS. Stanford, Calif.: Stanford University Press, 1972. 411 p.

1103 Gumperz, John J., and Hernandez-Chavez, Eduardo. "Bilin-
gualism, Bidialectalism and Classroom Interaction." In FUNC-
TIONS OF LANGUAGE IN THE CLASSROOM. Edited by C.B.
Cazden et al., eds., pp. 84-108. New York: Teachers College
Press, 1972.

1104 Gumperz, John J., and Hymes, Dell. "The Ethnography of
Communication." AMERICAN ANTHROPOLOGIST 66 (1964):
131-46.

1105 _____, eds. DIRECTIONS IN SOCIOLINGUISTICS: THE ETH-
NOGRAPHY OF COMMUNICATION. New York: Holt, Rinehart
and Winston, 1972. 276 p.

1106 Hall, Robert A., Jr. LINGUISTICS AND YOUR LANGUAGE.
New York: Doubleday, 1960. 265 p.

This brief, nontechnical work discusses a number of
problems related to language and linguistics.

1107 _____. PIDGIN AND CREOLE LANGUAGES. Ithaca, N.Y.:
Cornell University Press, 1966. 188 p.

The author emphasizes nature and history, structure and
relationships as well as linguistic, social, and political
significance.

1108 Harris, M.B., and Hassemer, W.C. "Some Factors Affecting the
Complexity of Children's Sentences, the Effects of Modeling,

Age, Sex and Bilingualism." JOURNAL OF EXPERIMENTAL CHILD PSYCHOLOGY 13 (1972): 447-55.

1109 Haugen, Einar. "Language and Immigration." NORWEGIAN-AMERICAN STUDIES AND RECORDS 10 (1938): 1-43.

1110 _____. "The Analysis of Language Borrowing." LANGUAGE 20 (1950): 210-31.

1111 _____. THE NORWEGIAN LANGUAGE IN AMERICA: A STUDY IN BILINGUAL BEHAVIOR. 2 vols. Philadelphia: University of Pennsylvania Press, 1953. 695 p.

1112 _____. "Problems of Bilingual Description." GENERAL LINGUISTICS 1 (1955): 1-9.

This article is a concise statement on the problems of description and on its place in aiding linguistic research: for example, the comparison of Norwegian and English.

1113 _____. THE ECOLOGY OF LANGUAGE. Stanford, Calif.: Stanford University Press, 1972. 346 p.

1114 _____. "Bilingualism, Language Contact, and Immigrant Languages in the United States: A Research Report, 1966-70." In CURRENT TRENDS IN LINGUISTICS. Edited by Thomas Sebeok, pp. 505-91. The Hague: Mouton, 1973.

1115 Hayes, John R., ed. COGNITION AND THE DEVELOPMENT OF LANGUAGE. New York: John Wiley and Sons, 1970. 382 p.

1116 Hernandez-Chavez, Eduardo, ed. EL LENGUAJE DE LOS CHICANOS: REGIONAL AND SOCIAL CHARACTER OF LANGUAGE USED BY MEXICAN AMERICANS. Arlington, Va.: Center for Applied Linguistics, 1975. 256 p.

Twenty articles representing a historically articulated collection on the major aspects of the relationships of Spanish and English in the American Southwest are included in this work.

1117 Hill, Archibald A. "The Typology of Writing Systems." In PAPERS IN LINGUISTICS IN HONOR OF LEON DOSTERT. Edited by William M. Austin, pp. 92-99. The Hague: Mouton, 1967.

The author classifies writing systems in three main divisions (discourse systems, morpehmic systems, and phonemic systems) according to the size of the unit of utterance on which is based.

1118 Hilton, Darla C. "Investigation of Internalization and Phonological Rules in Monolingual and Bilingual Children." M.A. disseration, University of Texas, 1969. 122 p.

1119 Huxley, Renira. "Development of the Correct Use of Subject Personal Pronouns in Two Children." In ADVANCES IN PSYCHOLOLINGUISTICS. Edited by Giovanni B. Flores d'Arcais and William J.M. Lavelt, pp. 141-57. Amsterdam: North-Holland Publishing Co., 1970.

1120 Hymes, Dell. LANGUAGE IN CULTURE AND SOCIETY: A READER IN LINGUISTICS AND ANTHROPOLOGY. New York: Harper and Row, Publishers, 1964. 764 p.

This work contains useful articles on linguistic anthropology; linguistic equality, diversity, and relativity; grammatical categories; cultural focus and semantic field; speech; social structure and speech community; processes and problems of change; relationships in time and space; and historical perspective.

1121 _____. "Bilingual Education: Linguistic vs. Sociolinguistic Bases." In BILINGUALISM AND LANGUAGE CONTACT. Edited by James E. Alatis, pp. 69-76. Washington, D.C.: Georgetown University Press, 1970.

1122 _____. FOUNDATIONS IN SOCIOLINGUISTICS: AN ETHNOGRAPHIC APPROACH. Philadelphia: University of Pennsylvania Press, 1974. 274 p.

1123 _____, ed. STUDIES IN THE HISTORY OF LINGUISTICS: TRADITIONS AND PARADIGMS. Bloomington: Indiana University Press, 1974. 380 p.

1124 Hymes, Dell, and Bittle, William E., eds. STUDIES IN SOUTHWESTERN ETHNOLINGUISTICS: MEANING AND HISTORY IN THE LANGUAGES OF THE AMERICAN SOUTHWEST. Studies in General Anthropology, no. 3. The Hague: Mouton, 1967. 467 p.

1125 Imhoof, Maurice I., ed. SOCIAL AND EDUCATIONAL INSIGHTS INTO TEACHING STANDARD ENGLISH TO SPEAKERS

OF OTHER DIALECTS. Bloomington: Indiana University School of Education, 1971. 138 p.

Imhoof presents a series of lectures on various aspects of the language problems of inner-city children. Included here are papers by Roger W. Shuy, "Sociolinguistic Strategies for Studying Urban Speech," and Joshua A. Fishman, "Attitudes and Beliefs About Spanish and English Among Puerto Ricans."

1126 Ingram, D. "Transitivity in Child Language." LANGUAGE 47 (1971): 888-910.

1127 Jakobovits, Leon A., and Miron, M.S. READINGS IN THE PSYCHOLOGY OF LANGUAGE. Englewood Cliffs, N.J.: Prentice-Hall, 1967.

1128 James, C.B.E. "Bilingualism in Wales: An Aspect of Semantic Organization." EDUCATIONAL RESEARCH 2 (1960): 123-36.

1129 Jesperson, Otto. LANGUAGE, ITS NATURE, DEVELOPMENT, AND ORIGIN. New York: Henry Holt and Co., 1922. 448 p.

This work discusses the theory of linguistic development beginning with a history of linguistic science, then dealing with the child, the individual in the world, and the development of language.

1130 Jones, Randall, and Spolsky, Bernard, eds. TESTING LANGUAGE PROFICIENCY. Arlington, Va.: Center for Applied Linguistics, 1975. 146 p.

1131 Jorstad, D. "Psycholinguistic Learning Disabilities in Twenty Mexican-American Students." JOURNAL OF LEARNING DISABILITIES 4 (1971): 143-49.

1132 Kehlenbeck, Alfred P. AN IOWA LOW GERMAN DIALECT. Publication of the American Dialect Society, no. 10. Greensboro, N.C.: American Dialect Society, 1948. 63 p.

The historical background, phonology, morphology, syntax, loan-words, vocabulary, and other characteristics of the Low German dialect spoken by the trilingual (Low German-High German-English) people of four townships of Iowa is discussed by the author.

1133 Kernan, Keith T. "Semantic Relationships and the Child's Acquisition of Language." ANTHROPOLOGICAL LINGUISTICS
12 (1970): 171-87.

1134 Kessler, Ann C. "The Acquisition of Italian and English Syntax
in Bilingual Children." Ph.D. dissertation, Georgetown University, 1971. 257 p.

1135 Kessler, Carolyn. THE ACQUISITION OF SYNTAX IN BILIN-
GUAL CHILDREN. Washington, D.C.: Georgetown University
Press, 1971. 127 p.

1136 Kirk, S.A. "Ethnic Differences in Psycholinguistic Abilities."
EXCEPTIONAL CHILDREN 39 (1972): 112-18.

1137 Kloss, Heinz. "Types of Multilingual Communities: A Discussion
of Ten Variables." SOCIOLOGICAL INQUIRY 36 (Spring 1966):
135-45.

   The variables discussed in this article are: types of
   speech communities, number of languages used by individuals, types of personal and impersonal bilingualism,
   legal status, segments involved, type and degree of
   individual bilingualism, prestige of languages involved,
   degree of distance, indigenousness of speech communities, and attitude toward linguistic stability.

1138 Kolers, Paul A. "Bilingualism and Bicodalism." LANGUAGE
AND SPEECH 8 (1965): 122-26.

1139 Krear, Serafina [Elizabeth]. "The Role of the Mother Tongue
at Home and at School in the Development of Bilingualism."
ENGLISH LANGUAGE TEACHING 24 (1969): 2-4.

1140 Labov, William. LINGUISTICS ACROSS CULTURES: APPLIED
LINGUISTICS FOR LANGUAGE TEACHERS. Foreword by Charles
C. Fries. Ann Arbor: University of Michigan Press, 1957. 141 p.

   Written in nontechnical language, this book demonstrates
   the role that descriptive linguistics can play in practical language teaching including comparison of sound
   systems, grammatical structures, vocabulary systems, and
   values of contrastive studies.

1141 Labov, William; Lambert, Wallace [E.]; and Andersson, Theodore.
"Relacion entre el apprendizaje de una lengua extranjera y el
vernaculo." EDUCACION 11 (1962): 11-41.

Three papers presented in Spanish at the Conferencia Sorbe la Ensenanza de Lengua held at San Juan, Puerto Rico, discusses the relation between the native tongue and the acquisition of a second language.

1142 Labov, William, et al. A PRELIMINARY STUDY OF THE STRUC-TURE OF ENGLISH USED BY NEGRO AND PUERTO RICAN SPEAKERS IN NEW YORK CITY. New York: Columbia University, 1965. 61 p.

The general aims of this study are (1) to determine the socially significant variables in English structure which distinguish black and Puerto Rican speakers from the rest of the New York City speech community, and (2) to define those structural and functional conflicts of the black and Puerto Rican vernaculars with standard English which may interfere with the acquisition of reading skills.

1143 Labov, William, et al. A STUDY OF THE NON-STANDARD ENGLISH OF NEGRO AND PUERTO RICAN SPEAKERS IN NEW YORK CITY: THE USE OF LANGUAGE IN THE SPEECH COM-MUNITY. New York City: Columbia University, 1968. 377 p.

The differences in the use of language in the black and Puerto Rican communities in New York City are covered. (Volume 1 discussed the differences in the structure of non-standard English and standard English.)

1144 Lamarche, Maurice M. "The Topic-Comment Pattern in the De-velopment of English among Some Chinese Children Living in the United States." Ph.D. dissertation, Georgetown University, 1972. 147 p.

1145 Lambert, Wallace E. LANGUAGE, PSYCHOLOGY, AND CUL-TURE. Stanford, Calif.: Stanford University Press, 1972. 267 p.

1146 Lambert, Wallace E.; Havelka, J., and Crosby, C. "The Influ-ence of Language Acquisition Contexts on Bilingualism." THE JOURNAL OF ABNORMAL AND SOCIAL PSYCHOLOGY 56 (March 1958): 239-44.

It was found that if the bilingual has learned his two languages in culturally distinctive contexts, "that the semantic differences between translated equivalents are comparatively increased."

1147 Lambert, Wallace E.; Havelka, J.; and Gardner, R.C. "Linguistic Manifestations of Bilingualism." AMERICAN JOURNAL OF PSYCHOLOGY 72 (March 1959): 77-82.

This is a study to develop a series of behavioral measures of bilingualism. This is helpful research in determining which is the dominant language in the individual.

1148 Lambert, Wallace E., and Rawlings, Chris. BILINGUAL PROCESSING OF MIXED-LANGUAGE ASSOCIATIVE NETWORKS. Montreal: McGill University, 1969. 14 p.

Compound and coordinate bilinguals, equally skilled in French and English, were compared for their ability to search out "core concepts" when given mixed-language clues.

1149 _____. "Bilingual Processing of Mixed-Language Associative Networks." JOURNAL OF VERBAL LEARNING AND VERBAL BEHAVIOR 8 (1969): 604-9.

1150 Laosa, L.M. "Bilingualism in Three United States Hispanic Groups: Contextual Use of Language by Children and Adults in their Families." JOURNAL OF EDUCATIONAL PSYCHOLOGY 67 (1975): 617-27.

1151 Lemaire, Herve B. "Franco-American Efforts on Behalf of the French Language in New England." In LANGUAGE LOYALTY IN THE UNITED STATES: THE MAINTENANCE AND PERPETUATION OF NON-ENGLISH MOTHER-TONGUES BY AMERICAN ETHNIC AND RELIGIOUS GROUPS, edited by Joshua A. Fishman et al., pp. 253-79. The Hague: Mouton, 1966.

This is an up-to-date description of the status of French in New England, with a full analysis of the elements that have contributed to their cultural survival.

1152 Lemus-Serrano, Francisco. "Mother-Tongue Acquisition and Its Implications for the Learning of a Second Language." Ph.D. dissertation, Claremont Graduate school, 1972. 219 p.

1153 Lenneberg, Eric H. BIOLOGICAL FOUNDATIONS OF LANGUAGE. New York: John Wiley and Sons, 1967. 489 p.

1154 _____, ed. NEW DIRECTIONS IN THE STUDY OF LANGUAGE Cambridge, Mass.: M.I.T. Press, 1964. 274 p.

1155 Leopold, Werner F. SPEECH DEVELOPMENT OF A BILINGUAL
CHILD: A LINGUIST'S RECORDS. 4 vols. Northwestern Uni-
versity Studies, Humanities Series, nos. 6, 11, 18, and 19.
Evanston, Ill.: Northwestern University Press, 1939-49.

This work is an observation and recording of the development of speech in a child to whom German and English were spoken with equal frequency from age two.
The first three volumes contain reports of vocabulary
growth, sound learning, grammar, and general problems
in the first two years, and vol. 4 contains the author's
diary of the study.

1156 Lieberson, Stanley. "Bilingualism in Montreal: A Demographic
Analysis." THE AMERICAN JOURNAL OF SOCIOLOGY 71
(July 1965): 10-25.

The author uses census data and linguistic indexes to
examine trends in the ability of Montreal's population
to communicate with one another between 1921 and
1961.

1157 Locke, William V. "Notes on the Vocabulary of the French-
Canadian Dialect Spoken in Brunswick, Maine." THE FRENCH
REVIEW 19 (May 1946): 420-22.

1158 _____. PRONUNCIATION OF THE FRENCH SPOKEN AT
BRUNSWICK, MAINE. Preface by J.M. Carriere. Greensboro:
University of North Carolina, American Dialect Society, 1959.
202 p.

This work is an important contribution to the study of
Franco-American speech.

1159 Lombardi, Thomas D. "Psycholinguistic Abilities of Papago Indian School Children." EXCEPTIONAL CHILDREN 36 (1970):
485-93.

1160 Lopez, Sarah Jane Hudelson. "The Use of Context by Native
Spanish-Speaking Mexican American Children When They Read
Spanish." Ph.D. dissertation, University of Texas, 1975. 159 p.

1161 McConnell, F. "Language Development and Cultural Disadvan-
tagement." EXCEPTIONAL CHILDREN 35 (1969): 597-606.

1162 McDowell, John Holmes. "The Speech Play and Verbal Art of
Chicano Children: An Ethnographic and Sociolinguistic Study."
Ph.D. dissertation, University of Texas, 1975. 432 p.

1163 Mace, Betty Jane. "A Linguistic Profile of Children Entering Seattle Public Schools Kindergartens in September, 1971, and Implications for Their Instruction." Ph.D. dissertation, University of Texas, 1972. 311 p.

1164 Mackey, William F. "Bilingualism and Linguistic Structure." CULTURE 14 (1953): 143-49.

This study describes the basic changes in linguistic structure due to bilingualism.

1165 _____. "Bilingual Interference: Its Analysis and Measurement." JOURNAL OF COMMUNICATION 15 (December 1965): 239-49.

This article is a thoughtfully written study which includes a helpful section on types of language behavior. It describes not only the meaning of interference and language borrowing but also a method for analyzing and measuring bilingual interference.

1166 _____. LANGUAGE TEACHING ANALYSIS. Indiana University Studies in the History and Theory of Linguistics. Bloomington: Indiana University Press, 1967. 562 p.

This is a comprehensive general work on foreign-language pedagogy.

1167 Macnamara, John. "The Bilingual's Linguistic Performance--A Psychological Overview." THE JOURNAL OF SOCIAL ISSUES 23 (April 1967): 58-77.

Mainly six topics are discussed in this article: the measurement of bilingualism, the distinction between coordinate and compound bilinguals, linguistic interference, language switching, and translation. It includes suggestions for future research.

1168 _____. "The Cognitive Strategies of Language Learning." In CONFERENCE ON CHILD LANGUAGE. PREPRINTS OF PAPERS PRESENTED AT CONFERENCE, CHICAGO, ILLINOIS, NOVEMBER 22-24, pp. 471-84. Quebec: Laval University, International Center on Bilingualism, 1971.

1169 McNeill, David. THE ACQUISITION OF LANGUAGE: THE STUDY OF DEVELOPMENTAL PSYCHOLINGUISTICS. New York: Harper and Row, 1970. 165 p.

1170 Martin, Jeanette P. A SURVEY OF THE CURRENT STUDY AND TEACHING OF NORTH AMERICAN INDIAN LANGUAGES. Arlington, Va.: Center for Applied Linguistics, 1975. 90 p.

1171 Martinez-Bernal, J.A. "Children's Acquisition of Spanish and English Morphology Systems and Noun Phrases." Ph.D. dissertation, Georgetown University, 1972. 312 p.

1172 Mazeika, E.J. "A Descriptive Analysis of the Language of a Bilingual Child." Ph.D. dissertation, University of Rochester, 1971. 273 p.

1173 Menarini, Alberto. "L'italo-americano degli Stati Uniti." [The Italian-American of the United States]. LINGUA NOSTRA 1 (October-December 1939): 152-60.

This thorough technical work is a study of the dialects spoken by Italian immigrants in the United States.

1174 Menyuk, Paula. "Alteration of Rules in Children's Grammar." JOURNAL OF VERBAL LEARNING AND VERBAL BEHAVIOR 3 (1964): 480-88.

1175 _____. "Syntactic Rules Used by Children from Preschool Through First Grade." CHILD DEVELOPMENT 35 (1964): 533-46.

1176 _____. SENTENCES CHILDREN USE. Cambridge, Mass.: M.I.T. Press, 1969, 197 p.

1177 Mickelson, N.I., and Galloway, C.G. "Cumulative Language Deficit among Indian Children." EXCEPTIONAL CHILDREN 36 (1969): 187-90.

1178 Miller, M.R. "The Language and Language Beliefs of Indian Children." ANTHROPOLOGICAL LINGUISTICS 12 (1970): 51-61.

1179 Miller, Robert L. THE LINGUISTIC RELATIVITY PRINCIPLE AND HUMBOLDTIAN ETHNOLINGUISTICS: A HISTORY AND APPRAISAL. The Hague and Paris: Mouton, 1968. 127 p.

1180 Montare, Alberto, and Boone, Sherle. "Language and Aggression: an Exploratory Study Amongst Black and Puerto Rican Youth." Paper presented at the Annual Meeting of the American Educational

Research Association, New Orleans, Louisiana, 25 February –
1 March 1973. 10 p. Mimeographed.

This work investigates the hypothesis that high level
language proficiency is associated with low observable
aggression and low language proficiency is associated
with high aggression. Conclusions indicate that (1)
Puerto Rican subjects had significantly lower scores
than black subjects on total language proficiency, and
(2) both verbal and total aggression results for the
Puerto Rican group were significantly greater than those
for the blacks.

1181 Nagy, Lois B. "Effectiveness of Speech and Language Therapy
as an Integral Part of the Educational Program for Bilingual Children." Ph.D. dissertation, International University, 1972. 273 p.

1182 Natalicio, Diana [S.]. "Formation of the Plural in English: A
Study of Native Speakers of English and Native Speakers of
Spanish." Ph.D. dissertation, University of Texas, 1969. 211 p.

1183 Natalicio, Diana S., and Williams, Frederick. REPETITION AS
AN ORAL LANGUAGE ASSESSMENT TECHNIQUE. Austin:
Center for Communication Research, University of Texas, 1971.
41 p.

1184 Nelson, Lowry. "Speaking of Tongues." AMERICAN JOURNAL
OF SOCIOLOGY 64 (November 1948): 202–10.

Retention rates for various foreign languages spoken in
the United States.

1185 O'Donnell, R.C.; Griffin, William; and Norris, R.C. SYNTAX
OF KINDERGARTEN AND ELEMENTARY SCHOOL CHILDREN:
A TRANSFORMATIONAL ANALYSIS. Champaign, Ill.: Na-
tional Council of Teachers of English, 1967. 212 p.

1186 Ott, Elizabeth H[aynes]. "A Study of Levels of Fluency and
Proficiency in Oral English of Spanish-Speaking School Beginners." Ph.D. dissertation, University of Texas, 1967. 149 p.

1187 Pap, Leo. PORTUGUESE-AMERICAN SPEECH: AN OUTLINE
OF SPEECH CONDITIONS AMONG PORTUGUESE IMMIGRANTS
IN NEW ENGLAND AND ELSEWHERE IN THE UNITED STATES.
New York: King's Crown Press, 1942. 223 p.

The author provides an outline of Portuguese language
history, economic conditions, culture, and social traits
in America.

1188 Parisi, Domonico. "Differences of Socio-Cultural Origin in the Linguistic Production of Pre-School Subjects." RASSEGNA ITALIANA DI LINGUISTA APPLICATA 2 (1970): 95-101.

1189 _____. "Development of Syntactic Comprehension in Preschool Children as a Function of Socioeconomic Level." DEVELOPMENTAL PSYCHOLOGY 5 (1971): 186-89.

1190 Parisi, Domenico, and Antinucci, Francesco. "Lexical Competence." In ADVANCES IN PSYCHOLINGUISTICS. Edited by P.O. d'Arcais and N. Levelt, pp. 197-210. Amsterdam: North-Holland Publishing Co., 1970.

1191 Paulston, Christina B. IMPLICATIONS OF LANGUAGE LEARNING THEORY FOR LANGUAGE PLANNING: CONCERNS IN BILINGUAL EDUCATION. Bilingual Education Series, no. 1. Washington, D.C.: Center for Applied Linguistics, 1974. 37 p.

1192 Peña, Albar Antonio. "A Comparative Study of Selected Syntactical Structures of the Oral Language Status in Spanish and English of Disadvantaged First-Grade Spanish-Speaking Children." Ph.D. dissertation, University of Texas, 1967. 152 p.

1193 Philips, Susan U. "Acquisition of Rules for Appropriate Speech Usage." In BILINGUALISM AND LANGUAGE CONTACT. Edited by James E. Alatis, pp. 77-101. Washington, D.C.: Georgetown University Press, 1970.

1194 _____. "Participant Structures and Communicative Competence: Warm Springs Children in Community and Classroom." In FUNCTIONS OF LANGUAGE IN THE CLASSROOM. Edited by C.B. Cazden et al., pp. 370-94. New York: Teachers College Press, 1972.

1195 Piaget, Jean. THE LANGUAGE AND THOUGHT OF THE CHILD. Cleveland: World Publishing Co., 1955. 276 p.

1196 Pialorsi, Frank Paul. "The Production and Recognition of Grammatical and Ungrammatical English Word Sequences by Bilingual Children." Ph.D. dissertation, University of Arizona, 1973. 119 p.

1197 Poulsen, M.K. "Automatic Patterning of Grammatical Structures and Auditory and Visual Stimuli as Related to Reading in Disadvantaged Mexican-American Children." Ph.D. dissertation, University of Southern California, 1971. 224 p.

1198 Ramirez de Arellano, Diana. EL ESPANOL: LA LENGUA DE PUERTO RICO. APRECIO Y DEFENSA DE NUESTRA LENGUA MATERNA EN LA CIUDAD DE NUEVA YORK. New York: New York City Board of Education, 1971. 39 p.

Ramirez believes that the institution of bilingual education in the city's schools is an important first step in elevating Spanish to the position it deserves as a means of instruction and communication. She discusses issues related to bilingual education such as use of instructional materials and improvement of self-concept.

1199 Rapier, J[acqueline].L. "Effects of Verbal Mediation upon the Learning of Mexican-American Children." CALIFORNIA JOURNAL OF EDUCATIONAL RESEARCH 18 (1967): 40-48.

1200 Raubicheck, Letitia. "Psychology of Multilingualism." VOLTA REVIEW 36 (January 1934): 17-20, 57-58.

Some thoughts on language, culture, second-language learning, and bilingualism are discussed by the author.

1201 Reinstein, Steven, and Hoffman, Judy. "Dialect Interaction Between Black and Puerto Rican Children in New York City: Implications for the Language Arts." ELEMENTARY ENGLISH 49 (1972): 190-96.

1202 Rodrigues, Raymond J. "A Comparison of the Written and Oral English Syntax of Mexican American Bilingual and Anglo American Monolingual Fourth and Ninth Grade Students (Las Vegas, New Mexico)." Ph.D. dissertation, University of New Mexico, 1974. 224 p.

1203 Rodriguez, Norma. "Language Skills and Attitude Toward Reading of Children Who Participated in the 'Adictos de la Lectura' Program in Puerto Rico." Ed.D. dissertation, 1974. 160 p.

1204 Salomone-Levy, Rosemary. AN ANALYSIS OF THE EFFECTS OF LANGUAGE ACQUISITION CONTEXT UPON THE DUAL LANGUAGE DEVELOPMENT OF NON-ENGLISH DOMINANT STUDENTS. New York Times Bilingual Bicultural Education in the United States Series. New York: Arno Press, 1978. 305 p.

The intent of this important study was "to assess the relative effectiveness of the separate versus the fused language acquisition context upon the bilingual behavior of first and second grade Italian dominant students participating in a bilingual education program and to further compare these to a similar group not participating in any form of bilingual instruction." In studying the problem, the author sought answers to basic questions: What is the relation between language acquisition context in bilingual education and dual language development; and what is the relation between bilingual education versus English monolingual education upon dual language development and use. Drawing upon recent research findings in the fields of psycholinguistics, social psychology, and sociolinguistics, Salomone-Levy addresses the task "of developing, implementing, and evaluating a bilingual education project and primarily the task of generating evidence in support of one approach to the education of the non-English dominant child." Originally, Ph.D. dissertation, Columbia University, 1976.

1205 Samuels, S. Jay. "Psychological and Educational Considerations in Early Language Learning." In NEW DIMENSIONS IN THE TEACHING OF FLES. Edited by F. Andre Paquette, pp. 211-31. New York: American Council on the Teaching of Foreign Languages, 1969.

1206 Sanches, Mary. "Features in the Acquisition of Japanese Grammar." Ph.D. dissertation, Stanford University, 1966. 143 p.

1207 Sanches, Mary, and Blount, Ben, eds. SOCIOCULTURAL DIMENSIONS OF LANGUAGE USE. New York: Academic Press, 1975. 411 p.

1208 Sapir, Edward. "Language and Thinking." In READING ABOUT LANGUAGE. Edited by Charlton Laird and Robert H. Gorrell, pp. 234-89. New York: Harcourt Brace Jovanovich, 1971.

1209 Sapir, Edward, and Swadesh, Morris. "American Indian Grammatical Categories." WORD 2 (1946): 103-12.

1210 Saporta, Sol., ed. with the assistance of Jarvis R. Bastian. PSYCHOLINGUISTICS: A BOOK OF READINGS. New York: Holt, Rinehart and Winston, 1961. 551 p.

This book is a collection of articles on the nature and function of language, approaches to the study of language, speech perception, the sequential organization and semantic aspects of linguistic events, and the relation of linguistic processes to perception and cognition.

1211 Saville[-Troike], Muriel R. "Interference Phenomena in Language Teaching: Their Nature, Extent, and Significance in the Acquisition of Standard English." ELEMENTARY ENGLISH 12 (March 1971): 396–405.

1212 Sharp, Derrick. LANGUAGE IN BILINGUAL COMMUNITIES. London: Edward Arnold, 1973. 214 p.

1213 Shriner, T.H., and Miner, L. "Morphological Structures in the Language of Disadvantaged and Advantaged Children." JOURNAL OF SPEECH AND HEARING RESEARCH 11 (1968): 605–10.

1214 Shuy, Roger W., and Fasold, Ralph W., eds. LANGUAGE ATTITUDES: CURRENT TRENDS AND PROSPECTS. Washington, D.C.: Georgetown University Press, 1973. 178 p.

1215 Silverman, Stuart H. "The Evaluation of Language Varieties." MODERN LANGUAGE JOURNAL 53 (April 1969): 241–44.

   This article discusses the following topics: "Bilingualism," "English (Second Language)," "Language Patterns," "Language Research," "Puerto Ricans," "Sociolinguistics," "Spanish Speaking," "Speech," "Tables (Data)."

1216 Skrabanek, R.L. "Language Maintenance among Mexican-Americans." INTERNATIONAL JOURNAL OF COMPARATIVE SOCIOLOGY 11 (1970): 272–82.

1217 Slears, Brian. "Aptitude, Content and Method of Teaching Word Recognition with Young American Indian Children." Ph.D. dissertation, University of Minnesota, 1970. 276 p.

1218 Slobin, Dan I. "Imitation and Grammatical Development in Children." In CONTEMPORARY ISSUES IN DEVELOPMENTAL PSYCHOLOGY. Edited by N.S. Endler, L.R. Boulter, and H. Osser, pp. 437–43. New York: Holt, Rinehart and Winston, 1967.

1219 _____. "Children and Language: They Learn the Same Way All Around the World." PSYCHOLOGY TODAY, May 1972, pp. 77–82.

1220 Smith, Frank, and Miller, G.A. THE GENESIS OF LANGUAGE: A PSYCHOLINGUISTIC APPROACH. Cambridge, Mass.: M.I.T. Press, 1966. 206 p.

1221 Spolsky, Bernard. "Linguistics in Practice: The Navaho Reading Study." THEORY INTO PRACTICE 14 (December 1975): 347-52.

This article discusses some linguistic studies that have formed a basis for beginning an experimental program for training bilingual Navaho elementary school teachers.

1222 Stedman, James M., and Adams, Russell L. "Achievement as a Function of Language Competence, Behavior Adjustment and Sex in Young, Disadvantaged Mexican-American Children." JOURNAL OF EDUCATIONAL PSYCHOLOGY 63 (1972): 411-17.

1223 Streiff, Virginia. READING COMPREHENSION AND LANGUAGE PROFICIENCY AMONG ESKIMO CHILDREN: PSYCHOLOGICAL, LINGUISTIC, AND EDUCATIONAL CONSIDERATIONS. New York Times Bilingual Bicultural Education in the United States Series. New York: Arno Press, 1978. 272 p.

One of the few comprehensive studies on Eskimo children, this work assesses the relationship between differential amounts of use of the resources of a regional library and media center upon reading comprehension and language proficiency among Eskimo children in twelve village schools in southwestern Alaska. A wide range of techniques and a broad context of educational endeavor, enhance the value of the findings.

1224 Terry, Charles E., and Cooper, Robert L. "A Note on the Perception and Production of Phonological Variation." MODERN LANGUAGE JOURNAL 53 (April 1969): 254-55.

This article includes the following topics: "Bilingualism," "English (Second Language)," "Language Research," "Phonological Units," "Phonology," "Puerto Ricans," "Reading Skills," "Spanish," "Speech Skills," "Word Frequency."

1225 Teschner, Richard V., ed. SPANISH AND ENGLISH OF UNITED STATES HISPANOS: A CRITICAL, ANNOTATED, LINGUISTIC BIBLIOGRAPHY. Arlington, Va.: Center for Applied Linguistics, 1975. 352 p.

1226 Tisch, Joseph LeSage. FRENCH IN LOUISIANA: A STUDY OF THE HISTORICAL DEVELOPMENT OF THE FRENCH LANGUAGE OF LOUISIANA. New Orleans: A.F. Laborde and Sons, 1959. 68 p.

This work is a study of the evolution of the Acadian-French, Creole-French, and patois negre French dialects of Louisiana, with an analysis of the factors leading toward a unified "Louisiana French" in the future. A sampler of Louisiana French is provided.

1227 Tremaine, Ruth V. SYNTAX AND PIAGETIAN OPERATIONAL THOUGHT: A DEVELOPMENTAL STUDY OF BILINGUAL CHILDREN. Washington, D.C.: Georgetown University Press, 1975. 131 p.

1228 Tucker, C.A. "The Chinese Immigrant's Language Handicap: Its Extent and Its Effects." FLORIDA FL REPORTER 7 (1969): 110–13.

1229 Turano, Anthony M. "The Speech of Little Italy." AMERICAN MERCURY 26 (July 1932): 356–59.

The author gives a brief description of the "peculiar patois" spoken by Italian communities in the United States.

1230 Valdman, Albert, ed. TRENDS IN LANGUAGE TEACHING. Foreword by Alfred S. Hayes. New York: McGraw-Hill, 1966. 298 p.

This book includes articles reporting the search for progress in foreign-language education during the years since the passage of the National Defense Education Act of 1958.

1231 Van Duyne, H.J., and Gutierrez, G. "The Regulatory Function of Language in Bilingual Children." JOURNAL OF EDUCATIONAL RESEARCH 66 (1972): 122–24.

1232 Vaughan, Herbert H. "Italian and Its Dialects as Spoken in the United States." AMERICAN SPEECH 1 (May 1926): 431–35.

1233 Viereck, Wolfgang. "German Dialects Spoken in the United States and Canada: A Bibliography." ORBIS 16 (1967): 549–68.

1234 Vogelin, C.F., and Schutz, Noel W., Jr. "The Language Situation in Arizona as Part of the Southwest Culture Area." In STUDIES IN SOUTHWESTERN ETHNOLINGUISTICS: MEANING AND HISTORY IN THE LANGUAGES OF THE AMERICAN SOUTHWEST. Edited by Dell H. Hymes and William E. Bittle, pp. 403–51. The Hague: Mouton, 1967.

A well-researched study which includes a section on bilingualism among the Indian groups in the Southwest.

1235 Vygotsky, L.S. THOUGHT AND LANGUAGE. Edited and translated from Russian by Eugenia Hanfmann and Gertrude Vakar. New York: John Wiley and Sons, 1962. 168 p.

This is a study of the interrelation of thought and language with a critical analysis of the two most influential theories about the development of language and thinking.

1236 Walker, Willard. "An Experiment in Programmed Cross Cultural Education: The Import of the Cherokee Primer for the Cherokee Community and for the Behavioral Sciences." Unpublished paper presented at Tahlequah, Oklahoma, March 1965, in connection with the Carnegie Corporation Cross-Cultural Education Project of the University of Chicago. Mimeographed. 10 p.

The author presents the rationale for the design of the Cherokee primer by noting such variables as the factors influencing motivation, the presentation of the information to be learned, the native learning and teaching patterns, and so forth.

1237 Walsh, Donald D. WHAT'S WHAT: A LIST OF USEFUL TERMS FOR THE TEACHER OF MODERN LANGUAGES. 3d ed. New York: Modern Language Association, 1965. 34 p.

The author includes explanatory information on about three hundred items dealing with fields whose special lexicon perplexes the language teacher: culture, linguistics, programmed instruction, the language laboratory, psychometry, psycholinguistics, and so forth.

1238 Weinreich, Max. "History of the Yiddish Language: The Problems and Their Implications." PROCEEDINGS OF THE AMERICAN PHILOSOPHICAL SOCIETY 103 (15 August 1959): 563-70.

1239 Weinreich, Uriel. LANGUAGES IN CONTACT: FINDINGS AND PROBLEMS. Preface by Andre Martinet. The Hague: Mouton, 1967. 150 p.

One of the most comprehensive accounts ever written on bilingualism from primarily two angles: its linguistic consequences and its relation to intelligence and personality.

1240 Wight, B.W., Sloniger, M.F., and Keeve, J.P. "Cultural Deprivation: Operational Definition in Terms of Language Development." AMERICAN JOURNAL OF ORTHOPSYCHIATRY 40 (1970): 77–86.

1241 Wilkinson, Andrew. THE FOUNDATIONS OF LANGUAGE: TALKING AND READING IN YOUNG CHILDREN. New York: Oxford University Press, 1971. 275 p.

1242 Williams, Frederick. PSYCHOLOGICAL CORRELATES OF SPEECH CHARACTERISTICS: ON SOUNDING "DISADVANTAGED." Madison: University of Wisconsin, 1969. 121 p.

1243 _____, ed. LANGUAGE AND POVERTY: PERSPECTIVES ON A THEME. Chicago: Markham, 1970. 274 p.

1244 Williams, George. SOME ERRORS IN ENGLISH BY SPANISH-SPEAKING PUERTO RICAN CHILDREN. Cambridge, Mass.: Language Research Foundation, 1972. 18 p.

The purpose of the investigation reported in this document is to determine the range of errors in the spontaneous speech of Puerto Rican children of intermediate English ability in order to provide specific information on phonetic and morphological deviations from standard English for use in curriculum development.

1245 Wolfram, Walt. OVERLAPPING INFLUENCE IN THE ENGLISH OF SECOND GENERATION PUERTO RICAN TEENAGERS IN HARLEM. Washington, D.C.: Center for Applied Linguistics, 1971. 460 p.

This work is an attempt to determine the relative influence of black English and Puerto Rican Spanish in the speech of Puerto Ricans raised contiguous to the black community in Harlem.

IX. TESTS, MEASUREMENT, AND EVALUATION

1246 Adkins, D.C.; Payne, F.D.; and Ballif, B.L. "Motivation Factor Scores and Response Set Scores for 10 Ethnic Cultural Groups of Preschool Children." AMERICAN EDUCATIONAL RESEARCH JOURNAL 9 (1972): 557-72.

1247 Ainsfeld, Elizabeth, and Lambert, Wallace E. "Evaluational Reactions of Bilingual and Monolingual Children to Spoken Language." JOURNAL OF ABNORMAL AND SOCIAL PSYCHOLOGY 69 (July 1964): 89-97.

> "Monolingual and bilingual French-Canadian children listened to tape recordings of children's voices, some in English, some in French, and rated each speaker's personality on 15 traits. Differences between the ratings assigned French and English voices of the subgroups were interpreted as indicative of differences in stereotyped reactions."

1248 Albright, Vatia Harrison. "A Comparison Between the Self-Concept of Mexican American Pupils Taught in a Bilingual Program and Those Taught in a Monolingual Program." Ed.D. dissertation, George Washington University, 1974. 81 p.

> A random sample of 100 students (20 from each grade, grades 1 through 5) were tested, using the Piers-Harris Children's Self-Concept Scale (P-H CSCS), with additional information coming from the Stanford Achievement Test, the Lorge-Thorndike Intelligence Test, and the Otis Quick-Scoring Mental Ability Test. Among the findings were: (1) with the exception of the first grade, students in the two programs did not vary significantly in their self-concept score, and (2) the variance of scores increase with each grade level for bilingual groups.

1249 American Institutes for Research in the Behavioral Sciences. EFFECTIVE READING PROGRAMS: SUMMARIES OF 222 SE-LECTED PROGRAMS. Palo Alto, Calif.: American Institutes for Research in the Behavioral Sciences, 1975. 262 p.

1250 _____. EVALUATION OF THE IMPACT OF ESEA TITLE VII SPANISH-ENGLISH BILINGUAL EDUCATION PROGRAM. Palo Alto, Calif.: American Institutes for Research in the Behavioral Sciences, 1977. 236 p.

> This work is an evaluation of thirty-eight Spanish-English projects in eleven states in 1975-76 which suggests that programs are producing mixed results. See RE-SPONSE TO AIR STUDY (Arlington, Va.: Center for Applied Linguistics, 1977).

1251 Anastasi, Anne, and Cordova, Fernando A. "Some Effects of Bilingualism Upon the Intelligence Test Performance of Puerto Rican Children in New York City." THE JOURNAL OF EDU-CATIONAL PSYCHOLOGY 44 (January 1953): 1-19.

> "Whether or not bilingualism constitutes a handicap, as well as the extent of such a handicap, depends upon the way in which the two languages have been learned . . . ."

1252 Anastasi, Anne, and De Jesus, Cruz. "Language Development and Nonverbal IQ of Puerto Rican Preschool Children in New York City." JOURNAL OF ABNORMAL AND SOCIAL PSY-CHOLOGY 45 (1953): 357-66.

> In this psychological study, measures of language de-velopment and "Goodenough Draw-a-Man IQ's" were obtained on twenty-five Puerto Rican boys and twenty-five girls attending day nurseries in New York City's Spanish Harlem; children were 4 to 5 years old.

1253 Armstrong, Roy Anthony. "Test Bias from the Non-Anglo View-point: A Critical Evaluation of Intelligence Test Items by Mem-bers of Three Cultural Minorities." Ph.D. dissertation, Univer-sity of Arizona, 1972. 163 p.

1254 Baecher, Richard Emeram. "An Exploratory Study to Determine Levels of Educational Development, Reading Levels and the Cognitive Styles of Mexican American and Puerto Rican American Students in Michigan." Ph.D. dissertation, University of Michi-gan, 1973. 226 p.

> Subjects in the fourth and fifth grades of a Pontiac, Michigan, bilingual program were studied for their edu-

cational potential. The study used self-reporting inventories and adapted subtests of the Iowa Tests of Basic Skills, in English and Spanish. Future research on the Spanish-speaking bilingual should develop approach of this study for further work on cognitive study.

1255 Bain, Helen Pate. "A Study of the Effectiveness of Language Reinforced by Simultaneous Action in Bilingual Educational Television Programs for Young Children." Ed.D. dissertation, University of Tennessee, 1974. 150 p.

The data for this dissertation were collected in seven cities. Among the findings were the following: (1) children who did not speak the language performed better when language was reinforced by simultaneous action, (2) children who understood the language also performed better when language was reinforced by simultaneous action. The results showed young bilingual children could perform as well as monolingual children.

1256 Braclay, Lisa Frances Kurcz. "The Comparative Efficacies of Spanish, English and Bilingual Cognitive Verbal Instruction with Mexican-American Headstart Children." Ph.D. dissertation, Stanford University, 1969. 372 p.

1257 Barik, H.C., and Swain, M[errill]. BILINGUAL EDUCATION PROJECT: INTERIM REPORT ON THE SPRING 1972 TESTING PROGRAMME. Toronto: Ontario Institute for Studies in Education, 1972. 141 p.

1258 _____. "Three Year Evaluation of a Large-Scale Early Grade French Immersion Program." LANGUAGE LEARNING 25 (1975): 1-30.

1259 Barnes, F. "A Comparative Study of the Mental Ability of Indian Children." M.A. dissertation, Stanford University, 1955. 131 p.

1260 Bates, Enid May Buswell. "The Effects of One Experimental Bilingual Program on Verbal Ability and Vocabulary of First Grade Pupils." Ed.D. dissertation, Texas Technical University, 1970. 101 p.

This study's main purpose was to compare the mean gain in English verbal ability of some first-grade Mexican and Anglo Americans in a bilingual program. There was no significant gain between those enrolled in the program and those not in it.

1261 Bayley, Nancy. "Comparisons of Mental and Motor Test Scores for Ages 1-15 Months by Sex, Birth Order, Race, Geographic Location, and Education of Parents." CHILD DEVELOPMENT 36 (June 1965): 379-411.

> Mental and motor test scores on a "relatively hetero-geneous" and representative population of infants aged one to fifteen months are analyzed to determine possible effects of such variables as race, sex, birth order, geographical location, or parental ability. Fifty-five percent of the sample were white (with a 5 percent Puerto Rican subsample), 42 percent black, and 2.3 percent other.

1262 Bebeau, D.E. "Administration of a TOEFL Test to Sioux Indian High School Students." JOURNAL OF AMERICAN INDIAN EDUCATION 9 (1969): 7-16.

1263 Bernal, Ernest M., Jr. "Concept Learning Among Anglo, Black, and Mexican-American Children Using Facilitation Strategies and Bilingual Techniques." Ph.D. dissertation, University of Texas, 1971. 123 p.

> Anglos did significantly better than ethnic minorities under standard administration of concept-learning tasks. Minority groups all scored significantly higher when facilitation strategies were used.

1264 Berney, Tomi Deutsch. "The Effects of Language Choice on the Task Success of Bilingual Children." Ph.D. dissertation, Yeshiva University, 1972. 161 p.

> It was hypothesized on the basis of earlier studies that the children would learn best in their native language. The highest scores were received by two other groups. Performance on school-like material appeared to be more strongly affected by regular language of instruction.

1265 Bianchino, Francis Stephen. "Televised and Recognized Adminis-trations of Objective Testing on a Disadvantaged Bilingual Primary School Population." Ph.D. dissertation, United States Interna-tional University, 1975. 129 p.

> Data analysis showed that the language factor was sig-nificant in test results. The mode of presentation was also significant. One of the main findings was that the nontelevised standardized scales administered in the Puerto Rican dialect resulted in significantly superior performance to the nontelevised English presentation.

1266 Blanco, George M. "The Role of Foreign Language Educators in Bilingual Education." In PROCEEDINGS, pp. 22-29. Texas Conference on Coordinating Foreign Languages. Austin: Texas Education Agency, 1976.

1267 _____. CROSS-DISCIPLINARY PERSPECTIVES IN BILINGUAL EDUCATION: EDUCATION REVIEW. Arlington, Va.: Center for Applied Linguistics, 1977. 28 p.

1268 Brooks, R.; Brandt, L.; and Wiener, M. "Differential Response to Two Communication Channels: Socioeconomic Class Differences in Response to Verbal Reinforcers Communicated with and without Tonal Inflection." CHILD DEVELOPMENT 40 (1969): 453-70.

1269 Broussard, Sue Evelyn Lemaire. "Comparison of Achievement Between High School Monolinguals and Bilinguals." Ph.D. dissertation, Louisiana State University, 1977. 67 p.

The comparisons for statistically significant differences (tested at .05) indicated, among others, that monolinguals tested at significantly higher levels than bilinguals on the English, reading, and spelling tests; that a significant difference existed for the English test in favor of monolinguals when subjects of average IQs were compared.

1270 Buriel, Raymond. "Cognitive Styles Among Three Generations of Mexican-American Children." JOURNAL OF CROSS-CULTURAL PSYCHOLOGY 6 (December 1975): 417-29.

This article is a comparison with a group of Anglo children. Eighty elementary school children chosen randomly (three generations Mexican Americans and one Anglo American).

1271 Cain, Mary Alexander. "A Study of Relationships Between Selected Factors and the School Achievement of Mexican-American Migrant Children." Ph.D. dissertation, Michigan State University, 1970. 138 p.

1272 Canedo, Oscar Octavio. "Performance of Mexican-American Students on a Test of Verbal Intelligence." Ph.D. dissertation, United States International University, 1972. 137 p.

1273 Capco, Clemencio S., and Tucker, G. Richard. "Word Association Data and the Assessment of Bilingual Education Programs." TESOL QUARTERLY 5 (1971): 335-42.

1274 Carringer, Dennis Clyde. "The Relationship of Bilingualism to the Creative Thinking Abilities of Mexican Youth." Ph.D. dissertation, University of Georgia, 1972. 84 p.

1275 Cervenka, Edward J. ADMINISTRATION MANUAL FOR THE INVENTORY OF SOCIALIZATION FOR BILINGUAL CHILDREN, AGES THREE TO TEN. "Administration Manual for Tests of Basic Language Competence in English and Spanish," Levels 1 and 2. Prepared for the Child Development Evaluation and Research Center (Southwest). Parts of the Final Report to the Office of Economic Opportunity. Austin: University of Texas, 1968. Mimeographed. 104 p.

    This work is a set of three batteries of experimental instruments developed for use in the study of bilingual programs and other compensatory education programs in Texas.

1276 Chang, Winona Lee. "A Comparison of Certain Structures Written in English by Monolingual and Bilingual Sixth Graders." Ed.D. dissertation, Boston University, 1971. 219 p.

1278 Christiansen, I., and Livermore, G. "A Comparison of Anglo-American and Spanish-American Children on the WISC." JOURNAL OF SOCIAL PSYCHOLOGY 81 (1970): 1-14.

1278 Cline, Marion, Jr. "Achievement of Bilinguals in Seventh Grade by Socioeconomic Levels." Ed.D. dissertation, University of Southern California, 1961. 195 p.

1279 Cohen, Andrew [D.]. "Bilingual Schooling and Spanish Language Maintenance: An Experimental Analysis." THE BILINGUAL REVIEW/LA REVISTA BILINGUE 2 (January-August 1975): 3-12.

    The author studied the effect of several years of bilingual schooling on language maintenance. Pupils, kindergartners at outset and first graders at the end, were given a pupil's language use inventory. Parents were given a home interview questionnaire. A language use observation instrument was used to get a direct measure of language use. Pupils going from kindergarten to first grade in the bilingual education program were using more Spanish over time than comparison pupils.

1280 Collymore, Raymond Quintin. "A Survey of the Educational Aspirations and Cultural Needs of the Negro and Mexican-American Students in Two Community Colleges in the State of Colorado." Ed.D. dissertation, University of Colorado, 1971. 194 p.

1281 Coombs, L. Madison, et al. THE INDIAN CHILD GOES TO SCHOOL: A STORY OF INTERRACIAL DIFFERENCES. Washington, D.C.: Department of the Interior, Bureau of Indian Affairs, 1958. 286 p.

This important study involved administering California Achievement Tests to 23,608 pupils attending federal, mission, and public schools, in eleven states. It offered further evidence that Indian pupils do not achieve as well in the basic skill subjects as white pupils and that they fall progressively behind the national norms as they continue in school.

1282 Cooper, James G. "Predicting School Achievement for Bilingual Pupils." THE JOURNAL OF EDUCATIONAL PSYCHOLOGY 49 (February 1958): 31-36.

This study demonstrated that the six intelligence tests examined predicted school success with a degree of accuracy ranging from moderate to high for the Territory of Guam's bilingual pupils.

1283 Cordasco, Francesco. "The New Bedford Project for Non-English Speaking Children." JOURNAL OF HUMAN RELATIONS 20 (1972): 326-34.

Studies the New Bedford, Massachusetts, Portuguese community.

1284 Cordasco, Francesco, and Alloway, David N. "Spanish-Speaking People in the United States: Some Research Constructs and Postulates." INTERNATIONAL MIGRATION REVIEW 4 (Spring 1970): 76-79.

This article is an overview of the needs of Spanish-speaking people, with notices of program evaluations, and research recommendations.

1285 Cortez, Emilio Gregory. "Games for Second Language Learning: A Comparison of Two Approaches for Teaching English to Puerto Rican Children." Ed.D. dissertation, Temple University, 1974. 134 p.

1286 Covey, Donald David. "An Analytical Study of Secondary Freshmen Bilingual Education and Its Effect on Academic Achievement and Attitude of Mexican American Students." Ed.D. dissertation. Arizona State University, 1973. 204 p.

The selected group studied was 200 qualified ninth grade Mexican-American students. They were given the Iowa

Test of Educational Development, the Stanford Diagnostic Reading Test (Level 2) and the Nebraska Attitude Inventory. Among the conclusions were the following: Mexican-American students in a bilingual program achieve higher in English and reading than those in the regular program, but they do not achieve significantly higher in mathematics.

1287 Crate, Carole Elaine. "An Investigation of the Effects upon Seventh Grade Students of a Three Week Inter-disciplinary Chicano Awareness Unit." Ph.D. dissertation, University of Texas, 1974. 129 p.

1288 Crawford, Carole Ann. "A Comparative Study of Two Experimental Humanities Programs for Mexican American University Students." Ph.D. dissertation, University of Michigan, 1975. 125 p.

1289 Cruz, Sylvia, et al. "Spanish-Speaking Students and the Language Factor in the MRT." INTEGRATED EDUCATION 13 (November-December 1975): 43-44.

The author discusses a study designed to examine the effects of the Metropolitan Readiness Test. One question asked is whether there are significant score differences in students in all-English and bilingual classes.

1290 Cummins, James. "Cognitive Factors Associated with the Attainment of Intermediate Levels of Bilingual Skills." MODERN LANGUAGE JOURNAL 61 (January-February 1977): 3-12.

This is a study of the relationship between cognitive processes and balanced bilingual skills. There might be a threshold level of bilingual competence which would need to be reached before bilingualism could positively affect cognitive functioning.

1291 Darcy, Natalie T. "The Performance of Bilingual Puerto Rican Children on Verbal and Non-Language Tests of Intelligence." JOURNAL OF EDUCATIONAL RESEARCH 45 (March 1952): 499-506.

The author discusses the importance of administering both the verbal and the nonlanguage type to yield a valid intelligence score of a bilingual population.

1292 _____. "A Review of the Literature on the Effects of Bilingualism Upon the Measurement of Intelligence." THE PEDAGOGICAL SEMINARY AND JOURNAL OF GENETIC PSYCHOLOGY 82 (March 1953): 21-57.

The author emphasizes the importance of the bilingual student's background in interpreting intelligence tests.

1293 _____. "Bilingualism and the Measurement of Intelligence: Review of a Decade of Research." THE JOURNAL OF GENETIC PSYCHOLOGY 103 (December 1963): 259-82.

This article is a highly critical review of literature on bilingualism as related to intelligence covering 1953-1963; it discusses studies related to age and background of students, instruments, verbal and nonverbal language, and teaching methods.

1294 Davidson, M. Ruth. "A Comparative Pilot Study of Two First-Grade Programs for Culturally-Deprived Mexican-American Children." Ph.D. dissertation, University of Texas, 1967. 242 p.

1295 Decker, Douglas Lester. "English and Spanish Story Recall of First Grade Spanish Dominant Pupils in Bilingual Programs." Ed.D. dissertation, Columbia University, Teachers College, 1976. 108 p.

This dissertation is on 144 first graders from 10 Title VII California projects. The study did not reveal any clear evidence that the particular task of story recall varied from one language to another. The treatment--story plus questioning--was administered in Spanish or English or some combination of the two.

1296 Del Castillo, Ricardo. "Reactions of Bilingual and Monolingual Speakers to Accented and Non-Accented Speech." Ph.D. dissertation, Adelphi University, 1975. 58 p.

1297 Di Lorenzo, L.G., and Salter, R. "Evaluative Study of Pre-kindergarten Programs for Educationally Disadvantaged Children: Followup and Replication." EXCEPTIONAL CHILDREN 34 (1966): 111-19.

1298 Dissemination Center for Bilingual Bicultural Education. EVALUATION INSTRUMENTS FOR BILINGUAL EDUCATION: AN ANNOTATED BIBLIOGRAPHY. Austin, Tex.: Dissemination Center for Bilingual Bicultural Education, 1975. 125 p.

This work lists 250 entries which include material from commercial and nonprofit sources as well as from Title VII funded programs. Instruments in eight languages, including English, are listed.

1299 Dixon, Carol N. PEER TEACHING AND LANGUAGE EXPERI-
ENCE APPROACH: APPROPRIATE STRATEGIES FOR THE BILIN-
GUAL/BICULTURAL CHILD. Phoenix, Ariz.: International Read-
ing Association, 1975. 7 p.

1300 Domenech, Daniel Anthony. "The Relationship Between the Language Dominance and Cultural Affinity of Hispanic Students in
Bilingual Programs." Ph.D. dissertation, Hofstra University,
1977. 96 p.

> A cultural affinity scale and basic inventory of natural
> language was used in this study with eighty-six Hispan-
> ic students (4th through 7th grade) in Nassau County,
> Long Island, New York, bilingual and bicultural classes.
> The subjects consistently expressed biculturalism.

1301 Dwyer, R.C., et al. "Evaluation of Effectiveness of a Problem-
Based Preschool Compensatory Program." JOURNAL OF EDUCA-
TIONAL RESEARCH 66 (1972): 153-56.

1302 Edwards, J., and Stern, C. "Comparison of Three Intervention
Programs with Disadvantaged Preschool Children." JOURNAL
OF SPECIAL EDUCATION 4 (1970): 205-14.

1303 Ehrlich, Alan [G.], comp. TESTS IN SPANISH AND OTHER LAN-
GUAGES AND NON-VERBAL TESTS FOR CHILDREN IN BILIN-
GUAL PROGRAMS: AN ANNOTATED BIBLIOGRAPHY. New
York: Hunter College, 1973. 127 p.

1304 Eichorn, Dorothy H., and Jones, Harold E. "Development of
Mental Functions--Bilingualism." REVIEW OF EDUCATIONAL
RESEARCH 22 (December 1952): 425.

1305 Ervin-Tripp, Susan [M.]. "Language and TAT Content in Bilinguals."
JOURNAL OF ABNORMAL AND SOCIAL PSYCHOLOGY 68
(May 1964): 500-507.

1306 Fishman, Joshua A. "The Measurement and Description of Widespread and Relatively Stable Bilingualism." MODERN LANGUAGE
JOURNAL 53 (March 1969): 152-56.

1307 Fishman, Joshua A., et al. "Guidelines for Testing Minority
Group Children." JOURNAL OF SOCIAL ISSUES 20 (April
1964): 129-45.

1308 Fitch, Michael John. "Verbal and Performance Test Scores in Bilingual Children." Ed.D. dissertation, Colorado State College, 1966. 70 p.

The purpose of this study is to evaluate the effects of increased exposure to the English language on verbal and nonverbal measures in bilingual children.

1309 Fournier, James Francis, Jr. "An Investigation of the Correlation Differences in Science Concepts Held by Fifth Grade Mexican and Anglo American Students: A Cross-Cultural Study." Ed.D. dissertation, University of Northern Colorado, 1975. 96 p.

1310 Frantz, Cecilia Aranda. "An Oral Language Development Program for Mexican-American Children: A Descriptive Study." Ph.D. dissertation, Arizona State University, 1975. 120 p.

1311 Frender, Robert; Brown, Bruce; and Lambert, Wallace E. "The Roles of Speech Characteristics, Verbal Intelligence and Achievement Motivation in Scholastic Success." Unpublished paper. Montreal: McGill University, November 1968. 20 p.

1312 Fraytes-Dieppa, Celeste. "Paired-Associate Learning with Spanish and English Mediation in a Bilingual Community." Ed.D. dissertation, Boston University, 1977. 68 p.

This study was set up to see whether verbal mediation facilities made verbal learning among bilingual children easier. Analysis of variance suggested that mediation significantly improved (p < .001) those in paired-associate lists. Vocabulary in Spanish and English did not provide evidence that Spanish proficient children learned Spanish lists better than English lists.

1313 Gaarder, A. Bruce. "The First Seventy-Six Bilingual Education Projects." In BILINGUALISM AND LANGUAGE CONTACT. Edited by James E. Alatis, pp. 163-78. Washington, D.C.: Georgetown University Press, 1970.

1314 Galvan, Robert Rogers. BILINGUALISM AS IT RELATES TO INTELLIGENCE TEST SCORES AND SCHOOL ACHIEVEMENT AMONG CULTURALLY DEPRIVED SPANISH-AMERICAN CHILDREN. New York Times Bilingual Bicultural Education in the United States Series. New York: Arno Press, 1978. 88 p.

This is a significant study in which Galvan investigated the relationship between intelligence test scores and school achievement as they relate to bilingualism among

Spanish-language-dominant children, and the possibilities of more accurately evaluating the intelligence of bilingual children. The children selected for the study were in the third, fourth, and fifth grades of a Dallas, Texas, elementary school. Conclusions reached indicated that the use of achievement tests for determining school achievement was generally not a satisfactory measure for bilingual children. The inadequacy of using verbal tests of intelligence when testing bilingual children suggests the use of nonverbal tests of intelligence which might serve as a better indicator of pupil functioning and school success.

1315 Garcia, Ramiro. "Bilingual Instruction: Its Relationship to Cognitive and Affective Development--With Implications for Educational Policy Decisions." Ph.D. dissertation, University of California, Los Angeles, 1977. 184 p.

This study compared the mathematics and reading achievement of two groups of Los Angeles pupils. There were 362 Mexican-American children in the study. Analyses indicated that the experimental group achieved higher in mathematical computations while the control group achieved a higher level of reading vocabulary than the experimental group.

1316 Gonzalez, J.M. "Coming of Age in Bilingual/Bicultural Education: An Historical Perspective." INEQUALITY IN EDUCATION 19 (February 1975): 5-17.

1317 Gordon, Susan B. "The Relationship Between the English Language Abilities and Home Language Experiences of First Grade Children, from Three Ethnic Groups, of Varying Socioeconomic Status and Varying Degrees of Bilingualism." Ph.D. dissertation, University of New Mexico, 1969. 238 p.

Language-modeling, which varied according to ethnicity SES (socioeconomic status) and language model type, was related to and predictive of English-language ability. The sample consisted of 155 first-grade children (Navaho, Pueblo, and Spanish American).

1318 Gray, Tracy Chrysis. "A Bicultural Approach to the Issue of Achievement Motivation." Ph.D. dissertation, Stanford University, 1975. 147 p.

1319 Greene, John F., and Zirkel, Perry A[lan]. "The Validation of an Instrument to Assess Attitudes Toward the Puerto Rican, Black-American and Anglo-American Cultures." Paper presented at

American Educational Research Association Annual Meeting, Chicago, April 1974. 1973. 20 p. Mimeographed.

The purpose of this study was to determine the reliability of the Tri-Cultural Attitude Scale (TAS). Conclusions drawn were that the TAS appears to be a positive step toward meeting the need for adequate effective assessment in bilingual and bicultural and other cultural pluralism educational projects in the early grades.

1320 Gutierrez, Lorraine Padilla. "Attitudes Toward Bilingual Education: A Study of Parents with Children in Selected Bilingual Programs." Ph.D. dissertation, University of New Mexico, 1972. 180 p.

A sixty-three-item questionnaire was given to both parents (in 110 pair) and the responses showed that there were few significant differences between socioeconomic groups. Those under thirty-five were more positive in their attitudes than the older parents. This sample showed parents strongly in favor of a bilingual society.

1321 Haugen, Einar. "Some Pleasures and Problems of Bilingual Research." INTERNATIONAL JOURNAL OF AMERICAN LINGUISTICS 20 (April 1954): 116-22.

Suggestions on how to conduct research in bilingualism.

1322 Hertzig, Margaret E., and Birch, Herbert G. "Longitudinal Course of Measured Intelligence in Preschool Children of Different Social and Ethnic Backgrounds." AMERICAN JOURNAL OF ORTHOPSYCHIATRY 41 (1971): 416-26.

1323 Hickey, T. "Bilingualism and the Measurement of Intelligence and Verbal Learning Abilities." EXCEPTIONAL CHILDREN 39 (1972): 24-28.

1324 Hill, Floyd Williams. "A Study of the Influence of Socialization Anxiety on the Achievement of First-Grade Mexican-American Children." Ph.D. dissertation, University of Texas, 1969. 251 p.

1325 Hill, Henry S. "The Effects of Bilingualism on the Measured Intelligence of Elementary School Children of Italian Parentage." Ph.D. dissertation, Rutgers University, 1935. 148 p.

1326 _____. "The Effects of Bilingualism on the Measured Intelligence of Elementary School Children of Italian Parentage." THE

JOURNAL OF EXPERIMENTAL EDUCATION 5 (September 1936): 75-78.

The author concludes that the effect of bilingualism on the intelligence of Italian children who hear and speak either English or Italian at home may be disregarded.

1327 Hoffman, Moses N.H. "The Measurement of Bilingual Background." Ph.D. dissertation, Columbia University, Teachers College, 1934. 76 p.

The author describes a strong measuring instrument, the "Bilingual Schedule," helping the educator deal more intelligently with many of the problems confronting bilingual children in school.

1328 _____. THE MEASUREMENT OF BILINGUAL BACKGROUND. Contributions to Education, no. 623. New York: AMS Press, 1973. 84 p.

This work discusses American-born children of Italian and Jewish immigrants, and describes a strong measuring instrument, the "Bilingual Schedule," helping the educator deal more intelligently with many of the problems confronting bilingual children in school.

1329 Hopkins, Thomas R. LANGUAGE TESTING OF NORTH AMERICAN INDIANS. Washington, D.C.: U.S. Department of the Interior, Bureau of Indian Affairs, 1967. 80 p.

1330 Hurt, M., Jr., and Mishra, S.P. "Reliability and Validity of the Metropolitan Achievement Tests for Mexican-American Children." EDUCATIONAL AND PSYCHOLOGICAL MEASUREMENT 30 (1970): 989-92.

1331 Huzar, Helen. "The Effects of an English-Spanish Primary-Grade Reading Program on Second- and Third-Grade Students." M.A. dissertation, Rutgers University, 1973. 83 p.

This study sought to determine whether there would be any significant difference in the scores on an English reading test between second and third grade students in the same school, but not in the program.

1332 James, Davis Leander. "A Survey of Fifty-Five ESEA Title VII Bilingual Education Projects in the State of California." Ed.D. dissertation, University of Southern California, 1976. 283 p.

1333 Jameson, Gloria R. "The Development of a Phonemic Analysis for an Oral English Proficiency Test for Spanish-Speaking School Beginners." Ph.D. dissertation, University of Texas, 1967. 189 p.

1334 Johnson, Bruce Edward. "Ability, Achievement and Bilingualism: A Comparative Study Involving Spanish-Speaking and English-Speaking Children at the Sixth Grade Level." Ed.D. dissertation, University of Maryland, 1962. 195 p.

1335 Johnson, D.L., and Johnson, C.A. "Comparison of Four Intelligence Tests Used with Culturally Disadvantaged Children." PSYCHOLOGICAL REPORTS 28 (1971): 209-10.

1336 Johnson, Granville B., Jr. "Bilingualism as Measured by a Reaction-Time Technique and the Relationship Between a Language and a Non-Language Intelligence Quotient." PEDAGOGICAL SEMINARY AND JOURNAL OF GENETIC PSYCHOLOGY 82 (March 1953): 3-10.

1337 Johnson, Pamela F., and Warner, Dennis A. "A Bilingual Teacher is Not Enough." INTEGRATED EDUCATION 15 (May-June 1977): 39.

   At the beginning of the school year all Spanish-speaking children were given the Wide Range Achievement Test. Forty Spanish-speaking children were assigned to teachers who had some ability with Spanish. Forty-one went to English-speaking teachers. The students instructed by bilingual teachers did not make greater progress.

1338 Jones, William R. "The Language Handicap of Welsh-Speaking Children: A Study of Their Performance in an English Verbal Intelligence Test in Relation to Their Non-Verbal Mental Ability and Their Reading Ability in English." THE BRITISH JOURNAL OF EDUCATIONAL PSYCHOLOGY 22 (June 1952): 114-23.

1339 _____. "The Influence of Reading Ability in English on the Intelligence Test Scores of Welsh-Speaking Children." BRITISH JOURNAL OF EDUCATION PSYCHOLOGY 23 (June 1953): 114-20.

   The author compares bilingual and monoglot groups in both the verbal intelligence test and the silent reading test.

1340 _____. BILINGUALISM AND INTELLIGENCE. Cardiff: University of Wales Press, 1959. 68 p.

This report discusses monoglot vs. bilingual groups, social and economic status, and concludes that bilingualism need not be a source of intellectual disadvantage.

1341 _____. "A Critical Study of Bilingualism and Non-Verbal Intelligence." BRITISH JOURNAL OF EDUCATIONAL PSYCHOLOGY 30 (February 1960): 71-77.

The author discusses findings that bilingualism need not be a source of intellectual disadvantages, and stresses the importance of a thorough examination of socioeconomic factors in any comparative study of monoglot and bilingual children.

1342 Jones, William R., and Stewart, W[illiam].A.C. "Bilingualism and Verbal Intelligence." THE BRITISH JOURNAL OF PSYCHOLOGY 4 (March 1951): 3-8.

This article discusses a comparative study of tests administered to 11-year-old monoglot and bilingual children in each child's native language (English or Welsh). Resulted in a highly significant difference in favor of the monoglot group.

1343 Jones, William R., et al. THE EDUCATIONAL ATTAINMENT OF BILINGUAL CHILDREN IN RELATION TO THEIR INTELLIGENCE AND LINGUISTIC BACKGROUND. Cardiff: University of Wales Press, 1957. 52 p.

This work discusses a rigorous investigation undertaken by the Collegiate Faculties of Education at Aberystwyth and Bangor, Wales, United Kingdom, at the request of the Welsh Joint Education Committee.

1344 Jonz, Jon. "Measuring Values in Multilingual Settings." TESOL QUARTERLY 10 (June 1976): 203-9.

This article discusses the values assessment instrument given to junior and senior high school students studying a second language. The instrument was in Spanish and English versions.

1345 Karabinus, R.A., et al. "Van Alystyne Picture Vocabulary Test Used with Six-Year-Old Mexican-American Children." EDUCATIONAL AND PSYCHOLOGICAL MEASUREMENT 29 (1969): 935-39.

1346 Karadenes, Mark. "A Comparison of Differences in Achievement and Learning Abilities between Anglo and Mexican-American Children when the Two Groups are Equated by Intelligence." Ph.D. dissertation, University of Virginia, 1971. 261 p.

1347 Karnes, M.B.; Teska, J.A.; and Hodgins, A.S. "The Effects of Four Programs of Classroom Intervention on the Intellectual and Language Development of Four-Year-Old Disadvantaged Children." AMERICAN JOURNAL OF ORTHOPSYCHIATRY 40 (1970): 58-76.

1348 Kelly, L.G., ed. DESCRIPTION ET MESURE DU BILINGUISME/ DESCRIPTION AND MEASUREMENT OF BILINGUALISM. Toronto: University of Toronto Press, 1969. 112 p.

1349 Keston, Morton J., and Jimenez, Carmina A. "A Study of the Performance on English and Spanish Editions of the Stanford-Binet Intelligence Test by Spanish-American Children." THE JOURNAL OF GENETIC PSYCHOLOGY 85 (December 1954): 263-69.

      The authors conclude that since bilingual children are able to perform better in the language in which they have received formal instruction, only the English edition should be used to better measure the children's intelligence.

1350 Killian, J.R. "WISC, Illinois Test of Psycholinguistic Abilities, and Bender Visual-Motor Gestalt Test Performance on Spanish-American Kindergarten and First Grade School Children." JOURNAL OF CONSULTING AND CLINICAL PSYCHOLOGY 37 (1971): 38-43.

1351 Kittell, Jack E. "Bilingualism and Language-Non-Language Intelligence Scores of Third-Grade Children." JOURNAL OF EDUCATIONAL RESEARCH 52 (March 1959): 263-68.

1352 _____. "Intelligence-Test Performance of Children from Bilingual Environments." ELEMENTARY SCHOOL JOURNAL 64 (November 1963): 26-83.

      In an experiment controlled on all levels, thirty-three monolingual and thirty-three bilingual children were tested in three areas in the third and fifth grade.

1353 Klineberg, Nettye V. "Bilingualism and Intelligence in 10-Year-Old Italian Girls." M.A. dissertation, Columbia University, 1932. 121 p.

1354 Koeller, Shirley Ann Lipian. "The Effect of Listening to Excerpts from Children's Stories About Mexican-Americans on the Self-Concepts and Attitudes of Sixth-Grade Children." Ph.D. dissertation, University of Colorado, 1975. 339 p.

1355 Kuttner, R.E. "Comparative Performance of Disadvantaged Ethnic and Racial Groups." PSYCHOLOGICAL REPORTS 27 (1970): 372.

1356 Lambert, Wallace E. "Measurement of the Linguistic Dominance of Bilinguals." THE JOURNAL OF ABNORMAL AND SOCIAL PSYCHOLOGY 50 (March 1955): 197-200.

1357 Lambert, Wallace E., et al. "Bilingual Organization in Free Recall." JOURNAL OF VERBAL LEARNING AND VERBAL BEHAVIOR 7 (1968): 207-14.

   Two groups of bilinguals, one French English and the other English Russian, were tested individually. Various results suggest that organization according to semantic categories is a more useful schema than is language for bilinguals.

1358 Laosa, L.M., Tapia, L. Lara; and Diaz-Guerrero, R. "Perceptual-Cognitive and Personality Development of Mexican and Anglo-American Children as Measured by Human Figure Drawings." DEVELOPMENTAL PSYCHOLOGY 10 (1974): 131-39.

1359 Lark, Alexander Hamilton Stevenson. "An Evaluation of a Program for Ethnic Minorities Who Will Teach in Urban Elementary School." Ph.D. dissertation, University of Southern California, 1974. 187 p.

1360 Legarreta-Marcaida, Dorothy. "An Investigation of the Use or Non-Use of Formal English-as-Second Language (ELS) Training on the Acquisition of English by Spanish-Speaking Kindergarten Children in Traditional and Bilingual Classrooms." Ph.D. dissertation, University of California, Berkeley, 1975. 127 p.

   This study, longitudinal in nature, studied the facilitative effects of four different program models on acquiring English and maintaining Spanish. The models were as follows: traditional with no ESL; traditional with ESL; bilingual, unbalanced language with no ESL; and bilingual, balanced language with no ESL; and bilingual, unbalanced with ESL. Bilingual, balanced language with no ESL produced the most significant gains.

1361 Lerea, Louis, and Kohut, Suzanne. "A Comparative Study of Monolinguals and Bilinguals in a Verbal Task Performance." JOURNAL OF CLINICAL PSYCHOLOGY 17 (January 1961): 49-52.

> In a study involving two experiment groups, thirty bilinguals and thirty monolinguals, matched in age, sex, intelligence, and socioeconomic status, they found bilinguals superior in the micro-utterance association (relearning) task and concluded that "bilinguals may possess a unique potential unacknowledged in past research."

1362 Lesser, George S.; Fifer, Gordon; and Clark, Donald H. MENTAL ABILITIES OF CHILDREN FROM DIFFERENT SOCIAL-CLASS AND CULTURAL GROUPS. Chicago: University of Chicago Press, 1965. 188 p.

1363 Levinson, B.M. "A Comparison of the Performance of Bilingual and Monolingual Native-Born Jewish Preschool Children of Traditional Parentage on Four Intelligence Tests." JOURNAL OF CLINICAL PSYCHOLOGY 15 (1959): 74-76.

1364 Lewis, D.G. "Bilingualism and Non-Verbal Intelligence: A Further Study of Test Results." BRITISH JOURNAL OF EDUCATIONAL PSYCHOLOGY 29 (1959): 17-22.

1365 Lewis, Hilda P., and Lewis, Edward R. "Written Language Performance of Sixth-Grade Children of Low Socioeconomic Status from Bilingual and Monolingual Backgrounds." THE JOURNAL OF EXPERIMENTAL EDUCATION 33 (Spring 1965): 237-42.

1366 Lugo, James Oscar. "A Comparison of Degrees of Bilingualism and Measures of School Achievement Among Mexican-American Pupils." Ph.D. dissertation, University of Southern California, 1970. 172 p.

1367 McCabe, A.R., et al. THE PURSUIT OF PROMISE. A STUDY OF THE INTELLECTUALLY SUPERIOR CHILD IN A SOCIALLY DEPRIVED AREA. New York: Community-Service Society of New York, 1967. 312 p.

> A report of an intensive two-year demonstration project conducted in East Harlem to examine the characteristics of intellectually superior disadvantaged children and their families, and to test the effectiveness of a demonstration service program employing group methods in encouraging the academic and social functioning of these children.

1368 McCanne, Roy. "A Comparison of Three Approaches to First Grade English Reading Instruction for Children from Spanish-Speaking Homes." Ed.D. dissertation, University of Denver, 1966. 291 p.

1369 McClinton, Johnnie W. "Effectiveness of a Bilingual Vocational-Technical Development Program." Ph.D. dissertation, University of Missouri, 1972. 113 p.

1370 McDowell, Earl Ernest. "A Methodological Study of Compound and Coordinate Bilingualism." Ph.D. dissertation, University of Nebraska, 1974. 143 p.

1371 McKay, Maryann. "Spoken Spanish of Mexican American Children: A Monolingual and Bilingual School Program." Ph.D. dissertation, Stanford University, 1975. 139 p.

> The study was conducted with ninety-six Mexican-American elementary school children in the San Francisco Bay Area. All were Spanish dominant. They were matched with forty-eight children from another school. All children saw a short movie without sound and talked about it individually with the interviewer. The children in the monolingual school produced more language and more structurally complex language. Apparently, Spanish is a school subject to the children in the program.

1372 Mackey, William F. "The Measurement of Bilingual Behavior." The CANADIAN PSYCHOLOGIST 7 (April 1966): 72-92.

> This paper is an attempt to supply a technique for the analysis and measurement of bilingual behavior.

1373 _____. "The Description and Measurement of Bilingualism/ Description et Mesure du Bilinguisme." THE LINGUISTIC REPORTER 9 (October 1967): 1-2.

> The author briefly sets forth the problems yet to be solved and research yet to be done in this area.

1374 _____. "The Typology, Classification and Analysis of Language Tests." LANGUAGE LEARNING 3 (August 1968): 163-66.

> The author discusses the above topics as they relate to the work of the International Center for Research on Bilingualism.

1375 Mackey, William F., and Noonan, James A. "An Experiment in Bilingual Education." ENGLISH LANGUAGE TEACHING 6 (Summer 1952): 125-32.

The authors describe a successful experiment in teaching Polish children aged six to fifteen an academic subject in English after only fifteen to thirty-five hours of instruction in English.

1376 Manuel, Herschel T. TESTS OF GENERAL ABILITY AND READING. INTER-AMERICAN TEST MATERIALS. Austin: University of Texas, 1963. 636 p.

The conclusions of this work indicated that the new series of Inter-American tests of general ability and reading were successfully developed.

1377 _____. DEVELOPMENT OF INTER-AMERICAN TEST MATERIALS. Austin: University of Texas, 1966. 109 p.

Two new tests were developed in parallel English and Spanish editions: the preschool test of general ability, and the level 1 test of reading Spanish; the editions of earlier tests were revised.

1378 Marjoribanks, K. "Ethnic and Environmental Influences on Mental Abilities." AMERICAN JOURNAL OF SOCIOLOGY 78 (1972): 323-37.

1379 Martinez, Gilbert Thomas. "Predicted Educational Achievement Management Model for Bilingual Bicultural Education Using a Goal Synthesis Process." Ed.D. dissertation, University of Southern California, 1972. 214 p.

California school districts funded by the U.S. Office of Education vary a good deal in their curriculum and management. Goal statements were gotten from forty-four Title VII bilingual-bicultural projects as one basis for constructing a management model. Findings suggest a model is needed, in the construction of which educators and parents should participate.

1380 Mazon, M. Reyes, and McRae, Susan C. BILINGUAL EDUCATION: ORAL LANGUAGE ASSESSMENT AS A PREREQUISITE. San Diego: California Institute for Cultural Pluralism, 1975. 81 p.

1381 Mead, Margaret. "Group Intelligence Tests and Linguistic Disability among Italian Children." SCHOOL AND SOCIETY 25 (April 16, 1927): 465–68.

> The Otis group intelligence tests (from A and B) were given to American and Italian children in grades 6 to 10. American children were found superior to Italian children on these tests.

1382 Medina, Amelia Cirilo. A COMPARATIVE ANALYSIS OF EVALUATIVE THEORY AND PRACTICE FOR THE INSTRUCTIONAL COMPONENT OF BILINGUAL PROGRAMS. New York Times Bilingual Bicultural Education in the United States Series. New York: Arno Press, 1978. 283 p.

> In this study, Medina sought to compare general evaluation theory, bilingual education evaluation theory, federal regulations and guidelines for the evaluation of bilingual programs, and a local educational audit to determine if there were significant differences among requirements and practice. Two important tasks were addressed: a comparative analysis was used to determine the degree of appropriateness of general theory of evaluation to bilingual program evaluation; and a comprehensive theoretical model was identified which could provide a set of criteria against which an actual evaluation could be analyzed. The conclusions of the study are important for all bilingual education programs, and Medina's recommendations represent a significant contribution to understanding and improving bilingual education program evaluation.

1383 Mejia, Raynaldo Daniel. "Bilingual Education: An Analysis of Local District Commitment and Development of an Index of Critical Requirements. " Ed.D. dissertation, University of Southern California, 1976. 139 p.

1384 Miller, Max D. "Patterns of Relationships of Fluid and Crystallized Mental Abilities to Achievement in Different Ethnic Groups." Ph.D. dissertation, University of Houston, 1972. 214 p.

1385 Mishra, S.P., and Hurt, M., Jr. "Use of Metropolitan Readiness Tests with Mexican-American Children." CALIFORNIA JOURNAL OF EDUCATIONAL RESEARCH 21 (1970): 182–87.

1386 Mitchell, A.J. "The Effect of Bilingualism in the Measurement of Intelligence." THE ELEMENTARY SCHOOL JOURNAL 38 (September 1937): 29–37.

The author concludes that Spanish-speaking children suffer from an inferiority in ability to think accurately in the adopted language.

1387 Modiano, Nancy. "National or Mother Tongue in Beginning Reading: A Comparative Study." RESEARCH IN THE TEACHING OF ENGLISH 2 (April 1968): 32-43.

This is a report of an experiment conducted among several Indian tribes in the Highlands of Mexico.

1388 Morris, Joseph. "What Tests Do Schools Use with Spanish-Speaking Students?" INTEGRATED EDUCATION 15 (March-April 1977): 21-23.

There is growing evidence concerning the inappropriateness of standard tests for Spanish-speaking children. Translation of tests do not necessarily make them more useful.

1389 Morrison, John R. "Bilingualism: Some Psychological Aspects." THE ADVANCEMENT OF SCIENCE 14 (March 1968): 287-90.

This essay is concerned with evaluation and research, this reviews types of useful tests, examples of good evaluation and research, and stresses the need for much more of both.

1390 Mosley, Ramon Thomas. "Development and Application of a Spanish-English Bilingualism Attitude Scale." Ph.D. dissertation, Texas A and M University, 1969. 86 p.

1391 Murphy, Marilyn. "The Effects of Modeling and Repetition upon the Acquisition of Three Standard English Patterns by Spanish-Speaking First-Grade Students." Ph.D. dissertation, University of New Mexico, 1973. 247 p.

1392 Najmi, Mohaned Abdul Khalique. "Comparison of Greeley's Spanish-American and Anglo-White Elementary School Children's Responses to Instruments Designed to Measure Self-Concepts and Some Related Variables." Ed.D. dissertation, University of Northern Colorado, 1962. 105 p.

1393 Nasseri, Gholamreza. "Self-Esteem, Test Anxiety and General Anxiety Among Students of Three Ethnic Groups in Grades Nine Through Twelve." Ed.D. dissertation, Northern Illinois University, 1975. 173 p.

1394 New York City. Board of Education. DEVELOPING A PRO-
GRAM FOR TESTING PUERTO RICAN PUPILS IN THE NEW
YORK CITY PUBLIC SCHOOLS. New York: Board of Education,
1958. 146 p.

> This work covers the following areas for developing a
> program for testing Puerto Rican pupils: (1) testing
> ability to understand spoken English, (2) scales for rat-
> ing ability to speak English and to understand spoken
> English, (3) testing ability to read English, (4) testing
> skill in arithmetic computation, (5) testing intelligence,
> (6) collecting personal and educational background in-
> formation, and (7) issues in developing a program for
> testing pupils of Puerto Rican background.

1395 [New York City]. Morris High School. STUDY OF PUERTO
RICAN GRADUATES, MORRIS HIGH SCHOOL, JUNE 1971.
New York: Migration Division, Commonwealth of Puerto Rico,
1963. 25 p.

> The purpose of this study was to determine the follow-
> ing: (1) number and percent of Puerto Rican student
> graduates, (2) number and percent of Puerto Rican stu-
> dents enrolled in academic, commercial, and general
> programs, (3) the scholastic honors, awards, and schol-
> arships received by Puerto Rican students, (4) scholastic
> averages, (5) the language studied while in high school,
> and (6) plans after graduation.

1396 Offenberg, R.M. "Evaluation of a Bilingual Evaluation." READ-
ING IMPROVEMENT 10 (1974): 271-78.

1397 Olesini, Jose. "The Effect of Bilingual Instruction on the
Achievement of Elementary Pupils." Ph.D. dissertation, East Texas
State University, 1971. 80 p.

1398 Ott, Elizabeth Haynes. "A Study of Levels of Fluency and Proficiency in Oral English of Spanish-Speaking School Beginners."
Ph.D. dissertation, University of Texas, 1967. 192 p.

1399 Palmer, Leslie, and Spolsky, Bernard, eds. PAPERS IN LAN-
GUAGE TESTING 1967-1974. Washington, D.C.: TESOL,
1975. 227 p.

> This work is a collection of papers on the subject of
> language testing from the International Seminar on Lan-
> guage Testing, San Juan, 1973, and from the TESOL
> QUARTERLY.

1400 Parrish, Bert Willey. "The Effects of Experimental Background upon the Informal Reading Inventory Diagnosis of Anglo-American and Mexican-American Ninth-Grade Students." Ed.D. dissertation, Arizona State University, 1974. 123 p.

1401 Patterson, Charles I. "A Comparison of Performances of Mexican and American Children in a Bicultural Setting on Measures of Ability, Achievement and Adjustment." Ed.D. dissertation, Michigan State University, 1960. 150 p.

1402 Paul, Daniel L. "The Effect of Integrated Grouping and of Studying Minority Culture in Reducing Cultural Cleavage in Elementary Classrooms." Ed.D. dissertation, Western Michigan University, 1973. 175 p.

> The question examined was whether prejudice could be significantly reduced by studying the minority culture and integrating ethnic groups. The samples were in Holland, Michigan, schools. Among the findings that existed in both groups were that studying the minority culture did not significantly reduce prejudice, and that ethnic contact in class did not significantly reduce prejudice.

1403 Peal, Elizabeth, and Lambert, Wallace E. "The Relation of Bilingualism to Intelligence." PSYCHOLOGICAL MONOGRAPHS: GENERAL AND APPLIED 76 (1962): 1-23.

> A study of the effect of bilingualism on intellectual functioning, this famous paper marks a new period in bilingual research.

1404 Pike, Earl Oswald, Jr. "Observationally-Induced Question-Asking Behavior in Disadvantaged Mexican-American Children." Ph.D. dissertation, University of Oregon, 1971. 131 p.

1405 Pintner, Rudolf. "The Influence of Language Background on Intelligence Tests." JOURNAL OF SOCIAL PSYCHOLOGY 3 (1932): 233-40.

> The author suggests that a bilingual environment may prevent some individuals from ever really indicating their maximum intelligence on a verbal group intelligence test.

1406 Pintner, Rudolf, and Arsenian, Seth. "The Relation of Bilingualism to Verbal Intelligence and School Adjustment." THE JOURNAL OF EDUCATIONAL RESEARCH 31 (December 1937): 255-63.

The authors discuss the bilingual (Yiddish and English) children of New York.

1407 Pomerantz, Norman Eliot. "An Investigation of the Relationship Between Intelligence and Reading Achievement for Various Samples of Bilingual Spanish-Speaking Children." Ed.D. dissertation, New Mexico State University, 1970. 123 p.

1408 Poole, M. Juliana, Sister. "The Development of a Spanish Language Version of the Slosson Intelligence Test." Ed.D. dissertation, University of Rochester, 1974. 128 p.

1409 Purdy, J.D. "Associative Learning Rates of Second, Fourth and Sixth Grade Indian and White Children Using a Paired-Associate Learning Task." Ph.D. dissertation, University of Oklahoma, 1966. 313 p.

1410 Puthoff, Faye Tucker. "The Development of Norms for Bilingual First-Grade Children's Responses to the Hand Test and Peabody Picture Vocabulary Test." Ed.D. dissertation, University of Oklahoma, 1972. 66 p.

1411 Quijano, Teresa. "A Cross-Cultural Study of Six Differences among First-Graders on a Verbal Test." M.A. dissertation, Texas Women's University, 1968. 141 p.

1412 Ramirez, Arnulfo Gonzalez. "The Spoken English of Spanish-Speaking Pupils in a Bilingual and Monolingual School Setting: An Analysis of Syntactic Development." Ph.D. dissertation, Stanford University, 1974. 154 p.

1413 Ramirez, Arnulfo Gonzalez, and Politzer, Robert L. "The Acquisition of English and the Maintenance of Spanish in a Bilingual Education Program." TESOL QUARTERLY 9 (June 1975): 113-24.

English and Spanish versions of an oral proficiency test were given to Spanish-surnamed children at grades K, one and three, and given in a bilingual education program. Achievement in English seems unrelated to maintenance of Spanish for bilingual children.

1414 _____. A REVISED SPANISH/ENGLISH ORAL PROFICIENCY TEST. Palo Alto, Calif.: Stanford Center for Research and Development in Teaching, 1975. 45 p.

1415 Ramirez, Maria Irene. "A Comparison of Three Methods of Teaching the Spanish-Speaking Student." Ed.D. dissertation, East Texas State University, 1971. 88 p.

1416 Randle, Janice Ann Whitehead. "A Bilingual Oral Language Test for Mexican American Children." Ph.D. dissertation, University of Texas, 1975. 206 p.

A description of the development of the test is preceded by a critical survey of tests used to measure aspects of language development in bilingual children. The most interesting independent variable proved to be the school attended. Children from the inner-city barrio schools had lower scores in English than those in a more heterogeneous community.

1417 Rapier, Jacqueline L. "Effects of Verbal Mediation Upon the Learning of Mexican-American Children." CALIFORNIA JOURNAL OF EDUCATIONAL RESEARCH 18 (January 1967): 40-46.

These experiments support Jensen's earlier findings (1961) that the low IQ of Mexican Americans is of a different nature than the low IQ of Anglo Americans, and thus Mexican Americans require different kinds of educational treatment.

1418 Redlinger, Wendy Eloise Anderson. "Bilingual Language Development in Preschool Mexican-American Children." Ph.D. dissertation, University of Arizona, 1977. 182 p.

In 1973, fifty-two bilingual children were tested with Mazeida's "Receptive Language Inventory for Monolingual (Spanish or English) or Bilingual Children 12-36 Months of Age" and a follow-up study of forty-three of them was made by the author. The great majority of the children did not show a double deficit in linguistic abilities. Most of them understood both languages well but only a few could label common items in Spanish.

1419 Reeder, Alfred Wayne. "A Comparative Study of Mexican-American Elementary Students in Open and Traditional Classrooms." Ed.D. dissertation, New Mexico State University, 1975. 157 p.

1420 Rhue, Sara A. "An Investigation of the Number Abilities of a Group of Bilingual Mexican-American Children in Grade One." Ph.D. dissertation, University of Iowa, 1950. 117 p.

1421 Richardson, Mabel Wilson. "An Evaluation of Certain Aspects of the Academic Achievement of Elementary Pupils in a Bilingual Program: A Project." Coral Gables, Fla.: The University of Miami, 1968. 72 p. Mimeographed.

> This is a study of the Coral Way Elementary School (Dade County, Florida) bilingual program, with a review of previous literature on the philosophy of language teaching.

1422 Rinaldi, John Raymond. "An Evaluation of Two Counselor Preparation Models and Their Impact upon the Activities and Perceptions of Chicano Counselors." Ed.D. dissertation, Texas Technical University, 1975. 154 p.

> The purpose of the study was to compare the attitudes, activities, supervisors', and self-ratings of two groups of school counselors, E.P.D.A. trained Chicago counselors, and non-E.P.D.A. trained Chicano counselors. No statistically significant differences were found.

1423 Rivas, Tony Ernest. "The Relationship Among Selected Variables and Achievement of Selected Spanish Surname Pupils and Schools in the Los Angeles City Unified School District." Ph.D. dissertation, Brigham Young University, 1976. 137 p.

1424 Rivera, Carmen Elena. "Academic Achievement, Bicultural Attitudes and Self-Concepts of Pupils in Bilingual and Non-Bilingual Programs." Ph.D. dissertation, Fordham University, 1973. 194 p.

1425 Rodgers, Judith Reed. "An Approach to the Evaluation of Bilingual-Bicultural In-Service Training Programs." Ph.D. dissertation, University of Colorado, 1977. 259 p.

> The evaluation model had thirteen components, among which were: change in the participants' cultural attitudes; relationship between sex, age, ethnicity and cultural knowledge, and familiarity scores; and ratings of workshop instructors. The findings revealed that the workshop affected a significant change (.05 level) in cultural attitudes and cultural knowledge as well as similarity.

1426 Roessel, Robert A., Jr., et al. "An Overview of the Rough Rock Demonstration School." JOURNAL OF AMERICAN INDIAN EDUCATION 7 (January 1968): 1-6.

1427 Rogers, Dorothy Patricia Brady. "Personality Traits and Academic Achievement Among Mexican-American Students." Ph.D. dissertation, University of Texas, 1971. 138 p.

1428 Rohner, Ronald P. "Factors Influencing the Academic Performance of Kwakiutl Children in Canada." COMPARATIVE EDUCATIONAL REVIEW 9 (1965): 331-40.

1429 Ross, Bruce M. "Preferences for Non-Representational Drawings by Navaho and Other Children." JOURNAL OF CROSS-CULTURAL PSYCHOLOGY 7 (June 1976): 145-56.

1430 Saldate, Marcario. "Factors Influencing Academic Performance of High and Low Achieving Mexican American Children." Ph.D. dissertation, University of Arizona, 1972. 85 p.

1431 Sandler, L., et al. "Developmental Test Performance of Disadvantaged Children." EXCEPTIONAL CHILDREN 39 (1972): 201-8.

1432 Savard, Jean-Guy. "A Proposed System for Classifying Language Tests." LANGUAGE LEARNING 3 (August 1968): 167-74.

   The author describes four stages needed in the development of an open classification system.

1433 Seago, D.W., and Koldin, T.S. "Comparative Study of the Mental Capacity of Sixth Grade Jewish and Italian Children." SCHOOL AND SOCIETY 22 (October 31, 1925): 564-68.

1434 Silverman, Robert Jay; Noa, Josylyn K.; and Russell, Randall H. ORAL LANGUAGE TESTS FOR BILINGUAL STUDENTS: AN EVALUATION OF LANGUAGE DOMINANCE AND PROFICIENCY INSTRUMENTS. Portland, Ore.: Center for Bilingual Education, Northwest Regional Educational Laboratory, 1976. 142 p.

1435 Simms, Ernest George. "The Effects of Bilingualism on the Structure of the Intellect." Ed.D. dissertation, Boston University, 1977. 273 p.

   Data for the study was gotten from eighteen of the Guilford Structure of the Intellect Tests. The tests showed bilinguals performing better than monolinguals on seven of the nineteen tests, and the latter performed significantly better on three tests. It could be predicted that bilinguals would score 29.1 points better than

monolinguals on total test score when IQ effects have
been held constant.

1436 Simoes, Antonio, Jr., ed. THE BILINGUAL CHILD: RESEARCH
AND ANALYSIS OF EXISTING EDUCATIONAL THEMES. New
York: Academic Press, 1976. 272 p.

1437 Skoczylas, Rudolph V. "An Evaluation of Some Cognitive and
Affective Aspects of a Spanish-English Bilingual Education Program." Ph.D. dissertation, University of New Mexico, 1972.
168 p.

A small-scale sociolinguistic survey of participants and
their families was undertaken to see whether bilingually
taught children have lost in linguistic, academic or cognitive growth. One major conclusion was that they
showed no evidence of either intellectual inferiority or
superiority after two years of being taught bilingually.

1438 Snow, Albert J. "American Indian Ethno-Science: A Study of
the Many Farms Science Project." JOURNAL OF AMERICAN
INDIAN EDUCATION 12 (October 1972): 5-11.

1439 Southwest Educational Development Laboratory. EVALUATION
OF MIGRANT EDUCATION IN TEXAS: FINAL REPORT. A
Research Report from the Texas Migrant Educational Development
Center. Austin: Southwest Educational Development Laboratory,
1968. 163 p.

Based on on-site observations at ninety schools throughout Texas, this report determines the educational opportunities available for children of migratory agricultural
workers in Texas and evaluates the educational programs
for migrants in Texas schools.

1440 Spence, A.G.; Mishra, S.P.; and Ghozeil, S. "Home Language
and Performance in Standardized Tests." ELEMENTARY SCHOOL
JOURNAL 21 (March 1971): 309-413.

1441 Spolsky, Bernard, et al. A MODEL FOR THE DESCRIPTION,
ANALYSIS AND EVALUATION OF BILINGUAL EDUCATION.
Navajo Reading Study Progress Report no. 23. Albuquerque:
University of New Mexico, 1974. 48 p.

1442 Stephens, Garth Floyd. "An Analysis of the Organization, Administration, and Management of Selected California Elementary

Title VII Bilingual-Bicultural Programs." Ed.D. dissertation, University of Southern California, 1976. 178 p.

1443 Stern, H.H. "Bilingual Education: A Review of Recent North American Experience." MODERN LANGUAGES 50 (1973): 57-62.

1444 Stewart, Peter John. "A Descriptive Study of the Implementation of Five Component Elements of Randomly Selected Title VII Bilingual-Bicultural Programs." Ph.D. dissertation, University of Maryland, 1976. 461 p.

Most Title VII programs have made provisions for implementing specific objectives of component elements (students, teacher, and others) but there has been a good deal of variation in implementation. Some programs have made an effort to implement all five elements.

1445 Streiff, Paul Robert. DEVELOPMENT OF GUIDELINES FOR CONDUCTING RESEARCH IN BILINGUAL EDUCATION. New York Times Bilingual Bicultural Education in the United States Series. New York: Arno Press, 1978. 198 p.

Using the theoretical framework of organizational theory, Streiff investigated the problem involving federal funding of innovative programs under the Bilingual Education Act enacted by the Congress in 1967. Specifically, the study sought to determine if the federal guidelines were adequate for the evaluation of bilingual education projects and, in a related sense, the role of the federal government as a major change agent through the funding of innovative educational programs mandated by Congress. The conclusions suggest "high levels of uncertainty, confusion about goals, approaches and methods," and Streiff formulates revised guidelines with recommendations for next steps in assessing the possibility of their acceptance.

1446 Sumner, Gerald C., et al. FEDERAL PROGRAMS SUPPORTING EDUCATIONAL CHANGE. THE PROCESS OF CHANGE INNOVATIONS IN BILINGUAL EDUCATION. Santa Monica, Calif.: Rand Corp. 1975. 153 p.

1447 Swanson, E., and DeBlassie, R. "Interpreter Effects on the WISC Performance of First Grade Mexican-American Children." MEASUREMENT AND EVALUATION IN GUIDANCE 4 (1971): 172-75.

1448 Talbott, Brian Leigh. "The Relationship Between Oral Proficiency and Achievement in a Bilingual-Bicultural Elementary School." Ph.D. dissertation, University of Idaho, 1976. 103 p.

This study examined 413 students in grades one through six.

1449 Tanguma, Ramon Hector. "Bilingual Education: The Effects of Selected Variables on the Achievement in Selected School Subject Areas of Mexican-American Fifth- and Sixth-Grade Students." Ph.D. dissertation, University of Texas, 1977. 359 p.

This dissertation showed that pupils in an elementary school in rural Texas achieved significantly more under bilingual instruction than under all-English instruction in the three areas of language arts, mathematics, and reading. The study suggests that bilingual instruction would be effective for the fifth and sixth grade, a pupil population which has not succeeded academically in the past.

1450 Taylor, Thomasine Hughes. "A Comparative Study of the Effects of Oral-Aural Language Training on Gains in English Language for Fourth and Fifth Grade Disadvantaged Mexican-American Children." Ph.D. dissertation, University of Texas, 1969. 152 p.

1451 Tilley, Sally Davis. "An Analysis of Q-Sort Ranking of Goals and Objectives in Bilingual Education." THE BILINGUAL RE-VIEW/LA REVISTA BILINGUE 3 (September-December 1976): 221-28.

This is an investigation of priority rankings of goals and objectives of bilingual education by directors of bilingual education programs. Directors distinguish, it was concluded, between TESOL and bilingual education programs. High on the list of their goals was interaction between the bilingual community and the school, and helping pupils academically and in terms of self-concept.

1452 _____. "The Relationship Between Self-Concept and Oral English Language Production of Anglo and Hispanic Primary-Grade Students in a Metropolitan Bilingual Program." Ph.D. dissertation, University of New Orleans, 1977. 106 p.

Some of the study's results are (1) there is no relationship between self-concept scores and oral English-language production scores of primary grade Anglo and Hispanic students when they are in one group, and (2)

the relationship between self-concept scores and oral
English-language production scores of primary grade
Anglo and Hispanic students is related to the students'
ethnic background.

1453 Tindol, Judith Ann. "Pilot Project: An Assessment Program for
the Development of Oral Language with Mexican-American Children in the Alpine Kindergarten." Ed.D. dissertation, East Texas
State University, 1975. 97 p.

1454 Trueba, Henry T. CONTROVERSIAL ASPECTS OF BILINGUAL
EDUCATION. Paper presented at Lecture Series on Chicano
Research Perspectives, 10 April 1975. Bloomington: Indiana
University, 1975. 13 p.

1455 [Ulibarri, Horacio, et al.] BILINGUAL RESEARCH PROJECT:
FINAL REPORT. Albuquerque: University of New Mexico,
College of Education, 1969. 183 p.

1456 U.S. General Accounting Office [GAC]. BILINGUAL EDUCA-
TION: AN UNMET NEED. Report to the Congress. Washington, D.C.: U.S. Government Printing Office, 1976. 28 p.

1457 U.S. Office for Civil Rights. TASK FORCE FINDINGS SPECI-
FYING REMEDIES AVAILABLE FOR ELIMINATING PAST EDUCA-
TIONAL PRACTICES RULED UNLAWFUL UNDER LAU V. NICHOLS.
Washington, D.C.: Department of Health, Education and Wel-
fare, 1975. 27 p.

1458 U.S. Office of Education. "Bilingual Education Proposed Regulations." FEDERAL REGISTER 4 (8 April 1976): 69

1459 Velasquez, Gilbert J. "Evaluation of a Bilingual Bicultural Education Program." Ph.D. dissertation, United States International
University, 1973. 218 p.

1460 Walden, Toini Antilla. "The Classification Skills of Five, Six,
and Seven Year Old Bilingual, Biliterate and Monolingual Children." Ed.D. dissertation, University of Southern California,
1973. 154 p.

One of the conclusions in this study is that children
who participate in an intervention program use more
and a greater variety of modes of grouping than children who do not have intervention.

1461 Walsh, John F., and D'Angelo, Rita. "IQ's of Puerto Rican Head Start Children on the Vane Kindergarten Test." JOURNAL OF SCHOOL PSYCHOLOGY 9 (1971): 173-76.

> Comparisons between Vane's standardization sample and the Puerto Rican group yielded no significant differences in full-scale scores. On the vocabulary subtest, Puerto Rican subjects earned lower mean scores. On the non-verbal subtests, they scored higher than the normative group.

1462 Wanat, Stanley F., ed. ISSUES IN EVALUATING READING. Arlington, Va.: Center for Applied Linguistics, 1977. 69 p.

1463 Weffer, Rafaela del Carmen Elizondo de. "Effects of First Language Instruction in Academic and Psychological Development of Bilingual Children." Ph.D. dissertation, Illinois Institute of Technology, 1972. 88 p.

> The purpose of the study was to assess what kind of impact bilingual education had on selected Spanish-speaking first graders in eleven Illinois school districts. The children were tested with an innovative method of "bilingual testing" where English and Spanish were alternately used. Children taught bilingually achieved in English, mathematics, and language as well as those in the comparison group.

1464 Wooden, Sharon Lee Anderson. "A Study of the Effectiveness of Three Approaches to the Teaching of Reading to Spanish-Speaking Disadvantaged Pupils in the First Grade." Ed.D. dissertation, New Mexico State University, 1969. 131 p.

1465 Woolley, Joanne Norris. "The Development of a Realistic Vocabulary List for Use with Primary Children in Spanish/English Bilingual Classes." Ed.D. dissertation, University of Southern California, 1974. 163 p.

1466 Wortham, Sue Clark. "A Survey and Comparison of Beginning Reading Instruction Practices in English versus Spanish for Mexican American Children in First Grade Classrooms in Texas." Ph.D. dissertation, University of Texas, 1976. 249 p.

> The investigator designed a questionnaire for fifty first-grade reading teachers who reported on their teaching strategies in reading. Among the conclusions are that 68 percent of the Mexican-American children were delayed as compared with 39 percent of the Anglo chil-

dren. Only 28 percent of the Mexican-American children learned to read Spanish.

1467 Zimmerman, Irla Lee; Stiner, Violette G.; and Pond, Roberta L. "Language Status of Preschool Mexican-American Children--Is There a Case Against Early Bilingual Education?" PERCEPTUAL AND MOTOR SKILLS 38 (February 1974): 227-30.

A test of 253 Mexican-American children of preschool age suggests that arbitrarily placing youngsters in bilingual programs with prior assessment to establish their language needs could be less productive than immediate English instruction.

1468 Zirkel, Perry Alan. "Bilingual Education Programs at the Elementary School Level: Their Identification and Evaluation." THE BILINGUAL REVIEW/LA REVISTA BILINGUE 2 (January-August 1975): 13-21.

The subjects of this study were 275 Puerto Rican pupils in four cities where experimental bilingual education programs were established in 1970-71. A questionnaire was developed by the author to identify patterns of bilingual and control instruction in each classroom. Bilingual programs in two of the Connecticut cities which provided a major part of instruction in Spanish were found to have generally positive results.

1469 _____. AN EVALUATION OF THE EFFECTIVENESS OF SELECTED EXPERIMENTAL BILINGUAL EDUCATION PROGRAMS IN CONNECTICUT. West Hartford: University of Hartford, Connecticut Migratory Children's Program, 1972. 175 p.

This evaluation seeks to compare the experimental bilingual evaluation programs with control group children in three areas: gains in academic abilities in Spanish and English, gains in self-concept level, and attitudes that parents have toward themselves at the end of the year.

1470 _____. "The Why's and Ways of Testing Bilinguality Before Teaching Bilingually." ELEMENTARY SCHOOL JOURNAL 76 (March 1976): 323-30.

The author provides twenty-five oral and aural instruments for determining language dominance before a child is put into a bilingual program.

1471 Zirkel, Perry Alan, and Greene, John F. THE ACADEMIC ACHIEVEMENT OF SPANISH-SPEAKING FIRST GRADERS IN CONNECTICUT. Hartford: Connecticut State Department of Education, Bureau of Compensatory and Community Educational Services, 1971. 8 p.

> This study sought to show that the deficiencies Puerto Rican children show in verbal ability and academic achievement could be corrected if instruction were in Spanish.

1472 _____. "An Evaluation of the Effectiveness of Selected Experimental Bilingual Education Programs in Connecticut." Ph.D. dissertation, University of Connecticut, 1972. 175 p.

Appendix I

THE NATIONAL NETWORK OF CENTERS

FOR BILINGUAL EDUCATION

The National Network of Centers for Bilingual Education is designed to provide services primarily to bilingual educators in school districts and colleges or universities with bilingual education programs funded through the Office of Bilingual Education.

To provide these services the network is divided into three major components: (A) Dissemination and Assessment Centers, (B) Materials Development Centers, and (C) Training Resource Centers.

A. DISSEMINATION AND ASSESS-
MENT CENTERS

Assessment and Dissemination Center
California State University--Los
  Angeles
3151 State University Drive
Los Angeles, California 90032

Dissemination and Assessment Center
Lesley College and (Fall River Public
  Schools)
29 Everett Street
Cambridge, Massachusetts 02138

Dissemination and Assessment Center
  for Bilingual Education
Education Service Center--Region 13
Program Development Division
7703 North Lamar Boulevard
Austin, Texas 78752

B. MATERIALS DEVELOPMENT CENTERS

Alaskan Native Language Material
  Development Center
University of Alaska
Rural Education Affairs
2223 Spenard Road
Anchorage, Alaska 99503

Arizona Bilingual Material Development Center
University of Arizona
1434 East Second Street
Tucson, Arizona 85721

Asian American Bilingual Center
Berkeley Unified School District
2168 Shattuck
Berkeley, California 94704

Asian Bilingual Curriculum Development Center
Seton Hall University
4400 South Orange Avenue
South Orange, New Jersey 07079

Asian Bilingual Material Center
Kaufman and Broad Building
Suite 404
10801 National Boulevard
Los Angeles, California 90064

Bilingual Materials Development Center
6000 Camp Bowie Road
Ft. Worth, Texas 76107
(Applicant--Ft. Worth Independent
School District
3210 West Lancaster
Fort Worth, Texas 76107)

Midwest Office for Materials Development
Board of Trustees
University of Illinois
College of Education
Urbana, Illinois 61801

Multilingual–Multicultural Materials
Development Center
California State Polytechnic University
Pomona Office of Teacher Preparation
3801 West Temple Avenue
Pomona, California 91768

The National Center for the Development of Bilingual Curriculum--Dallas
Dallas Independent School District
Nathan Adams School
3700 Ross Avenue
Dallas, Texas 75204

National Materials Development Center For French and Portuguese
168 South River Road
Bedford, New Hampshire 03102
(Applicant--New Hampshire College
and University Council
2321 Elm Street
Manchester, New Hampshire 03104)

Native American Materials Development Center
407 Rio Grande Boulevard, Northwest
Albuquerque, New Mexico 87103
(Applicant--Ramah Navajo School
Board, Inc.
P.O. Box 248
Ramah, New Mexico 87321)

Northeast Center for Curriculum Development
City of New York Board of Education
Comm. School District #7
Bronx, New York 10456

Pacific Area Languages Materials Development Center
University of Hawaii
c/o Department of ESL
1890 East West Road
Honolulu, Hawaii 96822
(Jt. applicants--Departments of Education Hawaii, Trust Territory of
the Pacific Islands)

Spanish Curricula Development Center
7100 Northwest Seventeenth Avenue
Miami, Florida 33147
(Applicant--The School Board of
Dade County)
1410 Northeast Second Avenue
Miami, Florida 33132

C. TRAINING RESOURCE CENTERS

Berkeley Resource Center
Berkeley Unified School District
2168 Shattuck Avenue, 2d Floor
Berkeley, California 94704

Bilingual Education Technical Assistance Center
Tacoma School District #10
P.O. Box 1357
Tacoma, Washington 98401

Bilingual Education Training Resource Center
Institute for Cultural Pluralism
5544 1/2 Hardy Avenue
San Diego, California 92182
(Applicant--San Diego State University Foundation)
5300 Campanile
San Diego, California 92182

Bilingual Training Resource Center
University of Washington
College of Education
122 Miller Hall
Seattle, Washington 98195

Comprehensive Educational Assistance Center
California State University at Fullerton
800 North State College Boulevard
Fullerton, California 92634

Cross-Cultural Resource Center
California State University, Sacramento
Department of Anthropology
6000 "J" Street
Sacramento, California 95819

Federation of Bilingual Training Resource Centers
PWU Station, Box 23778
Denton, Texas 76204

Merit Center
Temple University
Ritter Hall Annex
Room 434
Broad Street and Montgomery Avenue
Philadelphia, Pennsylvania 19122

Midwest Resource Center for Bilingual Bicultural Education
Bilingual Education Service Center
500 South Dwyer Avenue
Arlington Heights, Illinois 60005
(Applicant--Township High School District #214
700 West Kensington Road
Mt. Prospect, Illinois 60056

New England Bilingual Training Resource Center
Boston University
School of Education
765 Commonwealth Avenue
Boston, Massachusetts 02215

New England Multilingual-Multicultural Teaching Resource Center
Providence School Department
Summit Avenue School
86 Fourth Street
Providence, Rhode Island 02906

Regional Bilingual Training Resource Center
City of New York Board of Education
Center for Bilingual Education
110 Livingston Street
Room 224
Brooklyn, New York 11202

South Central Bilingual Resource Center
Region 13 Education Service Center
7703 North Lamar Boulevard
Austin, Texas 78752

Southwest Bilingual Education Training Resource Center
University of New Mexico
College of Education
Albuquerque, New Mexico 87131

University of Southwestern Louisiana Bilingual-Bicultural Resource Center
University of Southwestern Louisiana
East University Avenue
Lafayette, Louisiana 70504

University of Utah Bilingual Resource Center
Academic Affairs
University of Utah
Salt Lake City, Utah 84112

Appendix II
THE NATIONAL CLEARINGHOUSE
FOR BILINGUAL EDUCATION

The National Clearinghouse for Bilingual Education was authorized in the Education Amendments of 1974, after years of continued support for its creation by the bilingual education community.

The National Institute of Education in cooperation with the Office of Bilingual Education in 1978 awarded a three-year contract to InterAmerica Research Associates in a joint venture with the Center for Applied Linguistics to operate the clearinghouse. The clearinghouse will provide a national coordinating mechanism for collecting, analyzing, and distributing information about bilingual education and related programs.

During the first year of operation (1978), the clearinghouse will provide the following services:

A toll-free number for direct communication with the clearinghouse.
Outside the Washington, D.C., metropolitan area, the number is:
1-800-336-4560.
In the Washington, D.C., metropolitan area, the number is:
703-522-0710.

Limited, no-cost on-line bibliographic searches when requested through the Title VII Center Network.

On-site sessions at the National Network Centers for Bilingual Education to orient center personnel on how to effectively use the clearinghouse.

The clearing house will also provide the following products during its first year:

A "Human Resources File in Bilingual Education." The purpose of the file will be to list resources concerning persons who are available to provide consultant services in the area of bilingual education. Safeguards will be used to comply with the Freedom of Information Act. Anyone interested in being included in the file should contact the clearinghouse for more information.

A "resource Guide in Bilingual Education." The purpose of the guide will be to list resources in bilingual education.

A national newsletter devoted to the bilingual education community. Legislative issues, products, research, and resources affecting bilingual education will be discussed.

A "Conceptual Design" for the clearinghouse. The design will outline the clearinghouse's long-term goals and directions.

The long-term goals of the clearinghouse remain a high priority, and an advisory panel of recognized leaders in bilingual education will assist the clearinghouse staff in determining the future direction of the clearinghouse.

Direct all enquiries to the following address:

National Clearinghouse for Bilingual Education
1500 Wilson Boulevard
Suite 802
Rosslyn, Virginia 22209

AUTHOR INDEX

This index includes all authors, editors, compilers, translators, and contributors cited in the text. References are to entry numbers and alphabetization is letter by letter.

A

Aarons, Alfred C. 99, 1011
Abraham, Willard 100-101
Abrahams, Roger D. 102
Ada, Alma Flor 603
Adams, Russell L. 1222
Adkins, D.C. 1246
Adkins, P.G. 604
Adorno, William 103
Afendras, E.A. 1
Agheyisi, Rebecca 1012
Aguirre, Adalberto, Jr. 104
Ainsfeld, Elizabeth 1247
Ainsworth, C.L. 605, 898
Alano, Angeles C. 606
Alatis, James E. 200, 1013
Albright, Vatia Harrison 1248
Alexander, David J. 973
Alford, Gay 605
Allen, Harold B. 105, 852-53, 961
Allen, Virginia F. 2
Alloway, David N. 386, 1284
Altus, David M. 3
Alvarez, Juan M. 607
American Council of Learned
    Societies 1014
American Institutes for Research in
    the Behavioral Sciences 608,
    1249-50
Amsden, Constance 609

Anastasi, Anne 1251-52
Anderson, Nels 106
Anderson, Virginia 854
Anderson, Vivienne 610
Andersson, Theodore 4, 107-14,
    1141
Antinucci, Francesco 1190
Antonovsky, Aaron 611
Aran, Kenneth 387
Aranda, Paul 69
Arizona State University 612
Armstrong, Roy Anthony 1253
Arndt, Richard 388
Arnez, Nancy L. 899
Arnold, Richard D. 1015
Arredondo, Joe 613
Arsenian, Seth 115-16, 1406
Aspira 117, 614
Aucamp, A.J. 118
Austin, William M. 1117
Axelrod, Herman C. 119
Axelrod, Joseph 900

B

Babin, Patrick 5
Baca de McNicholas, Patricia 901
Backner, Burton L. 615
Baecher, Richard Emeram 1254
Badillo, Herman 120-21
Bain, Helen Pate 1255

Author Index

Author Index

Author Index

Author Index

Mitchell, A.J. 1386
Mitzman, Barry 273
Mobilization for Youth 58
Modiano, Nancy 344, 1387
Montare, Alberto 1180
Montgomery, Linda 745
Montgomery, P. 469
Montoya, Joseph M. 999
Moore, G. Alexander 746
Moore, Joan W. 534
Moore, S.G. 956
Moquin, Wayne 535
Morales, Frank Joseph 947
Moreland, Lilian 59
Morgan, Jean 93
Morris, Joseph 1388
Morrison, J. Cayce 274
Morrison, John R. 1389
Morrison, Karlene Elizabeth 536
Mosley, Ramon Thomas 1390
Mousley, Woodrow V. 747
Moyer, Dorothy Clauser 748
Moynihan, Daniel P. 465
Murphy, Marilyn 1391

N

Nagy, Lois B. 1181
Nahirny, Vladimir C. 537
Najmi, Mohaned Abdul Khalique 1392
Naremore, Rita C. 96
Nasseri, Gholamreza 1393
Natalicio, Diana 1182-83
National Advisory Council on Bilingual Education 275
National Conference on Bilingual Education 276
National Service Center 277
Nava, Alfonso Rodriguez 538, 973
Nava, Julian 539-42
Navarro, Eliseo 60
Naylor, Gordon Hardy 543
Nedler, Shari Evans 749, 880
Negron de Montilla, Aida 544
Nelson, Lowry 1184
Neville, A.R. 1092
New Mexico Department of Education 61
Newton, Anne 883

New York City. Board of Education 750-770, 881-82, 1394
New York City. Board of Education. Bilingual Resource Center, Brooklyn 62, 771-74
New York City. Board of Education. Division of General Education, Albany 775
New York City. Board of Education. Office of Bilingual Education 776
New York City. Morris High School 1395
New York Public Library, New York 63
New York State Education Department. Albany 777
New York University. Center for Field Research and School Services 778
Ney, James W. 64, 948
Nine-Curt, Carmen Judith 779
Noa, Josylyn K. 1434
Nogales, Luis G. 65
Noona, James A. 1375
Norbeck, Edward 185
Noreen, Sr. D.C. 780
Norris, R.C. 1185
Northeast Conference on the Teaching of Foreign Languages 278

O

O'Donnell, R.C. 1185
Offenberg, R.M. 1396
Office of Education. Division of Compensatory Education, Washington, D.C. 781
Ogletree, Earl J. 279
Ohannessian, Sirapi 66, 782, 884, 949
Oksaar, Els 280
Olave, Maria del Pilar de 603
Older, Edith 783
Olesini, Jose 1397
Olim, E.G. 281
Oliveira, Arnulfo Luis 950
Olneck, Michael R. 282
Olson, F. 956
Olton, R. 874
Onativia, Oscar V. 283
O'Neill, T. 408

Author Index

Read, Allen Walker 552
Readlinger, Wendy Eloise Anderson 1418
Reboussin, R. 553
Reeder, Alfred Wayne 1419
Regan, Timothy 795
Reinstein, Steven 1201
Revelle, Keith 77
Rexach, Maria G. 889
Reyes, Vinicio H. 305, 796
Reynolds, Florence E. 18
Rhue, Sara A. 1420
Rice, Roger 1000
Rich, Leslie 306
Richardson, Mabel Wilson 673, 1421
Rinaldi, John Raymond 1422
Rippee, Billy Dean 797
Ritzenthaler, Jeanette A. 798
Rivas, Tony Ernest 1423
Rivera, Carmen Elena 954, 1424
Rivera, Feliciano 528, 799
Rivera, Hugo H. 800
Rivera, Marie 801
Roberts, A.H. 54
Robinett, Betty Wallace 890
Rodgers, David 802
Rodgers, Judith Reed 1425
Rodgers, Ron 307
Rodrigues, Raymond J. 1202
Rodriguez, Armando 803
Rodriguez, Felicita 821
Rodriguez, Norma 1203
Rodriguez, Ray 308
Rodriguez, Valerio Sierra 554
Rodriguez Munguia, Juan C. 804
Roemer, Robert E. 309
Roessel, Robert A., Jr. 1426
Rogers, Dorothy Patricia Brady 1427
Rohner, Ronald P. 1428
Rojas, Pauline M. 805, 891
Ronch, Judah 206
Rosales, J.A. 806
Rosen, Carl L. 807
Rosenblatt, J. 555
Rosenthal, Alan G. 556
Rosier, Paul 808
Ross, Bruce M. 1429
Rothfarb, Sylvia 772
Russell, Randall H. 1434

Rustin, Stanley L. 809
Ryan, Ellen Bouchard 144

S

Salazar, Arturo 810
Salazar, Teresa Ann 78
Saldate, Marcario 1430
Salganik, Laura Hersh 310
Salomone-Levy, Rosemary 1204
Salter, R. 1297
Samuels, S. Jay 1205
Sanches, Mary 1206-7
Sanchez, George I. 79, 311
Sanchez, Gilbert 1001
Sanders, J.W. 466
Sandler, L. 1431
Santos, Ida 557
Sapir, Edward 1208-9
Saporta, Sol 1210
San Diego City Schools. California 811
Sanguinetti, Carmen 794
Santiago, Jorge 812
Savard, Jean-Guy 1432
Saville-Troike, Muriel R. 312, 313, 892-93, 1211
Schmidt, Graciela 324
Schmidt, L. 813
Schneider, Susan Gilbert 1002-3
Schrade, Arlene Ovidia 814
Schutz, Noel W., Jr. 1234
Schutzengel, Tirzah Gertrud 558
Schwartzberg, Herbert 815
Seago, D.W. 1433
Seaman, Paul David 314
Sebeok, Thomas A. 885, 1114
Seda, Eduardo 315
Seller, Maxine 316
Senn, Alfred 1014
Sexton, P. 469
Shapira, A. 525
Sharp, Derrick 1212
Sharp, John M. 156
Shasteen, Amos Eugene 559
Shaw, Frederick 317
Shedd, William B. 22
Sheldon, William D. 819
Shen, M. 1069

Author Index

Y

Yamamoto, Kaoru 381
Yarborough, Ralph M. 382
York, P.A. 846
Young, John 847
Young, R.G. 604
Yu, Connie Young 383

Z

Zamora, Gloria Lu Jean Rodriguez
    970-71

Zamora, Jesus Ernesto 848
Zarechnol, Michele 246
Zevin, Patricia Ernenwein 849
Zimmerman, B.J. 458
Zimmerman, Irla Lee 1467
Zintz, Miles V. 384, 972
Zirkel, Perry Alan 97-98, 183,
    471, 850-51, 1010, 1319, 1468-
    72
Zobel, Jan 385

TITLE INDEX

This index includes all titles of books, reports, and proceedings cited in the text. In some cases titles have been shortened. References are to entry numbers and alphabetization is letter by letter.

A

Academic Achievement of Spanish-Speaking First Graders in Connecticut, The 1471
Acquisition of Language, The 1169
Acquisition of Syntax in Bilingual Children, The 1135
Acquisition of Syntax in Children from Five to Ten, The 1040
Addresses and Reports Presented at the Conference on Development of Bilingualism in Children Varying Linguistic and Cultural Heritages 339
Administration Manual for the Inventory of Socialization for Bilingual Children, Ages Three to Ten 1275
American Bilingual Tradition, The 243
American Diversity 37
American Indian Education 3
America's Other Youth 469
Analysis of the Effects of Language Acquisition Context upon the Dual Language Development of Non-English Dominant Students 1204
Annotated Bibliography for Teachers of English as a Foreign Language 47

Annotated Selected Puerto Rican Bibliography 10
Annual Report (National Advisory Council on Bilingual Education, 1975) 275
Annual Report (National Advisory Council on Bilingual Education, 1976) 275
Annual Report (National Advisory Council on Bilingual Education, 1977) 275
Arapaho Child Life and Its Cultural Background 488
Art of Tesol, The 883
Assimilation through Cultural Understanding 623
Audio Visual Aids to Enrich the Curriculum for the Puerto Rican Child in the Elementary Grades 838

B

Background Materials, Methodology 66
Basic Occupational Language Training (BOLT) 300
Better Chance to Learn, A 354
Beyond the Melting Pot 465
Bibliografia Puertorriquena, 1493-1930 70

SUBJECT INDEX

In this index numbers refer to entry numbers, and underlined numbers refer to main areas within the subject. Alphabetization is letter by letter.

A

Absenteeism. See School attendance

Academic achievement and aspirations 282, 607, 649, 1311, 1421, 1424
  alienation and 429
  of American Indians 402, 553, 949, 1280
  anxiety and 1324
  bilingualism and 27, 115, 319, 1269, 1314, 1366, 1397
  birth order and 456
  of blacks 611
  effect of image-enhancement on 687
  English as a second language programs and 888
  of Italian Americans 350, 583
  of Kwakiutl children 1428
  language competence and 268, 512, 596, 1066, 1222, 1448, 1463
  of Mexican Americans 500, 576, 687, 823, 1222, 1271, 1286, 1324, 1330, 1346, 1366, 1401, 1427, 1430, 1449
  motivation and 553, 621, 1311, 1318
  parental influence on 576
  prediction of 1282, 1379
  psychological aspects of 596, 1463
  of Puerto Ricans 611, 1471

  reinforcement of 823
  relationship to intellectual ability 1384
  sociocultural aspects of 500, 839, 1278
  of Spanish-speaking Americans 839, 1278, 1314, 1334, 1423, 1437, 1469

Acculturation and assimilation 405, 486
  academic achievement and 429
  of American Indians 441, 560
  bibliography of 11, 21
  bilingual education and 241, 270
  of Chinese Americans 508
  of French-speaking Americans 561
  of Greek Americans 581
  of Hindustanis 437
  immigrant language maintenance and 203
  of Italian Americans 404, 579, 1020
  linguistical 1020, 1057
  of Mexican Americans 400, 438, 511
  of Puerto Ricans 21, 161, 448, 522, 623, 918
  role of political parties in 434
  Title III programs for 623

Adult education, bibliography of English as a second language programs in 35

Africa, Sub-Saharan, multilingualism in

laws and regulations concerning
171, 354–55, 362, 379,
647, 973–1010, 1457–58
research in 207, 264, 275, 326,
347, 353, 364, 707, 1321,
1436, 1445, 1455
see also Career education; Community colleges; Compensatory
education; Elementary education; English as a second
language; Higher education;
Historical perspectives in bilingualism; Instructional
materials; Intelligence levels
and tests; Interdisciplinary
education; Kindergarten;
Language and linguistics;
Preschool education; Psy-
chological perspectives in bilingualism; Sociocultural perspectives in bilingualism;
Secondary education; Teachers;
names of foreign languages
(e.g. Spanish language);
names of ethnic groups (e.g.
Mexican Americans)
Bilingual Education Act (1967) 27,
108, 164, 176, 361, 382,
1001, 1445
the American Indian and 353
1974 amendments to 1002–3
Puerto Ricans and 423
Bilingual Education Law (N.J.) 987
Bilingualism
cognitive skills and 185, 1069,
1290
creativity and 1274
defined 135, 224, 258–59, 261,
321
disadvantages of 373
effect of childhood 234, 365
effect on concept formation 558
history of 538, 552
identification of 233, 701
intellectual and academic achievement and 27, 115–16, 174,
198, 319, 381, 1239, 1251,
1269, 1314, 1323, 1325–26,
1340, 1353, 1366, 1386,
1397, 1403, 1405–6, 1435
bibliography of 1292–93

measurement and description of
1306, 1372–73
nationalism and 118, 242
personality and 185
racial attitudes and 496
role of the mother tongue in development of 1139, 1141,
1152
see also Multilingualism
Bilingual Project Forward–Adelante
666
"Bilingual Schedule" 1327–28
Birth order
influence on mental and motor
ability 1261
relationship to achievement 456
Blacks 332
academic achievement of 611
attitudes toward 1319
bibliography of 30, 43, 55, 80
concept learning by 125, 1263
curriculum and programs for 608,
611, 722, 777–78
compensatory education 636,
691
film workshops 610
Headstart programs 845
perceptual problems in 640
reading 639, 819, 827
guidance and counseling of 615
in higher education 1280
historical and sociocultural perspectives relating to 412,
465
birth order and achievement
relations in 456
children's writings in 499
cooperation and competition in
525
self-concept in 536
language of 961, 1142–43, 1180,
1201
in New Jersey 536
in New York City 412, 465,
499, 610, 777–78, 819,
848, 1142–43, 1201
in the social studies curriculum
661
values of 592
Boston

education for Puerto Ricans in 337
Greek Americans in 581
Bowdoin College 907
Bridgeport, Conn., Italian Americans
in 579
Buffalo, N.Y.
education of Spanish-speaking
Americans in 781
immigrant education in 316
Bureau of Indian Affairs. See U.S.
Bureau of Indian Affairs

C

California
assimilation of Hindustanis in 437
bilingual education in 103, 171,
231, 974, 996, 1332, 1442
public policy for 973
Mexican Americans in 103, 231,
548
minority character representation in
textbooks used in 523
prediction of educational achievement in 1379
see also Los Angeles; San Francisco
Camden, N.J., blacks and Puerto
Ricans in 536
Canada
attitudes toward immigrants in 498
bilingualism and biculturalism in
118, 129, 139, 178, 229,
334, 502, 591, 1014, 1060.
bibliography of 51, 59
see also Montreal; Quebec; Toronto
Cañada College (Redwood City, Calif.)
825
Canal Zone, bibliography of education
in 18
Cardenas, Jose A. 194
Career education, bilingual 308
Casa Italiana Educational Bureau,
publications of 22
Catholic schools 591
Center for Applied Linguistics, publica-
tions of 54, 64
Center for Urban Education 176
Cherokee Indians 189, 439, 655
bibliography of 44

English as a second language programs for 654
primers for 1236
Chicago
bilingual education in 219, 307
for Korean Americans 294
for Puerto Ricans 651, 733
for Spanish-speaking Americans
305
compensatory education programs
in 636
linguistical analysis of Greek
Americans in 314
Chicanos. See Mexican Americans
Child guidance, in community development programs 297
Child rearing
among Puerto Ricans 531
environmental influences on 470
Children as authors, blacks and
Puerto Ricans 499
Children's literature
bibliography of for Cherokee
Indians 44
bibliography of for Puerto Ricans
72
bibliography of for Spanish-speaking
Americans 67
in language arts programs 603
about Mexico and Mexican
Americans 748, 1354
Chinese Americans 121, 346, 381
acculturation and assimilation of
508
bibliography of 12, 80
English language development of
1144, 1228
historical and sociocultural perspectives relating to 489
family in 572
socialization in 508
language arts programs for 818
learning difficulties of 690
in Minnesota 508
in New York City 690
perceptual problems of 640
in the social studies curriculum
661

for Puerto Ricans 160, 253, 300, 651, 663, 729, 750-51, 754, 759, 763, 766, 854-55, 862, 871, 881, 889, 894, 1285
for Spanish-speaking Americans 792, 879, 890-91, 1360, 1391, 1463
testing and evaluation in 1262
value considerations in teaching of 866, 961
English language
auditory comprehension of 633
loanwords from in the Norwegian language 223
Puerto Rican proficiency in 753
relationship of proficiency in to self-concept 1452
relationship to the Spanish language 215
testing of school beginners in 1333
Environment
enhancing of 527
for Puerto Ricans 750-51, 754, 764
for Spanish-speaking Americans 605
influence on learning 462
intellectual development and 483, 1378
mother-child relationships and 470
Eskimos 27, 221, 353, 963, 993
English as a second language for 595, 890
preparation of for higher education 491
reading programs for and language proficiency of 1223
Ethnic groups, effect of teacher training on perception of 902. See also Immigrants; Minority groups; Race; names of ethnic groups (e.g. Mexican Americans)
Ethnic Heritage Program Act (1970) 27, 357
Ethnicity 267, 464
academic performance and 583
bibliography of 11, 46
in the development of self-concept 564

effect on teacher attitude change 1425
Ethnic studies programs 822
bibliography of colleges offering 7
bibliography of materials for teaching of 55
curriculum for 641
rationale for 315, 624
see also Bicultural education
Europe, Eastern, vernacular language usage in 352
Evangeline County, La., bilingual education in 693

F

Family
Japanese 495
language usage in the Arapaho 472
Mexican-American 569-70
Puerto Rican 389, 440, 471, 531, 753, 765, 918
Family rehabilitation programs 297
Farleigh Dickinson University (Rutherford, N.J.). Reading Conference 639
Film, in broadening communication skills 610. See also Audiovisual materials
Finland, bibliography of bilingualism in 59
Florida, bilingual education in 171
for Spanish-speaking Americans 890
see also Dade County, Fla.; Miami; Tarpon Springs, Fla.
Folklore, bibliography of Cherokee 44
Ford Foundation Project 891
Foreign language instruction 573, 653, 931, 1166, 1237, 1266
in elementary schools 319
integration of the Spanish culture into 814
job market needs and 291
law of 982
linkages to bilingual education 213
as a medium of academic subject instruction 840

Cherokee Indians and 44
Italian Americans and 83, 424
Mexican Americans and 83, 393,
    528, 535, 540-42, 550
Puerto Ricans and 9-10, 41, 67,
    70, 90, 158, 387, 420,
    448, 590
Spanish-speaking Americans and
    407
History, teaching of in Pennsylvania
    37. See also Spanish history
    and culture
Hoboken, N.J., Title III projects in
    623
Holland, Mich., bicultural education
    in 1402
Homework, in urban education 899
Hopi Indians 444
Housing
    in community development programs
    297
    of Puerto Ricans 389, 768
    of Spanish-speaking Americans 984
Hungarian Americans, foreign language
    usage by 237, 451
Hutterites 599

I

Illinois, bilingual education in 171,
    979
    for Spanish-speaking Americans
    231, 1463
    see also Chicago
Illinois Test of Psycholinguistic
    Abilities 1350
Immigrants
    attitudes toward in Canada 498
    children of 87, 169, 533, 932
        academic achievement of 282
        bibliography of 23, 25, 93
        education of 27, 419
        intelligence of 174
        psychological surveys of 131
    loyalty to mother tongue by 203
    political party activity of 430
    see also Ethnic groups; names of
        immigrant groups (e.g.
        Chinese Americans)
Immigration to the United States

bibliography of 11, 23
reevaluation of 357
Income, of Spanish-speaking Americans
    392, 984
Indianapolis, German bilingual schools
    in 368, 445
Indian Education Conference, seven-
    teenth 612
Indians, American. See American
    Indians
Indians (Eastern), assimilation of 437
Individualized instruction, for Mexican
    Americans 926
    in reading programs 609
    see also Self-study programs
Indonesia, vernacular language usage
    in 352
Initial Teaching Alphabet (ITA) 747
Inservice education. See Teachers,
    training of
Institutions
    bibliography of Puerto Rican 10
    preservation of Italian 579
Instructional materials 81, 233, 322,
    805, 848
    for American Indian education 949
    for educating Spanish-speaking
        Americans 207, 305,
        816-17
    in federally funded programs 187
    for Puerto Rican education 285,
        1198
    for the study of Puerto Rico 812
    see also Audiovisual materials;
        Individualized instruction
Integration. See Segregation and
    integration
Intelligence levels and tests 1261,
    1281, 1335-36, 1351-52,
    1431
    American Indians and 1259
    effect of language instruction on
        826
    environmental effects upon 483,
        1378
    Italian Americans and 1325-26,
        1353, 1381, 1433
    Jewish Americans and 1363, 1433
    Mexican Americans and 393,
        483-84, 1272, 1401, 1417,
        1447

Subject Index

Subject Index

vocational guidance and education in 755, 810
Segregation and integration 379
  role of language in 434
  role of political parties in 430
  of Spanish-speaking students 311
  see also Discrimination
Seguin, Tex., education of migrants in 218
Self-identity and concept 564, 613, 649, 796, 1393, 1424, 1457
  of American Indians 514
  of blacks 536
  of disadvantaged children 520, 562
  effect of image enhancement on 687
  effect of social reinforcement on 549
  English as a second language programs and 888
  film workshops to improve 610
  in guidance programs 621
  of Mexican Americans 401, 549, 554, 687, 692, 743, 1248, 1354
  of Puerto Ricans 536, 1198
  reading programs and 741
  relationship to oral English ability 1452
  relationship to the language of instruction 512
  of Spanish-speaking Americans 117, 621, 741, 1392, 1452, 1469
Self-study programs, in reading instruction for Mexican Americans 609. See also Individualized instruction
Semantics. See Language and linguistics
Seminole Indians 457
Senior, Clarence 86
Sex
  achievement as a function of 1222
  effect on teacher attitude change 1425
  grammatical complexity and 1108
  influence on mental and motor ability 1261

Sex roles, conflicts of among Puerto Ricans 809
Siblings, as teachers of preschoolers 111
Simulation methods, in bilingual and bicultural education 648
Sioux Indians
  English as a second language programs for 654, 1262
  handbook for teachers of 678
Slavic Americans 532, 1014
  foreign language usage by 237
Slosson Intelligence Test 1408
Social class
  academic achievement and 522, 560
  compensatory education programs and 636
  intellectual ability and 515, 1340-41, 1362
  language usage and 1034, 1100
  in response to verbal reinforcers 1268
  written language ability and 1365
Socialization. See Acculturation and assimilation
Social studies programs 660-62
  integration of the Spanish culture into 814
  for Mexican Americans 649, 674, 950
  for Puerto Ricans 632, 752, 758, 760-62, 770, 811
Sociocultural perspectives in bilingualism 27, 99, 102, 115-16, 118-19, 165, 176, 188, 197, 202, 207, 214, 229, 238, 241, 266-67, 270, 331, 351, 386-602, 867
  American Indians and 391, 402, 406, 439, 441, 444, 457, 462, 472, 480, 488, 493, 514, 521, 524, 545, 547, 553, 560, 574, 580, 593-95, 597, 601
  Amish and 455
  Armenian Americans and 592
  bibliography of 2, 7, 35-36
  blacks and 412, 456, 465, 499, 525, 536, 592

302

Subject Index

Tewa Indians, language of 1057
Texas
    bilingual education in 166, 171,
        231, 338-39, 563, 792,
        848, 1439, 1449
    compensatory education programs in
        1275
    German Americans in 1061, 1093
    migrant laborers in 1439
    statistical profiles of Spanish-
        speaking Americans in 392
    see also Corpus Christi, Tex.;
        Dallas; Del Rio, Tex.;
        Laredo, Tex.; Mercedes,
        Tex.; San Antonio, Tex.;
        Seguin, Tex.
Texas Foreign Language Association
    134
Texas Technological College 898
Textbooks
    bibliography of Spanish language
        9
    discrimination in 383
    Mexican Americans protrayed in
        784
    minority character representation
        in 523
    for teacher education 933
    for teaching Spanish-speaking
        Americans 117
Theater, community development pro-
    grams and the 297
Thought and thinking
    language and 1208, 1235
    social bases of 257
Time perception and perspective 391
Toronto, bilingual mathematics pro-
    grams in 677
Transitional Bilingual Education Act
    (Massachusetts) (1971) 804,
    980, 991
Tri-Cultural Attitude Scale (TAS)
    1319
Tutoring
    cross-age 724
    by peers 1299
    in vocabulary 726

U

Ukranian Americans, language

loyalty among 203
Underachievers, self-concepts and
    values of 692
Union of Soviet Socialist Republics
    bilingual education in 221, 478
    foreign language teaching in 876
    multilingualism in 222, 518
    see also Russian Americans
United Nations. Educational, Social,
    and Cultural Organization
    27, 351
U.S. Alcohol, Drug Abuse, and
    Mental Health Administration
    69
U.S. Bureau of Indian Affairs 27,
    122, 353, 375, 843, 949,
    993
U.S. Commission on Civil Rights 27,
    231, 354-55
U.S. Department of Health, Educa-
    tion and Welfare 69
U.S. Office of Education 55, 187
    Bureau of Research 364
Universities. See Community colleges;
    Higher education
Urban education 735, 746, 899
    bibliography of 76
    immigrant children and 27
    Mexican Americans and 674
    Puerto Ricans and 117
    sociology of 386
    Spanish-speaking Americans and
        279
    teacher education for 1359
    see also names of cities (e.g.
        New York City)
Urban speech 1125
Urban studies, curriculum for 641

V

Values
    of blacks 592
    consideration of in teaching
        English and language arts
        866, 961
    effect of language on 1022
    and language change among the
        Arapahos 472
    of Mexican Americans 473, 592,
        692

of Puerto Rican college students
809
of Spanish-speaking Americans
559, 1344
see also Attitudes
Van Alystyne Picture Vocabulary Test
1345
Vane Kindergarten Test 1461
Vernacular language usage
in education 27, 1062
global surveys of 352
see also Dialects
Vietnamese Americans, language arts
programs for 818
Virgin Islands, bibliography of education in 18
Visual perception, effect of language
interference on 1095
Vocabulary 563
effect of tutoring on 726
of Puerto Ricans 664
of Spanish-speaking Americans
1312
development of 1465
special aspects of in bilingual
programs 384
teaching of 787
testing and evaluation for 664,
1260, 1312
Vocational Education Act, amendments (1968) 976
Vocational training and guidance
programs 810, 1369
bilingual 362
for Puerto Ricans 253, 755, 765,
820
for Spanish-speaking Americans 621

see also Employment

W

Wales
bilingualism in 118, 1128
bibliography of 59, 91
educational attainment and
1343
English language capabilities of
Welsh-speaking children in
1338-39
Washo Indians, acculturation of 560
Weschsler Intelligence Scale for
Children 1277, 1350, 1447
Wisconsin
German Americans in 1014
Norwegian Americans in 442
Word recognition. See Reading pro-
grams
Writing
testing and evaluation of 1276,
1365
topology of systems of 1117

Y

Yaqui Indians, language of 1057
Yiddish language 1051
history of 1238
see also Hebrew language; Jewish
Americans

Z

Zoning, open enrollment and 767